Work and Well-Being

An Agenda for the 1990s

Edited by
Gwendolyn Puryear Keita and Steven L. Sauter

American Psychological Association
Washington, DC

Published by
American Psychological Association
750 First Street, NE
Washington, DC

Copies may be ordered from   OCT 2 0 1992
APA Order Department
P.O. Box 2710
Hyattsville, MD 20784

This book was typeset in Century by Easton Publishing Services, Inc., Easton, MD

Printer: Princeton University Press, Lawrenceville, NJ
Cover designer: Enigma Concepts Inc., Silver Spring, MD
Technical editor and production coordinator: Linda J. Beverly

First printing March 1992

Library of Congress Cataloging-in-Publication Data
Work and well-being: an agenda for the 1990s/edited by Gwendolyn Puryear Keita
and Steven L. Sauter.
    p. cm.
   Papers presented at a conference held in Washington, D.C. Nov. 15–17, 1990,
sponsored by the American Psychological Association and the National Institute
for Occupational Safety and Health.
   Includes bibliographical references and index.
   ISBN 1-55798-153-1 : $30.00
   1. Industrial psychiatry—Congresses. 2. Job stress—Congresses. I. Keita,
Gwendolyn Puryear. II. Sauter, Steven L. III. American Psychological
Association. IV. National Institute for Occupational Safety and Health.
RC967.5.W67 1992
158.7—dc20   91-43128
                                          CIP

The contents of this volume are reproduced as received from contributors. The opinions, findings, and conclusions are not necessarily those of the National Institute for Occupational Safety and Health, nor does mention of company names or products constitute endorsement by the National Institute for Occupational Safety and Health.

Printed in the United States of America

Contents

Foreword

Improved training, better job design, and reduction of stress in the workplace are important tasks that can contribute significantly to the promotion of health and well-being, and the prevention of work-related psychological disorders. To make headway on these tasks, an interdisciplinary approach will be required that coordinates the best efforts of psychologists with those of educators, engineers, and colleagues from other social and behavioral science disciplines. The American Psychological Association (APA) welcomes the opportunity that was realized in the *Work and Well-Being: An Agenda for the 1990s* conference of working with the National Institute of Occupational Safety and Health (NIOSH), and with psychologists and colleagues in other key professions in making the world a better place to work.

Psychologists have a long history of involvement in the study of human behavior in organizations. Hugo Munsterberg, APA President in 1898, conducted pioneering studies of industrial safety and accidents, and Robert Yerkes, 1917 APA President, directed the efforts of the team of psychologists who developed and validated sound psychometric instruments for personnel selection and classification in World War I (Offermann & Goving, 1990).[1] While psychologists continue to work on problems of occupational safety and health, we have not given such problems the attention that is warranted in a growing area of research and practice. This conference was both an attempt to change that situation and a first step in demonstrating that change.

Only a decade ago, Joseph Matarazzo, 1989 APA President, recognized behavioral health as a new interdisciplinary specialty within behavioral medicine, and identified a unique role for psychology within this specialty, which he labeled health psychology. In response to Matarazzo's challenge for psychologists to become more involved in health psychology, many answered this call and the frontiers of health psychology have continued to expand. We now have an APA Division of Health Psychology with more than 3,000 members. Together with Dr. Patrick DeLeon and Dr. J. Donald Millar, Director of NIOSH, Joe Matarazzo was instrumental in stimulating the collaborative effort that resulted in this highly successful conference. He is also primarily responsible for creating and providing effective leadership for the APA Science Directorate Task Force on Health and Behavior. Unfortunately, Dr. Matarazzo was unable to attend the conference, but he continues to challenge psychologists to become more involved in health-related issues.

Although industrial and health psychology are the two most obvious fields within our discipline with direct relevance for workplace wellness and occupational stress, other specialties within psychology also continue to make contributions to the health and well-being of our nation's workers. Clinical and counseling psychologists treat employees experiencing stress and psychological disorders in the workplace. Researchers in behavioral medicine and personality have identified var-

---

[1] Offermann, L. R., & Gowing, M. R. (1990). Organizations of the future: Changes and challenges. *American Psychologist, 45,* 95–108.

iables that influence vulnerability to stress, such as Type-A characteristics, hostility, and hardiness. And social psychologists have demonstrated the importance of stress buffers, such as social support, job role ambiguity, and the psychological climate of the workplace.

For their seminal role in organizing this conference, I would like to acknowledge the effective leadership of Dr. Gwendolyn Puryear Keita of the APA Public Interest Directorate, and Dr. Steven L. Sauter of the NIOSH Division of Biomedical and Behavioral Sciences. We are also indebted to Professors Stanislav Kasl, Frank Landy, and James Campbell Quick, chairs respectively of the Surveillance, Work Design, and Health Promotion Panels, for their outstanding contributions in developing the reports and conference presentations of their panels, and to Sonja Preston for her skill and dedication in coordinating the conference activities.

The APA is strongly committed to addressing issues of occupational safety and health as they relate to stress and well-being and psychological disorders in the workplace. This conference was but one indicator of that commitment.

Charles D. Spielberger, PhD
President, American Psychological Association
Director, Center for Research in Behavioral
Medicine and Health Psychology

Preface

The papers presented in this volume are part of the proceedings of a conference entitled *Work and Well-Being: An Agenda for the 1990s*, cosponsored by the APA and NIOSH. This conference was a historic event, marking the first APA/NIOSH collaboration.

Work and Well-Being: An Agenda for the 1990s was an interdisciplinary conference which brought together over 300 experts from the fields of psychology, occupational medicine, epidemiology, public health, and business. Included were researchers, policy analysts, managers, and medical and human resource specialists representing industry, labor, government, and academia. Participants hailed from the United States, Puerto Rico, Canada, England, Finland, and Sweden. Their objective ratings showed the conference to be a success as measured in terms of interest, impact, knowledge transfer, and networking.

The conference had two major phases. The first phase involved the finalization of an action plan to protect the psychological health of workers. This plan was based upon more general formulations contained in the NIOSH-proposed National Strategy for Prevention of Work-Related Psychological Disorders (this article, originally appearing in the *American Psychologist*, Vol. 45, No. 10, is reprinted in this volume). In the year preceding the meeting, 32 experts from the fields of psychology, occupational medicine, epidemiology, and public health were recruited to assist in crafting the action plan. This publication presents the results of this effort, along with additional reports providing a background for the meeting and action plan.

The NIOSH strategy for protecting the psychological well-being of workers emphasized the need to improve working conditions, to improve education and health service delivery pertinent to work-related psychological disorders, and to improve the surveillance of work-related psychological disorders and risk factors. Information dissemination, research, training, and policy development cross-cut each of these areas. Accordingly, three panels (comprised of the 32 experts) were organized to develop action plans in job design, education/mental health service delivery, and surveillance. These panels were chaired by Dr. Frank Landy, Dr. James Campbell Quick, and Dr. Stanislav Kasl, respectively.

The work process for each panel, although basically similar, varied somewhat between panels. Consistent throughout the panels was that, using the NIOSH strategy as a starting point, all of the panel chairs developed a position paper suggesting proactive steps in their respective areas of focus. Dr. Landy began by preparing a well-developed first draft of a job design position paper which was circulated to his panel members for review. Panelists' comments were incorporated into a revised document. Several interactions of this process occurred. The final revision, presented in this volume, was prepared in response to reactions from panelists and conference attendees following presentation of the paper at the conference. Panelists also prepared final written commentaries which are reproduced in this volume following the job design paper.

The paper on health promotion, education, and treatment was developed along a similar path, except that Dr. Quick sent his panelists a brief outline and requested input which was then utilized in preparation of the first draft of the paper. Again, multiple iterations of review and revision occurred. Panelists' final comments were fully incorporated into the final draft of the paper appearing in this volume and, therefore, are not shown separately.

Preparation of the surveillance paper followed a somewhat different procedure. Dr. Kasl prepared a major paper in near final form. After presentation of this paper at the conference and response of panelists and conference participants, the revised version of the paper (appearing in this volume) was prepared by Dr. Kasl. As with the Landy paper, final commentaries by the panelists are given following the paper.

Without exception, the papers provoked extensive discussion by conference participants. Wishing not to lose the many rich insights contained in these discussions, moderators for the panel sessions in which the papers were presented were asked to summarize the discourse during the sessions. These summaries are also presented in this volume for the job design and education/mental health service delivery sessions. For the surveillance session, the commentary by conference participants largely mirrored that of the panelists.

Beyond the three position papers and associated commentaries, this volume also contains the texts of several keynote papers delivered at the conference. These papers provide a backdrop and add urgency to the need to develop an effective action plan for protection of worker mental health. The papers by Drs. Sauter and Millar outline a decade of NIOSH concern and action relating to growing stress problems in the workplace. In an invited address, Dr. Lennart Levi discussed the relationship between occupational environment, psychosocial factors and worker health and well-being through an examination of the theoretical concepts, current research, and applications from Sweden. Finally, we reproduce in this volume "Sharon's Monologue" from *The Department*, by playwright Barbara Garson. This piece was delivered by actress Sharon Shambouger as part of a luncheon address on the second day of the conference. In delivery, it served as a powerful reminder of the group of individuals who were the focus of the conference itself—the worker. In the second phase of the conference, 15 paper sessions and over 30 poster presentations focused on recent scientific studies and developments addressing the causes, effects, and control of stress and associated mental health problems in the workplace. These reports are featured in a companion volume, *Stress and Well-Being: Assessments and Interventions for Occupational Mental Health*, edited by Drs. James Campbell Quick, Lawrence Murphy, and Joseph Hurrell.

We present these proceedings documents recognizing that psychological strain is quickly becoming one of the most prevalent, costly, and debilitating forms of occupational ill-health. We hope that they will be useful in alerting industry, labor, government, and academia to the need for action to protect and enrich the psychological well-being of the workforce, and in providing a schema for job and program design to achieve this end.

Gwendolyn Puryear Keita, PhD   Steven L. Sauter, PhD

Part I

Introductory Remarks

Remarks of C. Everett Koop for the Opening of the APA/NIOSH Conference on "Work and Well-Being: An Agenda for the 1990s"

Congratulations to the American Psychological Association and to the National Institute for Occupational Safety and Health of the U.S. Public Health Service. Their common vision and joint efforts to organize this significant conference is a much appreciated expression of leadership today. This conference on work and well-being is actually an extension of three earlier national meetings sponsored by NIOSH on work and health intended to work out, hammer and tong, a national strategy for the prevention of 10 leading occupational diseases and injuries. I want to express my thanks to the director of NIOSH ASG, Dr. J. Donald Millar, for his sustained efforts and faithful leadership in the pursuit of strategies for preventing diseases and injuries and for promoting health in the workplace. It is also appropriate to thank the many partners of NIOSH in labor, business, and academia who have been working steadily on these issues and challenges as well. Many of you I know personally, and I have come to appreciate your commitment and the fruit of your labors.

I am pleased to see that this conference will not only be specifically discussing occupational mental health and stress in the workplace, but also issues of work and health more broadly. We need more discovery and discussion in this area. We need to build on the foundation of understanding extant from traditional worksite health promotion programs. I say "build" because evaluation studies in this area have been plagued with methodological shortfalls and have, therefore, been inconclusive in their results and findings. In addition, knowledge gained from the research and evaluation enterprise has failed too often to be meaningful and useful for guiding policy decisions *in* and *for* the workplace. I hope you will address *this issue* as you think through agendae for the 1990s and beyond.

I also hope you will turn your collective attention to *minorities, women, and older workers* and to the *special* burden of stress on them in the workplace, and in society in general. Issues of race, gender, and aging continue to impact health and well-being disproportionately across the nation. I hope you will remember the link between work stress and family stress, the added burden of difficult economic times, the looming threat for many of unemployment, and the stressful necessity of working multiple jobs for the economic survival of so many of our families.

I am encouraged by your visible partnerships . . . between the academy, business, public health, labor, and the profession of psychology . . . between NIOSH and APA . . . between public health and psychology. These are meaningful, practical, appropriate, powerful partnerships. Such partnerships hold promise for real, substantive progress in carrying out an agenda for the 1990s . . . and beyond.

Finally, let me say that our nation needs a much larger sustained cadre of professionals who have a focused expertise on health in the workplace, who can serve the corporate business world, who can consult effectively with labor, who can teach with excellence, and carry out practical research in our academies. I encourage you to deliberate on this need, and to take deliberate action in support of investments in higher education investments . . . by both private and public sectors, beginning perhaps with doctoral and post-doctoral training of psychologists in work and health.

Alexander Graham Bell once said, "When one door closes, another opens; but we often look so long and so regretfully upon the closed door that we do not see the one that has opened for us." May you see the open doors today.

Thank you for the privilege of serving as your honorary chairman. Best blessings on what I know will be a first-rate, benchmark meeting.

J. Donald Millar

Public Enlightenment and Mental Health in the Workplace

In 1985 and 1986, when NIOSH developed strategies for preventing psychological disorders and other leading work-related diseases and injuries, one of our major concerns was whether the strategies would be put to use. The thinking was that, although these strategies looked good on paper, they would be worthless if action were not taken to implement them. Thus, this APA/NIOSH conference represents a major step forward in our quest to reduce the incidence of psychological disorders in the workplace, and it is certainly a very satisfying moment for NIOSH.

In 1982, when NIOSH first developed the list of leading work-related diseases and injuries (see Part Two of this book), the public was very skeptical about several of the categories. Two categories, *cardiovascular disease* and *psychological disorders* received a less than enthusiastic reception. However, today we have been vindicated, and few would argue the association of these categories with workplace stressors. Today mental disorders are the leading cause for social security disability claims in the United States. Dr. Steven Sauter, Chief of the Motivational and Stress Research Section of the NIOSH Division of Biomedical and Behavioral Sciences, will give us more insight into this remarkable development in a synopsis of the national strategy for preventing psychological disorders in the workplace (see Part Two of this volume). In anticipation of this, I want to present a brief background of the top 10 list itself.

When I was named director of NIOSH in 1981, the one painfully obvious thing that I discovered was the great need for focus within the occupational safety and health field. A very basic question had yet to be answered: *What are the most important safety and health problems faced by workers in this country?* Thus, with the help of many experts both inside and outside the field, NIOSH tried to answer this question by evaluating (a) the frequency of occurrence of the problem, (b) the severity of the problem in affected individuals, and (c) the amenability of the problem to prevention. This lead to the creation of the "Ten Leading Work-Related Diseases and Injuries."

NIOSH has taken a lot of heat for some of the inclusions on this list, and indeed there seem to be a few categories whose status as an "occupational" health threat remains open for debate. However, there is no doubt that job-related stress and other psychological disorders are rapidly becoming one of the most pressing occupational safety and health concerns in the country today.

The Emergence of Psychological Disorders as a Major Health Threat

Consider the following items:

- Workers' compensation payments have nearly doubled from $13.6 billion in 1980 to $27.4 billion in 1987 and are expected to top $90 billion by the turn of the century (U.S. Department of Commerce, 1990). Interestingly enough, the number of claims resulting from mental disorders has increased during that period of time as well (see Sauter, Part Two, this volume).
- A conference on "Depression in the Workplace" sponsored by the University of Pittsburgh was held June 12–13, 1990 in Pittsburgh, Pennsylvania, that revealed an interesting statistic: Approximately 1 in 10 workers are suffering from depression, and the cost to society and business is nearly $27 billion annually.
- The University of Wisconsin released a study in October 1990 on occupational stress in the telecommunications industry that indicated that electronic monitoring of workers exacerbates job stress (Smith, Carayon-Sainfort, Rogers, Lim & LeGrande, 1991). Similar results were found in a study published by the "9 to 5, Working Women Education Fund" (Danann, 1990).
- A Westinghouse Electric Corporation/University of Pittsburgh School of Medicine study determined that workers suffered from higher than expected rates of depression, and concluded that occupational physicians should scrutinize more closely the role stress plays in workers' mental health (Bromet et al., 1990).
- In 1984, Dr. Craig Wright at the Gehrmann Lecture of the American College of Occupational Medicine (ACOM) in New Orleans states that (a) the issue of greatest prominence to the workplace in the 1990s would be stress and (b) if XEROX had one thing to do to improve production, it would be to institute a marriage maintenance program, since divorce is "killing them." (The audience laughed at this latter remark, but, today, if you look in some of the magazines found in airplanes you will note courses advertised to train executives about marriage problems.)

It is obvious today that synergism plays an important role in the etiology of disease. Good examples include smoking in conjunction with asbestos exposures and smoking with radon gas exposures. What the worker brings to the job may be as important as what the job brings to the worker. In other words, we cannot ignore the role of multiple factors in disease causation. Stress off the job can play an important role with stress on the job. Thus, it is obvious that psychological disorders in the workplace have emerged as a major health concern in this country today.

Even though we feel somewhat vindicated, we would feel still better if we knew more. For instance, we need to know more precisely what is the true incidence of psychological disorders in this country. What is the extent of this epidemic? Like other problems in occupational health, the most difficult thing to determine is exactly how much of the problem is a direct result of conditions at the workplace and how much is the result of factors outside of the work environment. This is a major concern for all of us. How can we distinguish between occupational-induced stress, for example, and nonoccupational-induced stress? We must ensure that we have sound methodology for determining the difference between the two; otherwise, there might be questions raised concerning such issues as the validity of workers compensation claims for stress. Fortunately, researchers are working hard to upgrade surveillance procedures, and this will pay off for us down the road.

Another gray area in determining just how big of a role psychological disorders play in occupational health is the degree of impact on a person's *physical* health. Exactly how often does job stress lead to cardiovascular problems or other physical problems, like alcoholism? There is evidence to support this latter subject. A 1988 study from the Finnish Institute of Occupational Health concluded that "alcohol consumption among Finnish doctors seems to be higher than that of the general population in Finland, and heavy drinking seems to be associated with stress and burnout" (Olkinuora et al., 1988). Certainly, there is a connection here. But to what extent are these things related? That is the *basic* subject on which we must continue to do research.

As with occupational health causes, we cannot focus all of our attention directly on the workers. We must continue to learn more about the "management climate" as well. Do employees with high levels of stress work for tyrannical managers who run their staff like recruits in boot camp? For that matter, do employees with lower levels of stress work for managers with a more modern, laid-back approach? One book, *Healthy Work: Stress, Productivity, and the Reconstruction of Working Life* (Karasek & Theorell, 1990), examines the working environment at great length. One interesting excerpt from the book says that ". . . all stress models have one distinguishing feature: the environment is the source or the cause (albeit not the sole source), and the individual is the target or locus of effects" (p. 86). This passage makes a lot of sense, because it is totally consistent with the NIOSH philosophy: We are not in this business to find fault with the worker; all workers are human and therefore subject to making mistakes. We are interested in what is wrong with the work environment that could prompt some of those mistakes. We will certainly have more luck trying to change the work environment than trying to change human behavior so that workers will never make mistakes.

We are entering, then, a new age of work in America. The workplace is being adapted to create a better environment for workers in which to flourish. The idea is simple: A better work environment will enhance productivity. Critics might point to the rigid, but very productive, work environment of the Japanese as a contradictory paradigm, but it is known that stress is a major problem in that culture. What price do we pay for greater productivity? That is one of the questions that we are tackling, and the next decade or two should provide some interesting answers. One way that we can come together around this issue to enact prevention will be through creative partnerships such as the one represented by this meeting between APA and NIOSH. As I mentioned earlier, the prevention strategies were not created just to be looked at. Action is needed, and this meeting is a positive step in the right direction.

Part II

Proposed National Strategies for the Prevention of Leading Work-Related Diseases and Injuries: Psychological Disorders

Steven L. Sauter

Introduction to the NIOSH Proposed National Strategy

Occupational stress is emerging as one of the principal social and occupational health concerns of the 1990s. In response to this concern, NIOSH has developed a multipoint strategy for control of stress in the workplace, and now APA and NIOSH have joined forces in a national meeting to translate this strategy into practical action steps. Before highlighting the key provisions of the NIOSH strategy, however, I would like to provide some background on events of the 1980s that combined to make job stress such an important issue today.

The current focus on job stress appears to be driven in part by legal precedence, increased media attention, and evolving medico-social values giving greater priority to the psychological well-being of workers. But perhaps most important, and underlying these forces, are recent changes in the nature of work. As had been projected for some time, employment in service sectors of the economy outstripped employment in manufacturing jobs in the early 1980s (Bezold, Carlson, & Peck, 1986). For example, cashier work, janitorial work, truck driving, waitressing, and nursing are projected to be among the fastest growing jobs in the period 1985–1995 (Silvestri & Lukasiewicz, 1985). Social scientists predicted that the growth of these types of jobs may have implications for the health and well-being of the workforce. Part of the concern focused on possible declines in wages and health benefits; but perhaps more relevant were fears that working conditions in these types of jobs (e.g., hectic, repetitive tasks with little opportunity for skill use, learning, or advancement) were prescriptions for stress (see Karasek & Theorell, 1990).

Consistent with these expectations, a national trend toward increased worker compensation claims for job stress soon developed. This effect is especially apparent in California worker compensation data which show a rapid increase, beginning in 1981, in the rate of claims for mental problems, whereas compensation rates for all other types of claims continued a modest decline (California Workers Compensation Institute, 1990). According to the National Council for Compensation Insurance, by 1982, stress claims accounted for 11% of all worker illness compensation claims, and the costs exceeded the average cost of all other types of claims (National Council on Compensation Insurance, 1985).

A strikingly similar phenomenon occurred for Social Security disability awards. For years, disability due to circulatory or musculoskeletal disorders dominated these types of awards; but just as service employment surpassed manufacturing employment in the early 1980s, so, too, did Social Security awards for mental disorders surpass awards for musculoskeletal disorders. With a current prevalence rate of about 20–25%, awards for mental disorders are now more common than for any other type of disability; more so than awards for even circulatory problems (Social Security Administration, 1989). This effect is far more dramatic in the prime working years. Workers below age 50 experience as much as two to four times the disability for mental disorders as for musculoskeletal or circulatory problems (Social Security Administration, 1989).

In simple terms, all this translates to the fact that nearly 600,000 workers are disabled for reasons of psychological disorders. The fiscal, let alone emotional, burden is dramatic. Annual payments to these individuals can be estimated at about $5 billion,[1] with another $.5 billion in payments to their families and dependents. Lost wages can be estimated at nearly $10 billion.[2] Although the effects of job stress per se have not been isolated, some sources place the total annual cost of stress-related disorders in the $100 billion range.

To be completely candid, it is possible that worker compensation claims for stress may be tracking legal precedents more than changing working conditions, or they may reflect simply increased attention to a problem that has been with us since the dawn of industrialization. Also, it must be remembered that Social Security disability allowance recipients are not necessarily disabled for work-related reasons (although occupational differentials in types and prevalence of disability awards suggest an important occupational contribution).[3] Still, this does not diminish the importance of the issue. Regardless of etiology, the enormous prevalence and economic costs of psychological disorders in the workforce make this a problem that neither industry nor society at large can ignore.

Not only do national health and compensation data speak to the importance of psychological disorders as a pre-eminent occupational health problem, but so, too, do data from workers and managers themselves. Especially impressive in this regard are the results of the 1985 National Health Interview Survey. According to survey results, a projected 11 million workers report "health-endangering" levels of mental stress at work (Shilling & Brackbill, 1987). Only one other workplace hazard, loud noise, was reported to be more prevalent. From the management side, a recent survey of medical and personnel directors of Fortune 1000 firms revealed that over 70% of respondents rated mental health problems as fairly-to-very pervasive in the workplace (Warshaw, 1990).

The purpose of the APA/NIOSH conference, however, was not to detail the scope of job stress and psychological disorders as occupational health problems. Rather, the purpose was to accelerate efforts toward control of the problem. In this regard, special tribute is due to Dr. Millar and NIOSH Division Directors who, in the early 1980s—and without the benefit of the data available today—boldly ranked psychological disorders among the leading occupational injuries and diseases.

This action by NIOSH spawned a collective effort to develop a national strategy, or blueprint, for preventing work-related psychological disorders. The strategy was drafted initially by a NIOSH working group, and refined with input from The Association of Schools for Public Health, and from experts from the APA, labor, and industry. The final version of the strategy was published in the October 1990

---

[1]Based on average award costs for all types of disability.

[2]Based on private sector, nonsupervisory salaries.

[3]See, for example, Murphy (1991) and Social Security Administration (1988).

issue of the *American Psychologist* (Sauter, Murphy, & Hurrell, 1990; Part Two, this volume).

There are four cornerstones in this NIOSH blueprint for protecting the mental health of workers. The cornerstones include:

- well-designed jobs,
- surveillance systems to detect psychological disorders and underlying risk factors,
- education of workers and managers on the signs, causes, effects, and control of work-related psychological disorders, and
- improved mental health service delivery for workers.

With regard to *job design*, the strategy concluded that there is sufficient information on the nature of stressful working conditions to allow generic recommendations for designing psychologically healthy jobs. Included in the strategy are recommendations pertaining to the design of the following aspects of jobs: work pace, work autonomy, work schedule, work roles, job security and career development, the social environment at work, and the nature of tasks performed. In 1986, these suggestions were published by the Centers for Disease Control (CDC) (Centers for Disease Control [CDC], 1986). To the best of my knowledge, this represents the first time a comprehensive set of principles for organizational aspects of work has been issued by a federal body.

Of course, the working group also recognized that our knowledge of risk factors for job stress is far from complete and that continuing research is needed. Of special concern are unknown risks associated with:

- an aging workforce,
- rapid expansion of certain occupations (e.g., health care) where stress is already believed to be a significant problem,
- constrained opportunities for the increasing population of women and minorities in the workforce, and
- new electronic technologies such as computer automation, which hold potential for wide-ranging changes, both positive and negative, in the organization of work.

A second cornerstone of the NIOSH strategy is *surveillance*. The Strategy concluded that there was need for increased data gathering for purposes of detecting and reacting to emerging stress problems. As a related matter, additional epidemiologic investigation of suspected risk factors for job stress, including occupations at risk, and the health effects of job stress is also needed.

A major impediment to progress in this area is the expense and logisticis of such data gathering. To economize, some investigators have attempted to utilize existing national survey or administrative data, such as the National Health Interview Survey or the Social Security disability allowance file, for such purposes (e.g., see Murphy, 1991). Although these data sources have potential utility for surveillance and epidemiologic studies of job stress, they are not designed for this purpose and crucial data on working conditions and stress-related health outcomes are often missing.

To improve upon this situation, the NIOSH strategy recommends increased coordination between job stress researchers and agencies such as the National Center for Health Statistics (NCHS), the National Institute of Mental Health (NIMH) or the CDC, to help shape periodic health surveys by these institutions to improve their utility for surveillance and epidemiologic study of stress. Increased data collection, guided by stress specialists, at the industry level is also likely to yield dividends. However, significant progress may not be possible without specialized surveys of stress factors and health outcomes. Until such improvements in mechanisms for data collection are realized, answers to fundamental questions, such as the incidence of stress-related disorders, or the jobs and working conditions posing the greatest risk for stress, will remain uncertain.

Training is the third element of the NIOSH strategy. Prevention of work-related psychological disorders depends ultimately on the ability of workers and managers to:

- recognize signs of psychological strain,
- recognize underlying risk factors, and
- implement control measures.

Unfortunately, the resources to foster these skills are sparse and prospects for improvement are not fully encouraging. Government efforts such as funding of training programs for workers have not kept pace with the problem. Job stress is a subject still foreign to many professional and graduate training programs, particularly in the health sciences. Few medical schools require coursework in this area. Similarly, a 1983 study at Yale (Neale, Singer, Schwartz, & Schwartz, 1983) showed little corporate investment in employee training in the area of job stress.[4]

To counter this problem, the NIOSH strategy calls for the mobilization of key professional societies such as the APA, the Human Factors Society, and the American Occupational Medicine Association, to sharpen their focus and strengthen divisional or technical group activities in the area of work and mental health.

Shop floor and management training are also recommended. Courses, books, and resouces specifically designed for this purpose are badly needed. Accreditation bodies need to ensure that health and mental health care providers achieve a degree of competence in the area of work and mental health. As one example of a positive development of this nature, Dr. James Quick, in collaboration with the APA, was partially successful in including such training for primary health care providers among the *Year 2000 Health Objectives for the Nation* (Public Health Service, 1991).

Finally, the NIOSH strategy emphasizes the need for improved mental health services for workers. Although there has been an exponential growth in industry employee assistance and health promotion programs which provide a vehicle for these services, the vast majority of workers in America have no mental health services available through their employment. Additionally, mental health programs

---

[4]This situation appears to have improved in recent years. A recent national survey found that 26% of work sites offered some type of stress management program (Office of Disease Prevention and Health Promotion, 1989).

in industry have been criticized for a narrow focus on "problem" employees, drug abuse, and lifestyles risk factors, as opposed to risky working conditions.

In contrast, the NIOSH strategy calls for the development of mental health services for workers that:

- place a greater priority on primary prevention,
- are integrated into the overall occupational health care program,
- recognize the effects of work-related stressors, and
- provide mechanisms for intervention involving organizational change.

Fortunately, there is evidence that industrial mental health programs are evolving in this direction (Bezold et al. 1986; George-Perry, 1988).

Conclusions

The APA/NIOSH conference bears witness that this four-point NIOSH strategy has already had some impact. For the first time in the United States, scientists, practitioners, and policy-makers from industry, labor, government, and academia assembled in a national forum to discuss tactics to control job stress. The influence of the NIOSH strategy, however, has reached beyond the United States. The general framework of the strategy has been adopted by the Ontario Ministry of Labor Task Force on Occupational Stress. Additionally, the strategy has been published in Chinese (Chinese Industrial Safety and Health Association, 1990), and is also being reprinted in French by Health and Welfare Canada.

The next step, and the purpose of the conference, was to translate the strategy into a concrete action plan. To assist in this effort, Drs. James Quick, Stan Kasl, and Frank Landy, each backed by a panel of experts, analyzed the NIOSH strategy and developed position papers proposing specific interventions as well as needed research (Part Three, this volume). The APA/NIOSH conference then served as a forum for the critical review and revision of these position papers. In this regard, the conference presented a special opportunity and challenge—to develop a consensus statement which could have a sweeping influence on the future of occupational stress research, practice, and policy in this country.

References

Bezold, C., Carlson, R. J., & Peck, J. C. (1986). *The future of work and health.* Dover, MA: Auburn House.

California Workers' Compensation Institute. (1990, June). *Mental stress claims in California workers' compensation: Incidence, costs, and trends.* San Francisco, CA: Author.

Centers for Disease Control. (1986, October). Current trends: Leading work-related diseases and injuries. *Morbidity and Mortality Weekly Reports, 35*(9), 613–614, 619–621.

Chinese Industrial Safety and Health Association. (1990). Prevention of psychological disorders. *Industrial Safety and Health (Taiwan), 16*, 9, 18–26.

Karasek, R., & Theorell, T. (1990). *Healthy Work: Stress, productivity, and the reconstruction of working life.* London: Basic Books.

Murphy, L. R. (1991). Job dimensions associated with severe disability due to cardiovascular disease. *Journal of Clinical Epidemiology, 44*(2), 155–166.

National Council on Compensation Insurance. (1985). *Emotional stress in the workplace: New legal rights in the eighties*. New York: Author.

Neale, M. S., Singer, J. A., Schwartz, J. L., & Schwartz, G. E. (1983, March). *Yale-NIOSH occupational stress project*. Paper presented at the 4th Annual Meeting of the Society of Behavioral Medicine, Baltimore, MD.

Office of Disease Prevention and Health Promotion. (1989). *National survey of work site health promotion activities*. Washington, DC: U.S. Government Printing Office.

Public Health Service. (1991). *Promoting health/preventing disease: Year 2000 objectives for the nation*. Washington, DC: Public Health Service.

Sauter, S. L., Murphy, L. R., & Hurrell, J. J., Jr. (1990). Prevention of work-related psychological disorders: A national strategy proposed by the National Institute of Occupational Safety and Health (NIOSH). *American Psychologist, 45*(10), 146–158.

Shilling, S., & Brackbill, R. M. (1987). Occupational health and safety risks and potential health consequences perceived by U.S. workers. *Public Health Reports, 102,* 36–46.

Silvestri, G. T., & Lukasiewick, J. M. (1985, November). Occupational employment projections: The 1984–1995 outlook. *Monthly Labor Review,* 42–57.

Social Security Administration. (1988). *Characteristics of Social Security disability insurance beneficiaries* (SSA Publication No. 64-032). Washington, DC: Social Security Administration.

Social Security Administration. (1989). *Social Security Bulletin: Annual statistical supplement, 1989*. Washington, DC: U.S. Government Printing Office.

Warshaw, L. J. (1990). *Stress, anxiety and depression in the workplace: Report of the NYGBH/Gallup Survey*. New York: New York Business Group on Health.

Steven L. Sauter, Lawrence R. Murphy, and
Joseph J. Hurrell, Jr.

Prevention of Work-Related Psychological Disorders

A National Strategy Proposed by the National Institute for Occupational Safety and Health (NIOSH)

With regard to the *physical* health and safety of workers, the work environment is generally viewed as a threat or risk factor. Similarly, work can have adverse consequences for *mental* health, but it can also have an important positive impact. In Western society at least, work experience plays an integral role in psychological development and well-being.

This perspective is aptly expressed for Albert Camus (1955): "Without risk, all life goes rotten, but when work is soulless, life stifles and dies." Smith and Smith (1973) claimed that occupations can provide a framework for the organization of behavior. Gardell (1971) suggested that "due to influences exerted by the Protestant ethic and other culturally conditioned factors . . . it is probable that most people perceive work to be one of the most important life areas for the individual's general satisfaction" (p. 149). Psychoanalytic theorists view work as a primary source of self-identity. Lazarus (1981) recounted Erikson's (1963) depiction of Biff, a character in Arthur Miller's *Death of a Salesman,* as suffering "ego-diffusion" for lack of ability to develop a sense of usefulness or productivity (p. 57). Hertzberg (1966), McGregor (1960), and Argyris (1964) wrote of motivation, esteem, and self-actualization through work. Lazarus saw another psychologically healthful function of work: a form of coping and refuge and a haven against problems, loneliness, and depression. Several studies on termination from work tend to bear our such tenets. Linn, Sandifer, and Stein (1985) found increased levels of somatization, depression, and anxiety in the unemployed, as well as increased visits to the doctor, medication use, and days in bed.

These considerations add significance to the prevention of work-related psychological disorders and distinguish such efforts from efforts toward the prevention of other occupational injuries and diseases; that is, the promise is not only reduced

Other members of the working group included Charles Althafer, Linda Cahill, Alexander Cohen, Michael Colligan, Bernadine Kuchinski, Joann Schloemer, Mitchell Singal, and Rebecca Stanivich.

morbidity, but the potential to actually enhance psychological growth and well-being.

Focus on the Strategy

Disorders of Current Interest

An initial hurdle in developing a national strategy to prevent psychological disorders is a semantic one. The very expression *psychological disorders* connotes a category of problems encompassing a wide array of social, behavioral, and biomedical conditions with diverse and often unknown etiologies. The focus of this strategy is on psychological disorders of general concern in the occupational health arena—those that are commonly investigated under the general rubric of "job stress"[1] and are believed to be amendable to workplace interventions. These are not necessarily conditions that are always identifiable under recognized systems of medical classification, such as the International Classification of Diseases (U.S. Department of Health, Education and Welfare [DHEW], 1968) or the *Diagnostic and Statistical Manual of Mental Disorders* (DSM-III) of the American Psychiatric Association (1980). Nevertheless, they can represent significant functional disturbances or risks for development of clinical disorders. These conditions include (a) affective disturbances such as anxiety, depression, and job dissatisfaction, (b) maladaptive behavioral and life-style patterns, and (c) chemical dependencies and alcohol abuse.

The strategy is less concerned with the area of chronic mental illness because occupational causation of those illnesses is not well documented. Furthermore, those problems frequently require removal from the work force or hospitalization, making workplace interventions for their control difficult. The strategy is not concerned with disturbances of psychological functions attributable to organic, genetic, or neurologic pathogenesis, although such mechanisms do not preclude a workplace basis (e.g., exposure to neurotoxic chemicals). Some of these problems are treated in other NIOSH prevention strategies, for example, the prevention strategies for neurotoxic disorders and disorders of reproduction (National Institute for Occupational Health and Safety [NIOSH], 1988). Finally, many acute and chronic somatic disorders are widely accepted as having a basis in job stress, notably cardiovascular disease (CVD). Beyond the recognition of CVD and other somatic disturbances as potential manifestations or sequelae of psychological disorders, the present strategy

---

[1]There is little consensus or consistency in the interpretation and use of the terms *stress* or *job stress* (sometimes connoting causal factors, sometimes outcomes, and sometimes intermediary processes). It is beyond the intent of this article to resolve the ambiguity. To avoid misinterpretation, an effort is made here to use more precise language. However, for economy of expression the terms *stress* and *job stress* are used sparingly in the text to refer to a body of literature or field of study concerned principally with the adverse physical and mental health effects of psychosocial aspects of work. These terms and their variations (e.g., stressors, negative stress, stressful) also appear enclosed in quotes throughout the text in reference to source literature, but only where the original report does not allow replacement with a less ambiguous term.

is confined to disorders in the psychological—behavior domain. (CVD is the subject of a separate NIOSH prevention strategy, NIOSH, 1985.)[2]

Occupational Connection and Prevention Focus

The occupational involvement in psychological disorders is not a matter of dispute in the mental health community. "Psychosocial stressors," specifying "occupational stress," as a major diagnostic axis is listed in the DSM-III. The present prevention strategy is particularly concerned with psychological disorders that bear a relation to working conditions. At the same time, the strategy acknowledges the interplay of work and nonwork factors in the etiology of psychological disorders and the difficulty of attributing psychological disorders exclusively to either domain. Accordingly, the strategy not only focuses on the understanding and control of job factors that contribute to psychological disorders in workers, but through promotion of improved workplace mental health services, strives also to remedy workers' psychological disorders regardless of a clear occupational basis.

This approach is consistent with current perspectives on the domain of occupational medicine. In the 1983 George H. Gehrmann Lecture of the American Occupation Medicine Association, Collings (1984) noted a "relentless" trend toward a "fuzzier and fuzzier" boundary between the occupational and nonoccupational in terms of etiology and treatment of disease (p. 511). Collings asserted that no medical condition escapes the influence of eight hours of daily work. Moreover Hilker (Hilker & Asma, 1975), speaking as medical director of Illinois Bell, declared that industry has both a responsibility and business interest (citing costs of personnel and productivity problems) in rehabilitating employees for psychological disorders. Hilker also suggested that rehabilitative efforts may be more effective when conducted in an occupational (as opposed to a community) setting.

Scope of Psychological Disorders as a National Health Problem

Currently, no surveillance system exists to adequately gauge the national scope of psychological health disorders. The best estimate to date of the magnitude of psychological disorders as a national health problem stems from data in the NIMH Epidemiologic Catchment Area study (Freedman, 1984). In this study, 17,000 community residents at five regional sites were interviews using the Diagnostic Interview Schedule (DIS) (Robins, Heltzer, Croughan, Williams, & Spitzer, 1981). The results are sobering. First reports indicate a six-month prevalence of psychological disorders about equal to the prevalence of hypertension. Specifically, from 17% to 23% of adults were found to have been afflicted with one or more of over a dozen major psychological disorders listed in the DSM-III; from 7% to 15% of adults were

---

[2]Although somatic disease is excluded from this strategy, specific attention should be given to the increasing body of evidence linking physical illness and psychological factors. Recent developments in the field of psychoimmunology are most striking. A review by Marx (1985) described pervasive anatomic and biochemical links between the immune and nervous systems to explain the influence of mood on susceptibility to disease. Suggested declines in immune function even with "commonplace stressors" are of particular interest (Kiecolt-Glaser, 1985; Kiecolt-Glaser, Speicher, Holliday, & Glaser, 1984).

found to have had one or more of the various anxiety disorders alone, and rates for substance abuse were 6% to 7%. Lifetime prevalence rates were considerably higher (29% to 38% for major disorders). Psychological disorders were most common among adults during the prime working age of 25 to 44 years. These findings reinforce earlier estimates of a population prevalence rate for psychological disorders approaching 25% (President's Commission on Mental Health, 1978).

Other indicators affirm the importance of psychological disorders as a growing national problem. Research by NIOSH has shown that mental disorders were the third most disabling condition among Social Security Administration (SSA) disability allowance recipients for the period 1975–1976, preceded only by musculoskeletal injuries and circulatory diseases (Fishback, Dacey, Sestito, & Green, 1986). Fully 11% of all SSA disability allowances were for mental disorders. By 1988, mental disorders had become the most prevalent disabling condition among SSA disability allowance recipients, accounting for 21% of all allowances (Social Security Bulletin, 1989). In a 1985 study of medication use, Valium was the fourth most commonly prescribed drug in the United States ("Top 200 Drugs," 1985). Two of the three most frequently prescribed drugs are specific for the treatment of hypertension, a condition that can have a psychological component. In general, psychotherapeutic agents accounted for one fourth of all outpatient prescriptions in 1984 (Baum, Kennedy, Knapp, & Faich, 1985).

Patterns observed in the use of health services add to the evidence. In a National Ambulatory Medical Care Survey of office visits to internists during 1980–1981, Cypress (1984) found that 3.3% of all visits resulted in diagnoses of mental illness. The percentage was nearly double for the 25- to 44-year age group. According to a 1980 study of patient needs in community primary care centers, the most common request for health care involved psychosocial problems (Good, Good, & Massi, 1983). A study among members of a health maintenance organization in the Washington, DC area found that the health education topic "anxiety and stress" was most preferred by members of both sexes (Nickalson, Donaldson, & Oh, 1983).

Complementing this finding, the results of the 1985 National Health Interview Survey showed that 75% of the general population reported experiencing at least "some stress" in the two weeks preceding the survey. About one half of the respondents reported "a lot" or "moderate amounts" of stress during this period (Silverman, Eichler & Williams, 1987). Economic impact is another measure. Costs for direct care of mental illness are reported to exceed $36 billion annually ("Giving Mental Health," 1986).

Psychological Disorders as an Occupational Health Concern

Epidemiologic and health care data on costs are accumulating to provide an increasingly clear picture of the occupational relevance—both cause and costs—of psychological disorders.

Occupational gradients with respect to mental health have long been known. Mental disturbances are most heavily concentrated among workers with lower income, lower educational level, fewer skills, and less prestigious jobs (Fried, 1975; Langner & Michael, 1963). Similar gradients are apparent for alcoholism (Fillmore

& Caetano, 1982; Guralnick, 1963). Quinn and Staines (1979) found an appreciable drop in job satisfaction among U.S. workers during the 1970s. Virtually all occupational and demographic subclasses were affected. Results of the 1985 National Health Interview Survey (Shilling & Brackbill, 1987) revealed that an estimated 11 million workers reported health-endangering levels of "mental stress" at work. Only one other hazardous work condition (loud noise) was found to be more prevalent.

Findings in other Western industrialized countries reinforce the U.S. experience. Data collected during the 1970s indicated that about one fourth to one third of Swedish workers viewed their work as often "stressful" or reported moderate to high levels of "stress" at work (Bolinder & Ohlstrom, 1971; Wahlund & Nerell, 1976). In a nationwide Canadian study (Canadian Mental Health Association, 1984), 60% of the workers studied reported they had experienced "negative stress" at work within the previous year and 35% reported "adverse psychological effects." Only 11% reported adverse physical effects. Again, such reactions were most common in the age range of 25 to 44 years.

Going beyond these generalizations, more precise analyses reveal that specific occupations and job factors present particular risks. Health professionals (e.g., physicians, dentists, nurses, and health technologists) have higher than expected rates of suicide (Guralnick, 1963; Milham, 1983) and of alcohol and drug abuse (Hoiberg, 1982). Nurses and other health care workers have increased rates of hospital admissions for mental disorders (Gundersson & Colcord, 1982; Hoiberg, 1982) and elevated admission rates to mental health centers (Colligan, Smith, & Hurrell, 1977). Burnout is particularly prevalent among health, human service, and teaching professionals (Maslach, 1982). A wide range of working conditions have been associated as job-risk factors of adverse affective states and job dissatisfaction. Examples include role stressors (Jackson & Schuler, 1985) and demands in excess of control (Karasek, Schwartz, & Theorell, 1982). Further discussion of job-risk factors is provided in the section on job design.

Data on workers' compensation provide a particularly striking indicator of the magnitude of psychological disorders as an occupational health issue. In general, claims for psychological disorders that result from job experiences multiplied over the 1970s. According to Lublin (1980), the State of California alone received 3,000 to 4,000 psychiatric injury claims in 1979, one half of which resulted in monetary awards. The prevalence of one specific type of claim, "gradual mental stress," has shown a dramatic increase in recent years.[3] The California Workers' Compensation Institute (1983, cited in National Council on Compensation Insurance, 1985, p. 5) reported that such claims more than doubled from 1980 to 1982, whereas claims for all other disabling injuries actually decreased by more than 10%. According to a study by the National Council on Compensation Insurance (1985), claims for gradual mental stress alone account for about 11% of all claims for occupational disease. That study also showed that in the period from 1981 to 1982, costs of

---

[3]The expression *gradual mental stress* is used in the field of workers' compensation insurance to refer to cumulative emotional problems that stem mainly from exposure to adverse psychosocial conditions at work. Emotional problems related to a specific traumatic event at work—such as witnessing a severe accident—or to work-related physical disease or injury are not included.

workers' compensation for gradual mental stress reached, and then surpassed, the average cost of claims for other occupational disease.

Total costs for psychological disorders in terms of medical services, employment, and productivity are far more elusive. Several sources agree, however, that such costs in the United States run in the tens of billions of dollars annually (Harwood, Napolitano, Kristiansen, & Collins, 1984; Wallis, 1983; Yates, 1979). These sources suggest that adding in the cost of physical health problems related to psychological disorders brings the total bill to $50–$100 billion annually.

Emerging trends in the economy, in technology, and in the demographic characteristics of the work force may result in increased risk for psychological disorders. Some of the more evident trends, with a description of their implications, follow.

1. Of the 20 fastest growing occupations, one half are related to the health and computer fields. A 26% increase is projected for health services in the decade 1985–1995, with an increase of 33% for registered nurses and 29% for nurses' aides, orderlies, and attendants (Silvestri & Lukasiewicz, 1985). As noted earlier, health service professionals, and nurses in particular, have consistently shown elevated risks for psychological disorders. Regarding the computer field, Bezold, Carlson, and Peck (1986) have cited data indicating that computers and robots will probably affect 7 million factor jobs and 38 million office jobs. According to these observers, the projected effects will include job displacement, deskilling, and lower paying jobs, each of which has implications for psychological well-being.

2. Of every 10 new jobs between 1985 and 1995, 9 will be in the service sector (Bureau of Labor Statistics, 1985), an area already shown to be at increased risk for psychological disorders (Colligan et al., 1977). Furthermore, workers in routine service jobs will probably not gain the compensation and benefits awarded to workers in the traditional industrial and manufacturing jobs (Bezold et al., 1986; Pederson, Sieber, & Sundin, 1986).

3. Of every 10 new jobs between 1985 and 1995, 6 will be filled by women, and the proportion of women will continue to increase to 46% of the work force (Fullerton, 1985). Because of role demands and constrained occupational opportunities, this trend may have an adverse impact on mental health.

4. According to Silvestri and Lukasiewicz (1985), the five occupations with the greatest number of new jobs by 1995 will be cashiers, registered nurses, janitorial workers, truck drivers, and waiters and waitresses. Many jobs in this cluster provide limited opportunity for growth and development, and limited availability of benefits.

Conceptual Basis for the Prevention Strategy

A prevention strategy for health disorders must take account of both causal mechanisms and factors that perpetuate the disorders. Generic approaches tend to focus on the interplay of host, agent, and contextual factors. One such approach, the Canadian Health Field Model, which has received wide attention as a framework for understanding and attacking the causes of ill health, is particularly suited as the basis of a prevention strategy for psychological disorders (Lalonde, 1974).[4] The Quebec Social and Family Affairs Council (1984) reported the most current interpretation of the Canadian Health Field Model, identifying three main categories of variables: (a) individual factors (physiological and psychological characteristics as determined by biological and hereditary factors); (b) environmental factors (aspects of the physical, social, economic, and working environments); and (c) health care systems (quantity, arrangement, and nature of health care).

This model views health as a process of adjustment between the individual and the environment. Psychological disturbances are considered a manifestation of imbalance between the individual and the environment and are eased or exacerbated depending on the health care available. The Quebec interpretation departs from the original formulation (Lalonde, 1974) in its treatment of one category of variables; unhealthy behaviors or lifestyles. In the original model, these factors are considered as acts of deliberate exposure to risks, whereas in the Quebec interpretation they more accurately represent consequences of stress.

This model of the health process is consistent with formulations in the contemporary theory on stress and with empirical observations. The basic concept in most current approaches to job stress embodies an unfavorable interaction between worker attributes and job conditions that leads to psychological disturbances and unhealthy behaviors and ultimately to physiological ill health (Caplan, Cobb, French, Harrison, & Pinneau, 1975; Cox, 1978; Gardell, 1971; Karasek et al. 1982; Levi, 1981). Research findings confirm this view on a general level. Both physical and psychosocial job characteristics have been shown to play a role in the etiology of work-related psychological disturbances. These factors operate in concert with other factors—such as stressful life events or familial demands and support—and with the physical and psychological traits, capacities, and needs of the workers (personality, age, gender, experience, learning, etc.). The interplay among these variables is complex, however, and the relative influence of the different classes of variables is not thoroughly understood.

The current understanding of psychological health processes, as described earlier, suggests key elements in a prevention strategy for work-related psychological disorders. These elements include abatement of known job (environmental) risk factors, research to improve understanding of these risk factors, surveillance to detect and track risk factors and to identify occupational groups at risk, and education to improve the recognition of risk factors and their control. At the same time, efforts are needed to improve mental health services for workers.

Components of the Prevention Strategy

Various methods of preventing work-related psychological disorders are classified here into four somewhat distinct categories of action: (a) job design to improve working conditions; (b) surveillance of psychological disorders and risk factors; (c)

---

[4]The Canadian Health Field Model was adopted in 1979 by the U.S. Surgeon General for analyzing the 10 leading causes of death in the United States (U.S. Department of Health, Education and Welfare, 1979), and in 1985 by NIOSH for developing a strategy to combat work-related musculoskeletal injury (NIOSH, 1985).

information dissemination, education, and training; and (d) enrichment of psychological health services for workers.

The following discussion covers the limits of current knowledge and practice and the strategic (prevention) initiatives that derive as consequences in each area. Research is considered under each activity as needed. To help facilitate implementation, the recommendations are stated in concrete terms that identify the specific actors and actions needed, whenever possible. Several recommendations, however, by their nature defy such specificity (e.g., general policy matters, generic research, and broad class of organizations or activities).

Job Design To Improve Working Conditions

The literature on occupational stress and health identifies a wide range of working conditions, both physical and psychosocial, that pose a threat to psychological well-being. Physical aspects include neurotoxic agents and physical and ergonomic characteristics of the task and workplace. The NIOSH (1974, 1977) National Occupational Hazard Survey estimated that nearly 12.5 million U.S. workers face exposure to metals and organic compounds (mercury, lead, solvents, etc.) known to cause psychological disorders. Psychological problems secondary to the physical disorders that arise from poor ergonomic conditions are increasingly apparent, as seen in recent research on office automation (Grandjean, 1983). Prevention efforts for controlling health problems, including psychological effects, that result from exposure to neurotoxic and physical and ergonomic risk factors are treated in separate NIOSH strategies for preventing leading work-related diseases and injuries (NIOSH, 1985, 1988).

With respect to job design, the present strategy focuses principally on psychosocial factors. Although *psychosocial* has not been succinctly defined in reference to working conditions, in general usage it connotes the social environment at work, organizational aspects of the job, and the content and certain operational aspects of the tasks performed. Unlike neurotoxic agents and ergonomic hazards, hazards involving psychosocial factors respect no occupational boundaries. Thus, the potential for exposure to this class of health risks is ubiquitous, and a great many psychosocial factors have been identified as potentially hazardous. The most firmly established of these, in terms of quantity and convergence of evidence, are discussed in the following section.

Knowledge of Psychosocial Risk Factors: The Status Quo

Work load and work pace. Although some evidence exists that work load per se is associated with negative health outcomes (Theorell & Rahe, 1972), the load or rate does not seem to be as critical as the amount of personal control or discretion exercised over these demands. Evidence is growing that control is the decisive factor in determining the health consequences of work demands, so that adverse effects occur when control is not commensurate with demands (Sauter, Hurrell, & Cooper, 1989). Similarly, research on the degree of participation in making decisions suggests that emotional distress, lowered self-esteem, and job dissatisfaction result from non-participation of workers (Margolis, Kroes, & Quinn, 1974; Spector, 1986).

Research on machine-paced work (involving limited worker control of the job demands) has indicated, from the beginning, a link with adverse health effects. Reports from early field studies showed a variety of negative psychological reactions (job dissatisfaction, tension, etc.) in machine-paced work (Hurrell & Colligan, 1987; Salvendy & Smith, 1981). In a NIOSH-sponsored study of 23 occupations (Caplan et al., 1975), machine-paced assembly workers reported the highest levels of anxiety, depression, and irritation, as well as more frequent somatic complaints.

Work schedule. Substantial evidence indicates that the temporal scheduling of work can have a significant impact on psychological, behavioral, social, and physical well-being. Rotating shifts and permanent night work, in particular, have been linked to a variety of such disturbances (Johnson, Tepas, Colquhoun, & Colligan, 1981; Monk & Tepas, 1985; Rutenfranz, Colquhoun, Knauth, & Ghata, 1977). These shift-related complications have been attributed to a disruption of physiological circadian rhythms and social interactions resulting from a work schedule that is at odds with the normal diurnal activity cycle (Aschoff, 1981).

Role stressors. National survey data suggest that role ambiguity is prevalent in many organizations (Kahn, Wolfe, Quinn, Snoek, & Rosenthal, 1964). According to these data, men who experienced role ambiguity reported lower self-confidence, higher job tension, and lower job satisfaction. Role conflict has been similarly linked to job tension and dissatisfaction (Jackson & Schuler, 1985). Research has also linked role ambiguity to indicators of mental ill health, including depressed mood, dissatisfaction with life, tension, anxiety, and resentment (Caplan & Jones, 1975; Van Sell, Brief, & Schuler, 1981), and to adverse psychophysiological states such as increased heart rate and blood pressure (French & Caplan, 1970).

Career security factors. Several conditions associated with career development and job future (lack of job security, under- or overpromotion, fear of job obsolescence, and early retirement) have been related to adverse psychological effects (e.g., low job and life satisfaction, low self-esteem) as well as poor physical health (Kasl & Cobb, 1982; Margolis et al., 1974; Sutherland & Cooper, 1988).

Interpersonal relations. Poor relationships with colleagues, supervisors, and subordinates at work have been identified as important risk factors (Beehr & Newman, 1978; Davidson & Cooper, 1981; Pearse, 1977). Social relationships both at work and outside the workplace are most commonly viewed as playing a moderating role, and adverse effects of exposure to job risk factors are more likely or pronounced when relationships provide little support (Cobb & Kasl, 1977; Cohen & Willis, 1985; House & Wells, 1978). For example, a study of more than 1,000 male workers showed that support from supervisors and coworkers buffered the effects of job demands on depression and job dissatisfaction (Karasek et al., 1982). Other research indicates a more direct effect on social support in offsetting the effects of adverse working conditions (Ganster, Mayes, & Fusilier, 1986).

Job content. The nature of the tasks performed has critical implications for psychological well-being. In particular, narrow, fragmented, invariant, and short-cycle tasks that provide little stimulation, allow little use of skills or expression of creativity, and have little intrinsic meaning for workers have been associated with job dissatisfaction and poor mental health (Cox, 1985; Gardell, 1981; Levi, 1981).

Intervening variables. The effects of the aforementioned factors on psychological well-being must be considered in the context of situational and personal variables that originate outside the job. Although these outside factors are not amenable to control through job design, they should be recognized here because of their potential interaction with job factors. Life events and the Type A behavior pattern are two such variables. Risk factors outside the work environment such as family problems, financial difficulties, and major life changes have been linked to a host of physical and psychological disorders (Dohrenwend & Dohrenwend, 1974). Although the Type A behavior pattern (characterized by a sense of competitiveness, time urgency, and overcommitment) may be fostered by a stressful job, it is also possible that individuals with this tendency select themselves into particularly demanding jobs.

Recommendations for Controlling Psychosocial Risk Factors at Work

Although it cannot be said that an understanding of work-related risk factors for psychological disorders is complete or that further study is unwarranted, knowledge is sufficiently advanced to permit more concerted action toward the control of risk factors at the work site. Training and technology transfer, to be treated later in this article, is particularly important, as is continuing research to hone our knowledge further and to investigate emerging problems.

Motivational and leadership efforts are equally important, however, and are the primary subject of discussion here. Although government agencies and industry organizations have provided direction in the control of physical workplace hazards, psychosocial aspects of the job have received little attention. In particular, recommendations in this area have never been issued at the national level. The generalizations below are based on existing knowledge and converging opinion on risk factors, and are offered as candidates for such recommendations. The intent here is not to define specific actions for intervention because the nature of such actions will vary depending on several factors (e.g., industry, organizational level). Rather, the aim is to offer positive principles to guide the design of jobs in the interests of improving mental health. Although research has demonstrated these principles to be effective, some work situations may not be readily amenable to the needed interventions. Furthermore, the underlying risk factors can be interrelated, and successful intervention will require attention to more than one of these principles.

Work load and work pace. Demand (both physical and mental) should be commensurate with the capabilities and resources of individuals, avoiding underload as well as overload. Provisions should be made to allow recovery from demanding tasks or for increased job control under such circumstances. Increased control by the individual over the pace of work is one example of a positive step.

Work schedule. Work schedules should be compatible with demands and responsibilities outside the job. Recent trends toward flextime, a compressed work week, and job sharing are positive steps. When schedules involve rotating shifts, the rate of rotation should be stable and predictable and should be in a forward (day-to-night) direction.

Work roles. Roles and responsibilities at work should be well defined. Job duties need to be clearly explained, and conflicts in terms of job expectations should be avoided.

Job future. Ambiguity should not exist in matters of job security and opportunities for career development. Employees need to be clearly informed of promotional opportunities and mechanism for improving skills or professional growth within the organization, as well as impending organizational developments that may potentially affect their employment.

Social environment. Jobs should provide opportunities for personal interaction both for purposes of emotional support and for actual help as needed in accomplishing assigned tasks.

Content. Jobs should be designed to provide meaning, stimulation, and an opportunity to use skills. Job rotation or increasing the scope of work are examples of steps to improve narrow, fragmented work activities that fail to meet these criteria.

Participation and control. Individuals should be given the opportunity to have input on decisions or actions that affect their jobs and the performance of their tasks.

Research Needs

Other steps, beyond formulating and promulgating such recommendations, can help implement improved job design.

1. NIOSH can work directly with industry, through mechanisms for technical assistance or cooperative agreements, to study problematic situations and to develop and install solutions.
2. Intervention studies are needed to evaluate the effects of psychosocial job enhancement in terms of psychological well-being. These studies should also examine performance outcomes and related bottom-line measures that are important for motivating industry to action. Beyond an incentive to improve working conditions, research of this nature can also provide models and direction to help guide the implementation of psychosocial improvements.
3. More basic study is needed on the role of extraorganizational factors visà-vis job-design factors, as they affect psychological well-being. Continuing research is also needed to examine the impact of technologic developments

(e.g., increasing use of computer automation and the use of robots in the work processes) and their potential for adverse as well as positive effects on job design and subsequent psychological effects. Logically, organizations that develop and promulgate such technology should hear a responsibility in supporting the research effort.

As an important related issue, this research must come to grips with several methodologic problems associated with research on occupational stress. Important advances in research include (a) increased use of longitudinal prospective and follow-up research designs of psychological outcomes; (b) development of more standardized methods for assessing psychosocial risk factors on the job; (c) greater adherence to the use of standard psychometric instruments in assessing psychological outcomes; (d) more extensive use of collatoral measures both for working conditions (e.g., assessments by coworkers, managers, objective measurements) and the indicators of psychological health effects (e.g., self-reports, medical and personnel records, psychophysiological measures, performance, attendance, and supervisory and peer evaluations); (e) increased efforts through representative sampling procedures and replication to assure that the findings will have general application (e.g., the use of multiple work sites or industries in the investigation of a particular occupation or job dimension); and (f) increased use of advanced statistical methods, such as structural analysis, to improve the understanding of causal mechanisms and pathways.

Surveillance of Psychological Disorders and Risk Factors

Any strategy of preventing health disorders has a central need for ongoing surveillance of disorders and risk factors to detect and react to emerging problems and to evaluate intervention. Current surveillance systems are insufficient to identify work-related psychological disorders adequately or to aid in their prevention.

Surveillance: The Status Quo

Surveillance of psychological disorders. Although reports cited earlier in this article give some indication of the prevalence of psychological disorders as an occupational health problem, most are only suggestive at best. Many information sources lack the continuity, breadth, and specificity required for effective surveillance of occupational psychological disorders. However, two nationwide studies conducted by the National Center for Health Statistics (NCHS)—the National Health Interview Survey (NHIS) and the National Health and Nutrition Examination Survey (NHANES)—offer some potential for surveillance of psychological disorders. Although neither study was designed specifically for surveillance of psychological disorders, both collect limited data on psychological disorders, occupation, and industry. Thus far, however, these data bases have been used specifically for surveillance of occupational mental health. For example, NCHS does not routinely provide cross tabulations of psychological disorders by occupation or industry in its published reports.

The Epidemiological Catchment Area (ECA) program sponsored by NIMH represents a recent, comprehensive attempt to assess the prevalence of major psychiatric disorders as classified by the DSM-III (Freedman, 1984). This program involved interview surveys conducted in households at five sites across the country. Follow-up interviews at six-month and one-year intervals also made possible the determination of incidence rates for mental disorders. Although occupation and industry data were obtained in the survey, the collection process for this information was not standardized. Another limitation was that only current occupation, rather than occupational history, was recorded. Finally, NIMH has no plans to repeat the ECA survey at regular intervals.

Also at the national level, data from the Social Security Administration on disability allowances hold potential for tracking psychological disorders in relation to occupations. As noted earlier, NIOSH has used these data to investigate occupational differentials in disabling conditions. NIOSH is currently studying whether SSA allowance data can be used to track psychological disorders.

Workers' compensation systems at the state level have not been used extensively to track psychological disorders in relation to occupational factors.[5] Reasons for this include a lack of uniformity across the states in diagnostic criteria and in laws governing the compensability of psychological disorders. Moreover, these data are not easily retrievable.

Surveillance of job risk factors. The Quality of Employment Surveys sponsored by the Deparment of Labor in 1969, 1973, and 1977 constitute the only nationally representative effort to monitor working conditions and to explore quality-of-work-life issues (Quinn et al. 1971; Quinn & Shephard, 1974; Quinn & Staines, 1979). This series of household surveys solicited information on a broad range of factors that contribute to the quality of work life. Topic areas include job content, job security, participation, earnings and fringe benefits, and health and safety concerns. No such surveys have been conducted since 1977.

Recommendations for Improving Surveillance

The following recommendations are offered to improve existing practices for surveillance of occupational psychological disorders and for surveillance of occupational conditions that place workers at risk for psychological disorders.

National level. (a) The Department of Labor should reinstitute Quality of Employment Surveys in conjunction with NIOSH to monitor the prevalence of risk factors in the workplace. More extensive data on psychological disorders should be collected in these surveys. (b) NIOSH should work with NCHS to improve the usefulness of NCHS surveys for surveillance of occupational mental health. Similarly, input to the NIMH ECA program should be explored. (c) NIOSH should consider adding suicide and alcohol/drug abuse on the list of Sentinel Health Events (Occupational), thereby stimulating an awareness and recording of these events in

---

[5]California is one exception. Similar activities have also been undertaken by the National Council on Compensation Insurance, an organization linked to compensation insurance underwriters.

relation to occupational factors (Rutstein et al., 1983). (d) A national clearinghouse is needed to identify and disseminate information on sources of data that contain information on psychological disorders with respect to occupation.

State level. (a) Data on risk factors for psychological disorders could be collected and organized by industry or occupation through the Centers for Disease Control (CDC) Health Risk Appraisal Network with state health departments. (b) The National Association of State Mental Health Directors should initiate efforts to assemble data on psychological disorders for surveillance of occupational mental health. (c) Workers' compensation data bases should be evaluated to identify high-risk occupations or industries.

Industry level. (a) Health examinations of employees should note psychological health status to help detect emerging problems. Data on working conditions should be recorded at the same time so that organizational risk factors can be identified. (b) In general, data from health care providers (e.g., employee assistance programs [EAPs], company medical departments) should be used in aggregate (to assure confidentiality) for organizational or industry surveillance of psychological disorders and risk factors. (c) Assessments for workplace safety and industrial hygiene should be expanded to incorporate work-place risk factors for psychological disorders.

Information Dissemination, Education, and Training

Prevention of work-related psychological disorders ultimately depends on the qualifications and resources that permit individuals to recognize psychological disorders and the underlying risk factors, and enable them to implement control measures. Individuals who play a principal role in this capacity include workers, management personnel, labor and corporate safety and health personnel, and health professionals in the community. The specific informational and training needs of these individuals can vary according to their role, but should encompass awareness and appreciation of psychological disorders as an occupational health problem, understanding of work and nonwork risk factors, recognition of individual signs and organizational manifestations of psychological disorders, reduction of stressful working conditions and personal risks, and treatments of psychological disorders.

The Status Quo

Scientific concern with the subject of occupational mental health has grown steadily from its roots in the human relations movement of the 1930s. Despite a now vast literature in this area, however, the role of work experience in the etiology of psychological disorders has received little formal attention in educational programs of the medical, mental health, management, or occupational safety and health community. Only recently, for example, have occupational factors been classified as etiologic agents for psychological disorders by the American Psychiatric Association (1980). Education for occupational safety and health personnel has historically focused on physical and chemical hazards in the work environment, with little consideration for the potential mental health consequences of working conditions. At present, only one major scientific journal focuses on the general subject of job stress,[6] and practical or tutorial literature in this area is almost nonexistent.

A NIOSH-funded project conducted in 1982 provides a rather dismal picture of the training of workers in mental health issues (Neale, Singer, Schwartz, & Schwartz, 1983). Although extensive corporate development of employee health programs was noted in the 80 corporate and labor organizations studied, the investigators drew the following conclusions about training opportunities in the area of occupational stress:

> First, there has been little done to educate *blue collar workers* about workplace stressors of both a physical and psychosocial nature. Similarly, both labor and corporate organizations have invested little time or money toward training workers in how to change or cope with stressful conditions at work. (Neale et al., 1983, p. 2)[7]

The report also concluded that existing programs tend to be targeted at middle or executive management and maladaptive health behavior (e.g., substance abuse), and use brief presentations of "workshop" variety that do not undergo evaluation. Some notable exceptions to this pattern exist. For example, NIOSH maintains publication, training, and information-dessimination activities on occupational health issues, including occupational stress. Several labor institutes (e.g., University of Wisconsin School of Workers, Oakland Institute for Labor and Mental Health) have been involved with training and information dissemination in the areas of work and mental health. On balance, however, prospects are poor for advances in training and development of general human resources in occupational mental health. Regressive developments are even evident. For example, NIMH recently disbanded the short-lived Center of Work and Mental Health, a program focusing on work and mental health issues.

Recommendations

Needs are evident for increased training opportunities, increased information availability, and further dedication of relevant organizations regarding issues of work and mental health. Avenues and suggestions for improvement in each of these areas include the following.

Training, education, and the development of training and educational materials. Worker education is needed, principally about indicators of psychological disorders and job factors that increase the risk for psychological disorders. A need also exists for educating managers in the mental health consequences of poor job design and

---

[6]Taylor and Francis began publication of a periodical entitled *Work and Stress* in 1987. However, numerous other journals (e.g., *Journal of Applied Psychology, Journal of Occupational Psychology*) accept articles on job stress.

[7]This situation may be changing. A recent national survey found that 26% of work sites polled offered some type of stress management program (Office of Disease Prevention and Health Promotion, 1989).

for training managers in the work-related causes of psychological disorders and the necessary control measures. It is particularly important that such training and education reach top management and labor levels. The training and educational needs of occupational health care professionals include recognition of occupational risk factors for psychological disorders, and management practices that impact on occupational mental health. At the same time, mental health professionals in general need to be educated about occupational psychological disorders.

Both NIOSH and OSHA support several programs that can be more fully exploited for these purposes. Training and education opportunities for safety and health professionals can be increased in the general area of work and mental health in the context of NIOSH-funded university programs such as the Educational Resource Centers (ERCs) through NIOSH professional intramural direct-training courses or through cooperative agreements between NIOSH and schools of public health. Guidelines for ERCs could include a requirement for advanced education in occupational mental health issues. Certifying boards should be encouraged to include this content in qualifying examinations. In general, professional societies and accreditation organizations need to promote greater attention to occupational factors in training mental health personnel (e.g., clinical psychologists, psychiatrists, social workers) and occupational health personnel, particularly occupational nurses and physicians.

Increased training in job design, as it relates to psychological well-being, for management and engineering personnel could be promoted through the NIOSH projects Minerva and SHAPE (Safety and Health Awareness for Preventive Engineering), which are designed to enrich the curricula of business and engineering schools, respectively, in occupational health and safety topics. Industrial engineering programs, in particular, need to be targeted. The OSHA funding of labor centers and training-grant programs provides an important mechanism for enriching education at the worker level in the areas of work and mental health.

Funding under the foregoing mechanisms should be channeled not only to deliver training and education but also to develop training and educational materials. Although extensive theoretical and research literature exists in the job stress area, accumulated scientific knowledge has not been translated into applied information in the form of practical guidelines, procedures, and manuals. The need is perhaps most acute for worker-oriented educational materials.

Dissemination of information. NIOSH provides technical and reference information on occupational safety and health, including the subject of occupational stress, through its public-access data bases (NIOSH Document Information Directory System [NIOSHTIC]) and the NIOSH Publications Clearinghouse. Some of this information has been prepackaged in the form of special bibliographies by subject areas, for example, "health aspects in the use of video display terminals." The availability of this information is announced by direct mailings to relevant organizations. Access to both the information and the information referral service could be improved by announcements in select trade and scientific media, and via the NIOSH Exhibits Program at convocations of the mental health community and other relevant professional, industry, and labor organizations.

The NIOSH Exhibits Program promotes safety and health awareness through displays at meetings of major professional and labor organizations (e.g., American Public Health Association, American Occupational Health Conference, National Safety Council, American Industrial Hygiene Association, American Nurses Association, AFL-CIO Industrial Union Department). This program could provide a vehicle for promotional activities on work and mental health issues. Extension of this exhibits program to key organizations concerned with mental health issues (e.g., the American Psychiatric Association, the Society for Behavioral Medicine, the American Sociological Association, Association of Labor-Management Administrators and Consultants on Alcoholism, and other relevant state, volunteer, and private organizations) may reap important benefits.

Information on occupational factors in mental health can be disseminated at the industry level through communications and newsletters of trade associations and through the internal health newsletters that some large corporations maintain for distribution to their own employees (e.g., the Kimberly–Clark Health Management Bulletin). Efforts of this type should be encouraged because of the job-specific nature of many risk factors.

The subject of psychological problems in relation to work can be incorporated into the agenda of regular safety committee meetings at the worker-management level by disseminating information on problems and controls through meeting notes and labor newsletters. In addition, telephone networks such as TEL-MED and HEALTH LINES that provide public access to prerecorded health information, could disseminate information on work and mental health issues at the level of the individual worker.

Mobilization and coordination of relevant organizations. Professional organizations concerned with mental health should dedicate additional effort and resources to the subject of work and mental health. For example, the APA has no focal activity in this area. One positive step would be for organizations such as APA or the Human Factors Society to strengthen divisional or technical group activities in the area of work and mental health or to conduct focused symposia, paper sessions, or tutorials on this subject at their meetings. Equivalent activities focusing on psychological health outcomes could also be cultivated within professional organizations (e.g., the American Management Association) to deal with the design of jobs and work environments.

Many federal agencies and national professional organizations (e.g., NIOSH, NIMH, National Institute on Drug Abuse, National Institute on Alcohol Abuse and Alcoholism, and APA) offer resources in terms of information, technical expertise, sponsorship of meetings, and so on, bearing on work and mental health. Yet, little formal interaction exists among these organizations. Coordination of efforts or development of a more formal network among these organizations could result in improved resources and resource availability in the area of work and mental health. NIOSH and CDC should take the lead and explore mechanisms and subjects of interaction among relevant federal, state, and professional organizations concerned with work and mental health issues. NIOSH should also initiate a conference for state health and mental health departments to discuss and develop action plans that implement the recommendations of this strategy.

Enriching Psychological Health Services for Workers

Although improved job design and organizational practices can lead to improved psychological well-being among workers, such steps alone cannot fully eliminate the problems. The workplace is a microcosm of the general community, and the stresses and psychological disorders manifest in the community at large are also felt in the workplace. Regardless of the etiology, these problems are borne by industry through absenteeism, turnover, accidents, slippages in productivity, and health benefits. Roham (1982) has reported, for example, that a chemically addicted employee is 3.6 times as likely to be involved in an accident, has 2 1/2 times as many absences lasting eight days or longer, receives 3 times the average level of sick benefits, and is 5 times as likely to file a claim for workers' compensation. It is not surprising, therefore, that industry has responded with increased mental-health-related services for employees. Although such services play a critical role in the prevention mix, further attention to both their design and availability is needed.

Worksite-Based Mental Health Services: The Status Quo

To date, workplace treatment of health problems that have psychological dimensions has been accomplished primarily through EAPs or through referral to community health agencies. Neale et al. (1983) observed that EAPs represent a step in the right direction but often suffer because they focus more on treatment than prevention and are aimed primarily at reducing personnel and productivity problems, alcoholism, and chemical dependency, especially among blue-collar employees.

In recent years, EAPs have multiplied exponentially among U.S. firms. Walsh and Hingson (1985) cited data from the National Institute on Alcohol Abuse and Alcoholism indicating that the number of EAPs had grown from 6 in 1945, to 500 in 1973, to 4,400 in 1979–1980. However, the Association of Labor and Management Administrators and Consultants on Alcoholism estimated that in 1980 only about 12% of the U.S. work force had access to such programs, and availability was restricted primarily to employees of larger organizations. Public employees particularly are slighted in this regard (Bezold et al., 1986).

Quite apart from EAPs, health awareness and health promotion programs are also increasing in prevalence in industry. In contrast to EAPs, these programs are aimed more at the prevention of illness through education and the advocation of good health practices. Techniques of health risk appraisal may be used to examine life-style risk factors that can result in morbidity or premature mortality. Risk reduction programs, such as nutrition workshops, exercise and fitness activities, smoking cessation clinics, and stress management courses are offered to effect needed changes. However, these programs have typically been aimed at the white-collar work force, have been episodic, and have failed to emphasize occupational factors. Systematic follow-up and evaluation are rare (Neale et al., 1983).

EAPs and health promotion programs appear to be progressing toward a more comprehensive approach to worker health in which prevention and treatment activities are integrated to promote overall well-being (George-Perry, 1988). It is projected that these programs may grow to encompass family and community issues and organizational issues such as management style and environmental policies (Bezold et al., 1986).

Thus, although there is a steady movement toward more and improved work-site health opportunities, existing programs clearly have limitations. Moreover, the vast proportion of workers in America still have no mental health services available through their employment.

Recommendations for Improving Worksite-Based Mental Health Services

Because of the current limitations in occupational health services, the following recommendations are offered to assure workplace psychological health services that are at least minimally sufficient.

1. Working through existing and new interagency agreements, NIOSH, the Alcohol, Drug Abuse, and Mental Health Administration, and state mental health agencies should support such activities as (a) demonstration grants for mental health programs in industry; (b) development of innovative approaches to mental health services in industry; (c) program evaluation research; (d) development of communication networks linking industry, providers, and resource organizations; (e) educational efforts such as symposia and workshops on work-site mental health programs; and (f) direct consultation with industry or trade associations, individual businesses, and labor organizations to promote establishment of high quality service programs for work-site psychological health in all medium and large workplaces (e.g., in excess of 100 employees).

2. Mental health services should be integrated into the overall occupational health care program, whether on-site or external to the organization, and developed in a coordinated fashion with input from all relevant departments (e.g., medical, safety, personnel, risk management, line management). Key organizational characteristics of these services should include (a) joint management–worker input to program planning and administration; (b) ongoing services; (c) a formalized policy for referrals; (d) mechanisms for maintaining confidentiality of information; (e) guarantee of professional independence of providers; (f) specialized training to assure professional competence of staff; (g) access to these services through health benefit packages; and (h) access to the program by employees at all organizational levels.

    The scope and content of psychological health programs should be adjusted according to local factors such as the nature of the work performed and special needs of the work force. All such programs should offer, at a minimum, basic psychological support in areas common to any work force such as personal crisis management, alcohol and chemical dependency, marital and family counseling, and stress management. These services should have both treatment and primary prevention components. More specialized concerns such as impending retirement, lay off, relocation, and other job-specific problems may require additional effort and expertise. Mechanisms should be established for input by consultants in occupational mental health. These programs could provide a rich source of data through periodic feedback to the organization in aggregate form (to protect confidentiality) to help identify or rectify organizational problems.

3. Within small firms in which the establishment of on-site programs for psychological health services may not be feasible, a liaison or network should be established with local mental health or social service agencies to provide a bridge between troubled workers and treatment facilities. Formalized relationships should be developed so that routine referral is possible and mental health personnel from the agencies can be enlisted readily for specialized programs. State or local mechanisms should be developed to assist small firms in seeking these appropriate mental health services.

4. Local mental health and social service agencies should develop internal staff competence or seek consultation from appropriately skilled professionals on occupational mental health issues.

5. Further broadening of services in occupational psychological health, along the lines described earlier, is needed for federal, state, and municipal public employees.

6. In line with increasing judicial recognition of the occupational components of disabling emotional disorders (DeCarlo, 1985), health insurance benefits for treatment of such problems should be expanded and increased.

7. EAPs and health promotion programs should evolve to a higher state of awareness and practice, recognizing both occupational and nonoccupational factors as influential to health, and offering opportunities for both organizational and individual interventions to improve employee mental health.

References

American Psychiatric Association. (1980). *Diagnostic and statistical manual of mental disorders (3rd ed.)*. Washington, DC: Author.

Argyris, C. (1964). *Integrating the individual and the organization*. New York: Wiley.

Ashoff, J. (1981). Circadian rhythms: Interference with and dependence on work-rest schedules. In L. C. Johnson, D. I. Tepas, W. P. Colquhoun, & M. J. Colligan (Eds.), *The twenty-four hour workday: Proceedings of a symposium on variation in work—sleep schedules* (DHHS Publication 81-127, pp. 13–50). Washington, DC: U.S. Government Printing Office.

Baum, C., Kennedy, D. L., Knapp, D. E., & Faich, G. A. (1985, October). *Prescription drug use in 1984*. Paper presented at the American Public Health Association annual meeting, Washington, DC.

Beehr, T. A., & Newman, J. E. (1978). Job stress, employee health, and organizational effectiveness: A facet analysis, model, and literature review. *Personnel Psychology, 31*, 665–699.

Bezold, C., Carlson, R. J., & Peck, J. C. (1986). *The future of work and health*. Dover, MA: Auburn House.

Bolinder, E., & Ohlstrom, B. (1971). Stress pa Svenska arbetsplatser: En enkatstudie bland LO-medlemmasrna [Stress in the Swedish workplace: A study among LO membership]. Lund, Sweden: Prisma/LO.

Bureau of Labor Statistics (1985, November). *Bureau of Labor Statistics news*. Washington, DC: Author.

Camus, A. (1955). *The myth of Sisyphys*. New York: Knopf.

Canadian Mental Health Association (1984). *Work and well-being: The changing realities of employment*. Toronto, Ontario, Canada: Author.

Caplan, R. D., Cobb, S., French, J. R. P., Jr., Harrison, R. V., & Pinneau, S. R., Jr. (1975). *Job demands and worker health: Main effects and occupational differences* (DHEW NIOSH Publication No. 75-160). Washington, DC: U.S. Government Printing Office.

Caplan, R. D., & Jones, K. W. (1975). Effects of work load, role ambiguity, and Type A personality on anxiety, depression, and heart rate. *Journal of Applied Psychology, 60*, 713–719.

Cobb, S., & Kasl, S. V. (1977). *Termination: The consequences of job loss.* (DHEW NIOSH Publication No. 77-1261). Washington, DC: U.S. Government Printing Office.

Cohen, S., & Wills, T. A. (1985). Stress, social support, and the buffering. *Psychological Bulletin, 98,* 310–357.

Colligan, M. J., Smith, M. J., & Hurrell, J. J. (1977). Occupational incidence rates of mental health disorders. *Journal of Human Stress, 3,* 34–39.

Collings, G. H. (1984). Examining the "occupational" in occupational medicine. *Journal of Occupational Medicine, 26,* 509–512.

Cox, T. (1978). *Stress.* Baltimore, MD: University Park Press.

Cox, J. (1985). Repetitive work: Occupational stress and health. In C. L. Cooper & M. Smith (Eds.), *Job stress and blue collar work* (pp. 85–112). London: Wiley.

Cypress, B. K. (1984). *Patterns of ambulatory care in international medicine: The national ambulatory medical care survey. United States, January 1980–December 1981* (Vital and Health Statistics, Series 13, No. 80, Publication No. 84-1741). Washington, DC: U.S. Government Printing Office.

Davidson, M. J., & Cooper, C. L. (1981). A model of occupational stress. *Journal of Occupational Medicine, 23,* 564–570.

DeCarlo, D. T. (Ed.). (1985). Legal insight. *National Council on Compensation Insurance.* New York: National Council on Compensation Insurance.

Dohrenwend, B. S. & Dohrenwend, B. P. (1974). *Stressful life events: Their nature and effects.* New York: Wiley.

Erikson, E. H. (1963). *Childhood and society (2nd ed.).* New York: Norton.

Fillmore, K., & Caetano, R. (1982). Epidemiology of alcohol abuse and alcoholism in occupations. *Research Monograph No. 8–Occupational alcoholism: A review of research issues. Proceedings of a Workshop, May 1980, in Reston, Virginia* (DHHS Publication No. ADM 82-1184, pp. 21–88). Washington, DC: U.S. Government Printing Office.

Fischbach, T. J., Dacey, E. W., Sestito, J. P., & Green, J. H. (1986). *Occupational characteristics of disabled workers, 1975–1976* (DHHS NIOSH Publication No. 86-106). Washington, DC: U.S. Government Printing Office.

Freedman, D. X. (1984). Psychiatric epidemiology counts. *Archives of General Psychiatry, 41,* 931–933.

French, J. R., Jr., & Caplan, R. D. (1970). Psychosocial factors in coronary heart disease. *Industrial Medicine, 39,* 383–388.

Fried, M. (1975). Social differences in mental health. In J. Kosa & I. K. Zola (Eds.). *Poverty and health* (Rev. ed.). Cambridge, MA: Harvard University Press.

Fullerton, H. N., Jr. (1985). The 1985 labor force: BLS's latest projections. *Monthly Labor Reviews, 108,* 11, 17–41.

Ganster, D. C., Mayes, B. T., & Fusilier, M. R. (1986). Role of social support in the experience of stress at work. *Journal of Applied Psychology, 71,* 102–110.

Gardell, B. (1971). Alienation and mental health in the modern industrial environment. In L. Levi (Ed.), *Society, stress and disease: Vol. 1. The psychosocial environment and psychosomatic diseases* (p. 149). London: Oxford University Press.

Gardell, B. (1981). Autonomy and participation at work. In L. Levi (Ed.), *Society, stress and disease: Vol. 4. Working life* (pp. 279–289). Oxford, England: Oxford University Press.

George-Perry, S. (1988). Easing the cost of mental health benefits. *Personnel Administrator, 33,* 62–67.

Giving mental health its research due. (1986). *Science, 232,* 1065–1172.

Good, M. D., Good, B. J., & Massi, A. J. (1983). Patient requests in primary health care settings: Development and validation of a research instrument. *Journal of Behavioral Medicine, 6,* 151–168.

Grandjean, E. (Ed.). (1983). *Ergonomics and health in modern offices.* Philadelphia, PA: Taylor & Francis.

Gundersson, E. K. E., & Colcord, C. (1982). *Health risks in naval operations: An overview* (Report No. 82-1). San Diego, CA: Naval Health Research Center.

Guralnick, L. (1963). *Mortality by occupation and cause of death (No. 3), Mortality by industry and cause of death (No. 4), Mortality by occupational level and cause of death (No. 5) among men 20 to 64 years of age. v.s. 1950* (Vital statistics—special reports, Vol. 53). Washington, DC: U.S. Government Printing Office.

Harwood, H. J., Napolitano, D. M., Kristiansen, P. L., & Collins, J. T. (1984). *Economic cost to society of alcohol, drug abuse, and mental health: 1980* (Contract No. ADM 283-83-0002). Washington, DC: U.S. Government Printing Office.

Herzberg, F. (1966). *Work and the nature of man.* Cleveland, OH: World.

Hilker, R. J., & Asma, F. E. (1975). A drug abuse rehabilitation program. *Journal of Occupational Medicine, 17,* 351–354.

Hoiberg, M. S. (1982). Occupational stress and illness incidence. *Journal of Occupational Medicine, 24,* 445–451.

House, J. S., & Wells, J. A. (1978). Occupational stress, social support, and health. In J. S. House & J. A. Wells (Eds.), *Reducing occupational stress* (HEW Publication No. 78-140, pp. 8–29). Washington, DC: U.S. Government Printing Office.

Hurrell, J. J., Jr., & Colligan, M. J. (1987). Machine-pacing and shiftwork: Evidence for job stress. *Journal of Organizational Behavior Management, 8,* 159–175.

Jackson, S., & Schuler, R. (1985). A meta-analysis and conceptual critique of research on role ambiguity and role conflict in work settings. *Organizational Behavior and Human Decisions, 36,* 16–28.

Johnson, L. C., Tepas, D. I., Colquhoun, W. P., & Colligan, M. J. (Eds.). (1981). *The twenty-four hour workday: Proceedings of a symposium on variations in work-sleep schedules* (DHHS Publication No. 81–127). Washington, DC: U.S. Government Printing Office.

Kahn, R. L., Wolfe, D. M., Quinn, R. P., Snoek, J. D., & Rosenthal, R. A. (1964). *Organizational stress: Studies in role conflict and ambiguity.* New York: Wiley.

Karasek, R. A., Schwartz, J., & Theorell, T. (1982). *Job characteristics, occupational, and coronary heart disease.* (Final report on Grant No. R-01-OH00906). Cincinnati, OH: National Institute for Occupational Safety and Health.

Kasi, S. V., & Cobb, S. (1982). Variability of stress effects among men experiencing job loss. In L. Goldberg & S. Breznitz (Eds.), *Handbook of stress: Theoretical and clinical aspects* (pp. 445–465). New York: Wiley.

Kiecolt-Glaser, J. K. (1985, October). Stress and the immune function. In J. Hurrell (Chair), *Measures of job stress: A research methodology workshop.* Workshop conducted in New Orleans by the National Institute for Occupational Safety and Health.

Kiecolt-Glaser, J. K., Speicher, C. E., Holliday, J. E., & Glaser, R. (1984). Stress and the tranformation of lymphocytes by Epstein-Barr virus. *Journal of Behavioral Medicine, 7,* 1–11.

Lalonde, M. (1974). *Nouvelle perspective de la santé des Canadians: Un document de travail* [New perspectivies on the health of Canadians: A working document]. Ottawa, Ontario, Canada: Ministère de la Santé nationale et du Bien-être Social.

Langner, T., & Michael, S. (1963). *Life stress and mental health: The midtown Manhattan study.* New York: Free Press.

Lazarus, R. S. (1981). Some thoughts about stress and the working situation. In L. Levi (Ed.), *Society, stress and disease: Vol. 4, Working life* (pp. 54–58). Oxford, England: Oxford Univerity Press.

Levi, L. (1981). *Preventing work stress.* Reading, PA: Addison-Wesley.

Linn, M. W., Sandifer, R., & Stein, S. (1985). Effects of unemployment on mental and physical health. *American Journal of Public Health, 75,* 502–506.

Lublin, J. S. (1980, September 17). On-the-job stress leads many workers to file and win compensation awards. *Wall Street Journal.*

Margolis, B. L., Kroes, W. H., & Quinn, R. A. (1974). Job stress: An unlisted occupational hazard. *Journal of Occupational Medicine, 16,* 654–661.

Marx, J. L. (1985). The immune system "Belongs in the body." *Science, 227,* 1190–1192.

Maslach, C. (1982). *Burnout: The cost of caring.* Englewood Cliffs, NJ: Prentice-Hall.

McGregor, D. (1960). *The human side of enterprise.* New York: McGraw-Hill.

Milham, S., Jr. (1983). *Occupational mortality in Washington State, 1950–1979* (DHHS NIOSH Publication No. 83-116). Washington, DC: U.S. Government Printing Office.

Monk, T., & Tepas, D. A. (1985). Shiftwork. In C. L. Cooper & M. I. Smith (Eds.), *Job stress and blue collar work* (pp. 65–84). Chichester, England: Wiley.

National Council on Compensation Insurance. (1985). *Emotional stress in the workplace—New legal rights in the eighties.* New York: Author.

National Institute for Occupational Safety and Health. (1974). *National Occupational Hazard Survey: Vol. 1. Survey manual* (DHEW Publication No. 74–127). Rockville, MD: U.S. Government Printing Office.

National Institute for Occupational Safety and Health. (1977). *National Occupational Hazard Survey: Vol. II, Data editing and data base development* (DHEW Publication No. 77-213). Washington, DC: U.S. Government Printing Office.

National Institute for Occupational Safety and Health. (1985). Prevention of work-related musculo-skeletal injuries: A proposed synoptic strategy. In *Proposed national strategies for the prevention of leading work-related diseases and injuries, Pt. 1* (NTIS No. PB87-114740, pp. 17–34). Cincinnati, OH: Author.

National Institute for Occupational Safety and Health. (1988). Prevention of occupationally-generated illnesses: A proposed synoptic national strategy to reduce neurotoxic disorders in the U.S. workplace. In *Proposed national strategies for the prevention of leading work-related diseases and injuries. Pt. 2* (NTIS No. PB89-130348, pp. 31–50). Cincinnati, OH: Author.

Neale, M. S., Singer, J. A., Schwartz, J. L., & Schwartz, G. E. (1983, March). *Yale-NIOSH occupational stress project.* Paper presented at the 4th Annual Meeting of the Society of Behavioral Medicine, Baltimore, MD.

Nickalson, J. H., Donaldson, M. S., & Oh, J. E. (1983). HMO members and clinicians rank health education needs. *Public Health Reports, 98,* 22–226.

Office of Disease Prevention and Health Promotion. (1989). *National survey of work site health promotion activities.* Washington, DC: U.S. Government Printing Office.

Pearse, R. (1977). *What managers think about their managerial careers.* New York: AMACOM.

Pederson, D., Sieber, W., & Sundin, D. (1986). *Health care trends in United States industry: The changing nature of work and workforce.* Proceedings of the Third Joint U.S.-Finnish Science Symposium. Cincinnati, OH: National Institute for Occupational Safety and Health.

President's Commission on Mental Health. (1978). (Stock No. 040-000-00390-8). Washington, DC: U.S. Government Printing Office.

Quebec Social and Family Affairs Council. (1984). *Rapport du comite d'etude sur la promotion de la sante* [Report of the study committee for health promotion]. Quebec, Canada: Gouvernement du Quebec.

Quinn, R., Seashore, S., Kahn, R., Mangione, T., Campbell, D., Staines, G., & McCullough, M. (1971). *Survey of working conditions: Final report on univariate and bivariate tables* (Document No. 2916-0001). Washington, DC: U.S. Government Printing Office.

Quinn, R. P., & Shepard, L. (1974). *Quality of employment survey: Descriptive statistics, with comparison data from the 1969–70 survey of working conditions.* Ann Arbor: University of Michigan, Survey Research Center.

Quinn, R. P., & Staines, G. L. (1979). *The 1977 Quality of Employment Survey: Descriptive statistics, with comparison data from the 1969–70 and the 1972–73 survey.* Ann Arbor: University of Michigan, Survey Research Center.

Robins, L. N., Heltzer, J. E., Croughan, J., Williams, J. B. W., & Spitzer, R. E. (1981). *NIMH diagnostic interviews schedule: Version III* (Final report on Contract No. 278-79-00 17DB and Research Office Grant No. 33583). Rockville, MD: U.S. Department of Health and Human Services and National Institute of Mental Health.

Rohan, T. M. (1982). Pushers on the payroll: A nightmare for management. *Industry Week, 212,* 52.

Rutenfranz, J., Colquhoun, W. P., Knauth, P., & Ghata, J. N. (1977). Biomedical and psychosocial aspects of shift work. *Scandinavian Journal of Work Environment Health, 3,* 165–182.

Salvendy, G., & Smith, M. J. (Eds.). (1981). *Machine pacing and occupational stress.* London: Taylor & Francis.

Sauter, S. L., Hurrell, J. J., Jr., & Cooper, C. L. (Eds.). 1989. *Job control and worker health.* New York: Wiley.

Shilling, S., & Brackbill, R. M. (1987). Occupational health and safety risks and potential health consequences percieved by U.S. workers. *Public Health Reports, 102,* 36–46.

Silverman, M. M., Eichler, A., & Williams, G. D. (1987). Self-reported stress: Findings from the 1985 National Health Interview Survey. *Public Health Reports, 102,* 47–53.

Silvestri, G. T., & Lukasiewicz, J. M. (1985, November). Occupational employment projections: The 1984–95 outlook. *Monthly Labor Review,* 42–57.

Smith, K. U., & Smith, M. F. (1973). *Psychology: An introduction to behavior science.* Boston: Little, Brown.

Social Security Bulletin. (1989). *Annual statistical supplement, 1989* (DHHS Publication No. 13-11700). Baltimore, MD: U.S. Government Printing Office.

Sutherland, V. J., & Cooper, C. L. (1988). Sources of work stress. In J. J. Hurrell, L. R. Murphy, S. L. Sauter, & C. L. Cooper (Eds.), *Occupational stress: Issues and developments in research* (pp. 3–39). London: Taylor & Francis.

Spector, P. E. (1986). Perceived control by employees: A meter-analysis of studies concerning autonomy and participation in decision making. *Human Relations, 39,* 1005–1016.

Theorell, T., & Rahe, R. (1972). Behavorial and life satisfaction characteristics of Swedith subjects with myocardial infarction. *Journal of Chronic Disease, 25,* 139–147.

Top 200 drugs of 1984: 2.1% increase in refills pushes 1981 RxS 1.7% ahead of 1983. (1985, April). *Pharmacy Times,* pp. 25–33.

U.S. Department of Health, Education, and Welfare (1968). *Eighth Revision International Classification of Diseases Adapted for Use in the United States* (National Center for Health Statistics). Washington, DC: U.S. Government Printing Office.

U.S. Department of Health, Education, and Welfare. (1979). *Healthy people—The Surgeon General's report on health promotion and disease prevention* (Publication No. 79-55071. Washington, DC: U.S. Government Printing Office.

Van Sell, V., Brief, A. P., & Shuler, R. S. (1981). Role conflict and ambiguity: Intergration of literature and directions for future research. *Human Relations, 34,* 43–71.

Wahlund, I., & Nerell, G. (1976). *Work environment of white collar workers—Work, health, well-being.* Stockholm, Sweden: Central Organization of Salaried Employees.

Wallis, C. (1983, June). Stres: Can we cope? *Time,* pp. 48–54.

Walsh, D., & Hingson, R. (1985). Where to refer employees for treatment of drinking problems. *Journal of Occupational Medicine, 27,* 745–752.

Yates, J. E. (1979). *Managing stress.* New York: AMACOM.

Part III _____

Panel Papers and Comments

Health Promotion, Education, and Treatment Panel

Panel Members

James Campbell Quick, Chairperson, *University of Texas at Arlington, Arlington, TX*

Jordan Barab, *American Federation of County, State, and Municipal Employees, Washington, DC*

Joseph J. Hurrell, Jr., *National Institute for Occupational Safety and Health, Cincinnati, OH*

John M. Ivancevich, *University of Houston—University Park, Houston, TX*

A. David Mangelsdorff, *U.S. Army Health Care Studies and Clinical Investigation Activity, Health Services Command, Fort Sam Houston, San Antonio, TX*

Kenneth R. Pelletier, *Institute for Advancement of Health, San Francisco, CA*

Jonathan Raymond, *Gordon College, Wenham, MA*

Daniel C. Smith, *McDonnell-Douglas Corporation, Bridgeton, MO*

Veronica Vaccaro, *The Washington Business Group on Health, Washington, DC*

Steven Weiss, *National Heart, Lung, and Blood Institute, National Institutes of Health, Bethesda, MD*

James Campbell Quick

Health Promotion, Education, and Treatment

Section 1: Introduction

It is the intent of this paper to set out a strategy for enhancing individuals' mental, emotional, and psychological health as well as their stress management skills in the worksite. The paper is organized in five sections. Section 1 is an introduction to the problems associated with occupational mental health and work stress, to the rationale for the worksite as the point of intervention, and to the public health notions of prevention as the basis for action. Section 2 outlines the panel's strategy for promoting occupational mental health and stress management through education and treatment, with attention given to specific target populations. Section 3 reviews the need for evaluation research, including a discussion of relevant research dilemmas, criteria, and issues. Section 4 identifies the national constituents concerned with occupational mental health and work stress. National policy issues, responsibilities, and funding are addressed here. Section 5 is the conclusion.

The Problem

Eisenberg and Parron (1979) focused attention on the national burden of suffering produced by mental disorders in their contribution to the U.S. Surgeon General's report *Healthy People* (Hamburg, Nightengale, & Kalmar, 1979). Levi's (1979) contribution to the same report estimated 15% of the United States population is in need of mental health services at any one time. About the same time, the American Psychiatric Association (1980) classified occupational factors as etiologic agents for psychological disorders. Sauter, Murphy, and Hurrell (1990) reported that during 1980 there was a 6-month prevalence of psychological disorders about equal to that of hypertension. Three different studies have found that mental health treatment, the provision of mental health services, and/or treatment for distressful behaviors (i.e., alcohol and drug abuse) can reduce subsequent somaticizing and/or overutilization of other medical services (Cummings & VandenBos, 1981; Jones & Vischi, 1979; Mumford, Schlesinger, Glass, Patrick, & Cuerdon 1984).

The direct economic costs and lost output costs resulting from mismanaged stress and occupational mental health are substantial. Over a 20-year period, the Kaiser-Permanente Health Plan found that 60% of all physician visits were by patients who had nothing physically wrong with them and another 20% to 30% of physician visits were by patients who had physical illnesses (e.g., peptic ulcer and hypertension) with a stress-related component (Cummings & VandenBos, 1981). Yet, while 48 middle- to large-sized Fortune 1000 companies ranked "improve mental health" as the third highest health priority (Jacobson, 1988), a review of selected worksite health promotion program activities and supporting policies did not find mental health initiatives in the top six priorities (U.S. Government, 1989). Given these facts, attention needs to be brought to bear on improved stress management and occupational mental health.

Mullen (1988) is among those who have argued that there was an unrestrained growth in health care costs during the 1980s. Green and Kreuter (1990) maintain that health promotion policy may well have passed a cost containment era, having moved through the eras of resource development and redistribution. With business being the largest purchaser of health care services, the cost of health care has become a major concern for corporations during the 1980s. Can health care utilization at the national level be reduced through improved occupational mental health?

The chronic diseases, such as hypertension, have replaced the acute and infectious diseases in the United States during the twentieth century as the leading causes of death (Foss & Rothenberg, 1987; Green & Kreuter, 1990). This trend is likely to accelerate with the changing demographics (i.e., the aging adult population) within the United States during the 1990s and early twenty-first century. Stress and a range of psychosocial/behavioral risk factors are becoming increasingly important in chronic health disorders (Fielding, 1984; Pelletier, 1977; Quick & Quick, 1984).

While there are cases where organizations have attended to the mental and psychological well-being of their employees (e.g., Mobil Oil Corporation; see Moss, 1981), there has not been a focused, national strategy in the United States to advance the mental and psychological health of individuals in the workplace. Yet, humanitarian and utilitarian (i.e., financial and economic) motivations exist for such a national strategy (see Fielding, 1984; Ilgen, 1990), for the purposes of (a) performance enhancement in the worksite, (b) reduction in health care utilization, and (c) improvement of workforce health and well-being.

An often unstated and persistent threat or stigma associated with labels such as "mental health disorders," "mental illness," and "stress-related disorders" inhibit many from entering the public health battlefields of occupational mental health and stress management. Too often our language blames the victim and inhibits our collective capacity to formulate health promotion strategies to confront the complex issues of occupational mental health and stress management.

The Worksite

Ilgen (1990) has contended that health issues in the workplace are approaching crisis proportion and that the workplace provides a particularly fine setting within which to address health (see also Nathan, 1984a). Raymond, Wood and Patrick's (1990) work indicates that we may have overlooked the worksite as a prime locus of activity while advancing healthful lifestyles for the population in other loci of activity, such as the community or family. Fielding (1990) argues that the scientific base related to worksite health-promotion is thin and proposed 10 priority research challenges.

Behrens (1990) and Maloney (1990) push for health promotion with employee families because the family has an important influence on health practices. Green and Kreuter (1990) believe the community is the center of gravity for health promotion activities; and Pilisuk, Parks, Kelly, and Turner (1982) have reported on the success of the Galt Helping Network Project, a community-based program in mental health promotion that relies primarily on the use of natural helpers. Is our notion of "community" too narrow, however?

Military organizations and units are excellent illustrations of systems in which the intersection of community and occupational or work life occurs. Similarly, for many large corporations, the worksite is a central locus of activity, just as the military base is for operational units. Hence, for many in the working population, the worksite has become a key locus of "community," especially with the significant migration of women into the workforce and out of neighborhoods and suburbs.

As the largest purchasers of health services, corporations have at least one utilitarian motivation for concern with mental health issues in the worksite. In addition, increasing attention is being drawn to job stress and psychosocial factors as health risks for which the corporation has legal responsibility. While it is not always clear what liability the work organization has for managing, preventing, or compensating employees with regard to these risks (Ivancevich, Matteson, & Richards, 1985), some courts have held corporations responsible. For example, Ivancevich and his associates cite, among others, the case of *Carter v. General Motors* (1960), which accepted psychological illness as a disabling injury on the job. Finally, as the nation confronts a shortage of highly skilled labor, there is a strong motivation to care for the available labor resource.

The humanitarian and utilitarian motivations for work organizations to be concerned with the occupational mental health of its labor force are not mutually exclusive. Is the collision of profits and people inevitable (Winpisinger, 1987) or is there some common ground which may be found for humanitarian and utilitarian interests?

Prevention

While the "epidemiological revolution" of the nineteenth century is usually attributed to the development of the germ theory of disease and its application in public health, Green and Kreuter (1990, p. 323) trace it more directly to massive lifestyle changes in the European and North American populations. During the twentieth century, the population of the United States has relied upon public health notions (as employed in preventive medicine) and behavioral changes in lifestyles (e.g., exercise and fitness) to extend life expectancy at birth approximately 50%, from near 50 years at the turn of the century to 74.9 years as of 1985 (see Eisenberg & Parron, 1979; Levi, 1979; Quick, 1989; Quick & Quick, 1984; U.S. Government, 1988a).[1]

---

[1]For an extensive and detailed treatment of health promotion from a behavioral perspective, with a strong emphasis on disease prevention, see the Matarazzo, Weiss, Herd, Miller, & Weiss (1984) handbook, especially Chapter 1 (by Matarazzo), Chapter 9 (by DeLeon & VandenBos), and Section 11: Settings for Health Promotion.

Progress in the field of occupational health has at times been slow. According to Wegman and Fine, "The lack of steady improvement in identification and prevention of occupational disease stems from the continuous but uneven introduction of new industrial processes, materials, and products since the industrial revolution" (1990, p. 90). They then go on to indicate that the public health response to the occupational risks has been both uneven and lagged. Hence the need for timely and appropriate preventive action.

The three stages of prevention are generally well understood and accepted within the public health community, where specific applications can be made in the cases of acute and infectious diseases. However, the transference of these notions to the mental health arena is not always straightforward (see Eisenberg & Parron, 1979). For conceptual clarity, this paper employs the following prevention framework: *Primary prevention* concerns interventions aimed at eliminating, reducing, or altering worksite demands (stressors) and occupational mental health risks (e.g., task redesign programs). *Secondary prevention* concerns approaches designed to teach individuals new skills for managing inevitable or unavoidable worksite demands (stressors) and occupational mental health risks (e.g., corporate fitness programs and relaxation training). *Tertiary prevention* concerns treatment activities intended to alleviate suffering or dysfunction resulting from worksite demands (stressors) and occupational mental health risks (e.g., psychological counseling or traumatic stress debriefings). While primary prevention is always the preferred initial stage from a public health standpoint, individual traits and situational circumstances may not make that feasible. Secondary prevention (i.e., changing the person) seems to be the stage at which we most often begin.

Section 2: A Strategy for Education and Treatment

Physical fitness and exercise have been the centerpiece of corporate health promotion programs in the United States and Canada (Eakin, Gotay, Rademaker, & Cowell, 1988; Gebhardt & Crump, 1990; O'Donnell & Ainsworth, 1984). In this regard, the North Americans are ahead of the Europeans, Scandinavians, and Asians, both in the use of exercise and fitness for health promotion and in their use in a corporate wellness context (Collingwood, personal communication, July 3, 1990).[2]

The Scandinavian countries have been leaders in using notions from occupational health psychology to promote work redesign initiatives as opposed to lifestyle change initiatives. The former targets the demands which give rise to stress and risk in the worksite while the latter targets individual response, placing the burden of adjustment on the individual. A review of the most intensively researched programs, such as Johnson & Johnson's Live for Life, AT&T's TLC, Control Data's Staywell, and the Coors' Wellness Program shows a strong emphasis on lifestyle change (Weiss, Fielding, & Baun, 1990).

It is necessary to give attention to the adaptation and change of the worksite, with particular attention to the demands and stressors of that environment (Gardell, 1981, 1987; Ivancevich, Matteson, Freedman, & Phillips, 1990; Kryder, 1988; Levi,

---

[2]See Brengelmann (1990) for a report on some interesting developments taking place in West Germany.

1979; Quick & Quick, 1984; Winpisinger, 1987). That is why the Work Design Panel's contribution to a comprehensive strategy for mental health promotion and well-being in the worksite is so integral to, and the point of departure for, the efforts of the Health Promotion Panel. It is the Work Design Panel that will deal with the organizational, environmental, and task redesign issues of enhancing the psychological health of the worksite.

Prevention and treatment activities should be integrated into a comprehensive approach to promote individual's overall well-being (DeCarlo, 1985; Eisenberg & Parron, 1979). Unfortunately, the overall level of education and training received by workers in mental health issues has been found to be quite lacking (Neal, Singer, Schwartz, & Schwartz, 1983). Hence, the educational component is an essential foundation for the prevention strategy.

The Educational Component

There are three essential content areas to be addressed through education and training in the worksite. (We will address these areas and their relation to target populations in a later subsection.)

1. *Awareness and appreciation of psychological disorders* as occupational health problems in the workplace and their relationship to organizational-level outcomes.
2. *Understanding of work (and nonwork) risks and demands* which adversely impact occupational mental health.
3. *Recognition of individual signs and organizational symptoms* of mismanaged stress and impaired occupational mental health as early warning indicators of problems in the workplace.

The purpose of the educational and training component of this strategy will be to shape occupational health psychology attitudes and behavior, overcome stereotypes and stigmas, and promote early recognition and response to budding mental health disorders. Television, the mass media, computers, and other vehicles may be considered in elevating awareness and knowledge concerning mental health issues so as to ultimately change health behaviors (DeLeon & VandenBos, 1984; Flora & Maibach, 1989; Gustafson, Bosworth, Chewning, & Hawkins, 1987). The Surgeon General's campaign against smoking and the "Just Say NO" campaign against drugs are examples of mass educational programs targeting health behaviors. One of the key targets of this educational component are social norms which are the bases for individual behavior and action (Flora & Maibach, 1989).

For example, a beneficial social norm concerning exercise behavior has evolved in the United States over the last 20 years. It has been a key ingredient in the success of corporate exercise/fitness programs. On the other hand, a potentially destructive social norm concerns the value Americans place on individualism (Hofstede, 1980). The problem lies in the health risks associated with the social isolation which may be fostered by individualism (Gerpott, 1990; Hamburg & Killilea, 1979; House, Landis, & Umberson, 1988). Other cultures, notably China and Japan, place greater value on collectivism and the group. Hence, they do not foster social isolation.

The worksite education component should be supported by and extend from university-based graduate education programs, both at the masters and doctoral levels, in occupational health psychology and preventive stress management (Quick, 1988; Raymond et al., 1990). These programs need to blend the fields of mental health and psychology with training in public health. Curriculum development in the past 10 years in the schools of psychology, medicine, business, and public health should be the point of departure for this emerging university-based graduate education. The first required stress course at a medical school in the United States was developed by R. Nathan (1987), a clinical psychologist. Graduate courses in stress and work, self-regulation, behavioral epidemiology, and preventive stress management have been developed in departments of management, social work, and schools of public health (e.g., University of Houston, 1990; University of Texas at Arlington, 1990).

These graduate courses are part of an emerging educational curriculum which addresses a variety of questions through objective knowledge-based, self-assessment, and skill-based education (Quick, 1990; Stoto, Behrens, & Rosement, 1990) as well as through a strong emphasis on both theory, applied research, and practice (Raymond et al. 1990). The questions addressed include:

- What is the psychophysiology of stress?
- What is occupational mental health?
- What are the environmental and self-induced causes of stress?
- What are the environmental and self-induced risks to occupational mental health?
- What are the medical, psychological, and/or behavioral costs of distress and suboptimal mental health?
- How do we enable the individual to more successfully manage the demands of stressful environments?
- What lifestyle prevention and intervention strategies enhance stress management skills and mental health functioning?
- What developmental, cognitive, and social skills enhance individual resistance to environmental demands and mental health risks?

For the transference of a developed body of knowledge and skills to worksite educational settings, Pelletier and Lutz (1988, p. 10) developed a modularized program concept. Each program contained the following elements:

1. at least one stress management technique, such as diaphragmatic breathing;
2. one session per week;
3. a maximum session length of 45 minutes;
4. 12 to 15 participants;
5. peer led programs as well as professionally led ones;
6. homework, generalization skills, and follow-up;
7. evaluations to determine the program's efficacy; and

8. a curriculum that cannot be used as a substitute for correcting work design flaws.

As Raymond et al. (1990) have emphasized, education in occupational health psychology requires interdisciplinary collaboration and multidisciplinary approaches. While enhancing occupational mental health and stress management in the worksite may be rooted in occupational health psychology, public health, business administration, organizational behavior, and other disciplines may well need to be incorporated as the field grows.

The Treatment Component

Regardless of how effectively work design strategies are carried out and educational initiative pursued for purposes of primary and secondary prevention, there will be a need for treatment of those who suffer. The treatment component should involve the specification of mental health care and psychological treatment interventions/ services which may be made available to the specific organizational populations.[3]

The treatment component should be an extension of the educational component of the strategy. For example, Doherty (1989) argues that workers can be successfully treated for depression if employers recognize early warning symptoms and encourage treatment. While early detection and the encouragement of treatment require knowledge of symptoms as well as possible referral sources for treatment, the generally supportive nature of a work environment may play an importantly therapeutic role in and of itself. Education, treatment, and an emotionally supportive worksite can work together in fulfilling the strategy.

The treatment component here is not intended to deal with major mental health disorders such as severe mental deficiency, serious schizophrenias, and some of the serious developmental problems (Eisenberg & Parron, 1979). Rather, the targets are the range of affective and stress-related occupational mental health issues amenable to worksite or outpatient intervention. Key components of such treatment programs, using a variation of Pelletier and Lutz's (1988, p. 11) approach to stress management intervention in the worksite, would include:

- identification of symptomatic and high risk individuals (including screening out those with major mental disorders),
- appropriate referral and/or treatment of individuals,
- symptom-directed treatment by appropriate professionals,
- follow-up to assure treatment effectiveness, and
- evaluation of health improvement and cost efficacy.

Two concluding points are important here. First, further detail in the treatment component of the strategy must hinge, in part, on the input of the Surveillance

---

[3]The notion of 'treatment' usually refers to specific actions and/or techniques to be used in response to specific symptoms. It may be useful at this juncture to keep in mind the notion of lifestyle change interventions which are aimed at establishing a 'strong and resistant host' within the individual (see Weiss et al., 1990). These generalized forms of lifestyle change, as in the case of exercise, set the stage for good occupational mental health and stress management, and prevention is preferred to treatment.

Panel and their findings concerning incidence rates of affective and other mental health risk factors. Second, there are real "stigma" dilemmas here, as mentioned at the beginning of this paper, for individuals who become "identified" through the screening process mentioned above. Care with our language becomes very critical at this juncture.

Target Populations

Most organizations and worksites organize their employment populations based upon some combination of functional categories and hierarchical distinctions. Using this somewhat classical scheme for the identification of target populations within the worksite, we can create the following scheme:

1. *operating level employees*, either in manufacturing or service related industries;
2. *first line supervisors*, who straddle the interface between the operating and managerial levels in the system;
3. *middle management*, who connect the first level of supervision with the top level managerial team; and
4. *top level management*, who are strategically involved in the direction of the system.

Some argue that the health risks and health service needs of these hierarchical populations are quite different (Moss, 1981; Shostak, 1980; Winpisinger, 1987). While there may be validity in using this scheme, an alternative way of identifying and serving worksite populations needs to at least be considered.

For example, there is epidemiological evidence that significant differences in life expectancy, mortality, and morbidity exist in the country by race and sex (Matarazzo et al., 1984). Given the changing demographics of the worksite, it may be appropriate to organize educational and treatment initiatives to target populations based on risks and symptoms. This is the second place where the Surveillance Panel plays a crucial role in the overall national strategy. Hence, target populations from this perspective might be: women, minority groups, older workers (i.e., later career stages), those subject to reorganizations, single heads of households, and so forth.

While care must be exercised with regard to discrimination against protected classes of employees, there is evidence that differences do exist in the risks and symptoms among the target populations just identified (Hurrell, McLaney, & Murphy, 1990; Matarazzo et al., 1984; Matteson & Ivancevich, 1990; Nelson, Quick, & Hitt, 1989; U.S. Government, 1989; Verbrugge, 1989a, 1989b). Friedman and Gray (1989) recommended different and specific benefits packages for employees depending upon family and career cycle circumstances. They argued that employees have the need for greater education in these areas because their risks and needs are quite different.

Section 3: Evaluation Research

Funding the educational and treatment strategy outlined in the last section should depend on the establishment of evaluation research designs aimed at developing criteria data. The key questions driving this evaluation research component are: Is there a return on the human resource investment made in mental health education and treatment? and How should we measure the return?

The evaluation research studies of current fitness and wellness programs show that the payoff periods are often long and uncertain (Baun, Bernacki, & Tsai, 1986). In their evaluation of the Tenneco exercise program (random sample $N = 517$), Baun, Bernacki, and Tsai (1986) found lower illness absences among the exercisers, significantly lower ambulatory health care costs, and some apparent "absence proneness" among the nonexercisers. In evaluating the Live for Life Program at Johnson & Johnson, Bly, Jones, and Richardson (1986) used two health promotion groups ($N = 5,192$, and $N = 3,259$) and one control group ($N = 2,955$). The two health promotion groups in the Live for Life Program had (a) lower mean inpatient health care cost increases, (b) lower rates of increase in hospital days, and (c) no difference in outpatient and other health care costs.[4]

Health promotion programs with exercise and fitness as the central component are not the only type of programs to have been evaluated to date. Stern (1990) published a review of EAPs in terms of utilization, cost-benefit, and success rates. She reports that the often cited McDonnell Douglas study focused on the reduced health claims money saved and lower absentee rates of its EAP "graduates."

Fielding (1984) indicated that return on investment is usually approached from a cost-benefit standpoint or a cost-effectiveness perspective where the evaluation of health promotion programs are concerned. After reviewing four corporate health promotion/disease prevention programs, he concluded that, while no one successful model exists, some important keys for success are:

- long-term commitment,
- top management support,
- employee involvement,
- professional leadership,
- clearly defined objectives,
- careful planning, and
- family involvement.

While descriptive research of this nature may be a useful point of departure, building rigorous natural scientific as well as idiographic scientific designs will be essential. Excellent research designs and results can be achieved in field settings despite the occurrence of unplanned and uncontrolled events or the presence of a wide range of causal factors which affect individuals and organizational systems. Where attributing causality in field research is complicated and problematic, idiographic research designs may be employed.

Should health promotion programs of any kind use utilitarian and economic criteria alone in their evaluation? Warner, Wickizer, Wolfe, Schildroth, and Sam-

---

[4]See Nathan (1984b) for a presentation of the Johnson & Johnson Live for Life Program.

uelson (1988) were somewhat cautious and circumspect in reviewing the literature published through 1986 concerning the profitability claims of most health promotion programs. "The dearth of sound evidence on the economic merits of workplace HP (health plans) should not be interpreted as a negative assessment of the potential of such programs, however." (Warner et al., 1988, p. 106). Given the tremendous health and economic toll of preventable illness and the prospect of reducing the toll through changing behavior, they recommended the pursuit of a rigorous, research-based body of knowledge in this regard.

Humanitarian and utilitarian criteria are both important in the design of evaluation research programs. Specific criteria such as illness, absenteeism, and health care cost reflect the concern for individual health and well-being as well as organizational costs and performance. In addition, attention to the criteria of morbidity and mortality in the context of long-term evaluation of program impact is important (McLeroy, Green, Mullen, & Foshee, 1984).

Large scale evaluation programs which compare group-oriented, competitive, environmentally-based, and multiple risk factor programs must be developed (Mullen, 1988). The designs should be longitudinal in nature and developed in concert with work redesign proposals and epidemiological/surveillance evidence. Particular attention needs to be devoted to more comprehensive, as opposed to risk specific, programs given some of the etiological difficulties in the mental health arena (Eisenberg & Parron, 1979).

Section 4: Constituents and Responsibilities

In advocating health promotion as a public health strategy for the decade of the 1990s, Green and Kreuter (1990) proposed that a combined set of private sector, independent sector, federal, and global initiatives are essential for the execution of the strategy. The advancement of mental health in the worksite will require the combined efforts of at least six major constituents, each with differing interests and responsibilities.

The Constituents

The six major constituents with direct interests in occupational mental health promotion and stress management in the worksite are:

1. employees and employee groups,
2. private sector organizations,
3. health care providers,
4. health insurance companies,
5. federal and state government, and
6. universities and educational institutions.

Each of these constituents has a vested interest in the issue of occupational mental health and stress management in the worksite. Some of the interests are of a more humanitarian nature (e.g., employees and employee groups) while others are of a more utilitarian or financial nature (e.g., health insurance companies). All share some common ground in terms of their diverse, yet related, interests.

Educational institutions have a somewhat different set of interests in the issues of occupational mental health and stress management in the worksite. Their interests lie in the areas of curriculum development for health care and business professionals as well as research agendas related to the health risks, health promotion, program effectiveness, and so on.

The Responsibilities

For an educational and treatment health promotion strategy to be effective, the various national constituents must accept a combination of individual as well as shared responsibility for implementation and evaluation. The notions of partnership and collaboration are crucial in this regard. For example, partnerships can be formed between government agencies and academic institutions, private sector companies and labor unions, and insurers to design and implement research to:

- improve our understanding of health risk factors;
- develop valid, reliable measures for risk assessment; and
- evaluate the effectiveness of strategy components.

Pelletier, Klehr, and McPhee (1988a, 1988b) have reported on a combined effort of a consortium of private sector companies, such as AT&T and Bank of America, working collaboratively with the University of California at San Francisco in the Bay area for the purpose of health promotion. Doherty's (1989) report is based on the Depression/Awareness, Recognition, and Treatment (D/ART) Worksite Program project funded by NIMH. It is a good example of a private sector/government sector partnership which needs to be encouraged (U.S. Government, 1988b).

In the D/ART Program, employers are taking steps against untreated depression by impacting awareness and recognition as well as ensuring that appropriate and well-managed care is made available. Components of effective employer efforts include:

- employee education for health promotion/disease prevention,
- management training,
- employee assistance services,
- benefit redesign and management,
- data collection for decision making,
- integration of corporate health related services, and
- attention to organizational health.

Efforts such as these, where there is a sharing of interests, expertise, and resources, is essential to the long-term success of any national strategy for the advancement of mental health in the workplace. Natural alliances are most effective where mutual concerns provide the driving force for success.

The federal government, in collaboration with other constituents, must play an integral role in setting national policy with regard to mental health in the workplace, followed by publishing and promoting strategies for the fulfillment of the policy. Another role may be that of providing some incentives for program implementation, such as tax credits, while expecting other constituents to play important roles in direct funding of programs.

Section 5: Conclusion

While the population of the United States is not in the first rank of developed nations when it comes to life expectancy at birth, we have enjoyed much success in advancing the war on morbidity and mortality during the twentieth century: witness the 50% increase in life expectancy during the 1900s. It is now time to focus more attention on the mental health of our population, with specific attention to occupational mental health and stress management in the worksite. As Senator Cohen (1985) has argued, our public health enemies have shifted from the acute and infectious diseases to the chronic and debilitating ones. Cohen then goes on to say that the public health battlefield must now include the workplace as well as other public health settings. The quality of life, especially in the workplace, can be advanced through a health promotion strategy of education and treatment which is founded on the public health notions of prevention. At the same time, the individual and collective costs of this burden of suffering may be eased with the strategy's implementation. There are compelling humanitarian and utilitarian (i.e., financial and economic) motivations for the nation to establish such a mental health agenda in the workplace for the decade of the 1990s.

References

American Psychiatric Association. (1980). *Diagnostic and statistical manual of mental disorders (3rd ed.)*. Washington, DC: Author.

Baun, W. B., Bernacki, E. J., & Tsai, S. P. (1986). A preliminary investigation: Effect of a corporate fitness program on absenteeism and health care cost. *Journal of Occupational Medicine, 28*, 826–830.

Behrens, R. (1990). *Reaching families through worksite and community health promotion programs*. Washington, DC: Washington Business Group on Health.

Bly, J. L., Jones, R. C., & Richardson, J. E. (1986). Impact of worksite health promotion on health care costs and utilization. *Journal of the American Medical Association, 256*, 3235–3240.

Brengelmann, J. C. (1990). Work-site health promotion: The European experience, with particular emphasis on the Federal Republic of Germany. In S. M. Weiss, J. E. Fielding, & W. B. Baun (Eds.), *Health at work* (pp. 37–48). Hillsdale, NJ: Lawrence Erlbaum Associates.

Carter v. General Motors Corporation. (1960). 361 Michigan 577, 106 N.W. 2nd 105.

Cohen, W. S. (1985). Health promotion in the workplace: A prescription for good health. *American Psychologist, 40*, 213–216.

Cummings, N. A., & VandenBos, G. R. (1981). The twenty years Kaiser-Permanente experience with psychotherapy and medical utilization: Implications for national health policy and national health insurance. *National Policy Quarterly, 1*, 159–175.

DeCarlo, D. T. (Ed.). (1985). *Legal insight*. New York: National Council on Compensation Insurance.

DeLeon, P. H., & VandenBos, G. R. (1984). Public health policy and behavioral health. In J. D. Matarazzo, S. M. Weiss, J. A. Herd, N. E. Miller, & S. M. Weiss (Eds.), *Behavioral health: A handbook of health enhancement and disease prevention* (pp. 150–163). New York: John Wiley.

Doherty, K. (1989). The good news about depression. *Business & Health, March*, 1–4.

Eakin, J. M., Gotay, C. C., Rademaker, A. W., & Cowell, J. W. F. (1988). Factors associated with enrollment in an employee fitness center. *Journal of Occupational Medicine, 30*, 633–637.

Eisenberg, L., & Parron, D. (1979). Strategies for the prevention of mental disorders. In D. A. Hamburg, E. O. Nightengale, & V. Kalmar (Eds.), *Healthy people: The Surgeon General's Report on Health Promotion and Disease Prevention* (pp. 135–155). Washington, DC: U.S. Department of Health, Education, and Welfare.

Fielding, J. E. (1984). Health promotion and disease prevention at the worksite. *Annual Review of Public Health, 5*, 237–265.

Fielding, J. E. (1990). The challenges of work-place health promotion, In S. M. Weiss, J. E. Fielding, & A. Baun (Eds.), *Health at work* (pp. 13–28). Hillsdale, NJ: Lawrence Erlbaum Associates.

Flora, J. A., & Maibach, E. W. (1989). The role of media across four levels of health promotion intervention. *Annual Review of Public Health, 10*, 181–201.

Foss, L., & Rothenberg, K. (1987). *The second medical revolution: From biomedical to infomedical.* Boston: New Science Library.

Friedman, D. E., & Gray, W. B. (1989). *A life cycle approach to family benefits and policies.* New York: The Conference Board.

Gardell, B. (1981). Autonomy and participation at work. In L. Levi (Ed.), *Society, stress, and disease: Vol. 4. Working life.* Oxford: Oxford University Press.

Gardell, B. (1987). Efficiency and healthy hazards in mechanized work. In J. C. Quick, R. S. Bhyagat, J. E. Dalton, & J. D. Quick (Eds.), *Work stress: Health care systems in the workplace* (pp. 50–71). New York: Praeger.

Gebhardt, D. L., & Crump, C. E. (1990). Employee fitness and wellness programs in the workplace. *American Psychologist, 45*, 262–272.

Gerpott, T. J. (1990). Intracompany job transfers: An exploratory, two-sample study of the buffering effects of interpersonal support. *Prevention in Human Services, 8*, 113–137.

Green, L. W., & Kreuter, M. W. (1990). Health promotion as a public health strategy for the 1990s. *Annual Review of Public Health, 11*, 319–334.

Gustafson, D. H., Bosworth, K., Chewning, B., & Hawkins, R. P. (1987). Computer-based health promotion: Combining technological advances with problem-solving techniques to effect successful health behavior changes. *Annual Review of Public Health, 8*, 387–415.

Hamburg, B. A., & Killilea, M. (1979). Relation of social support, stress, illness, and use of health services. In D. A. Hamburg, E. O. Nightengale, & V. Kalmar (Eds.), *Healthy people: The Surgeon General's Report on Health Promotion and Disease Prevention* (pp. 253–276). Washington, DC: U.S. Department of Health, Education, and Welfare.

Hamburg, B. A., Nightengale, E. O., & Kalmar, V. (1979). *Healthy people: The Surgeon General's Report on Health Promotion and Disease Prevention.* Washington, DC: U.S. Department of Health, Education, and Welfare.

Hofstede, G. (1980). *Culture's consequences: International differences in work related values.* Beverly Hills, CA: Sage Publishers, Inc.

House, J. S., Landis, K. R., & Umberson, D. (1988). Social relationships and health. *Science, 241*, 540–545.

Hurrell, J. J., Jr., McLaney, M. A., & Murphy, L. R. (1990). The middle years: Career stage differences. *Prevention in Human Services, 8*, 179–203.

Ilgen, D. R. (1990). Health issues at work: Opportunities for industrial/organizational psychology. *American Psychologist, 45*, 273–283.

Ivancevich, J. M., Matteson, M. T., Freedman, S. M., & Phillips, J. S. (1990). Worksite stress management interventions. *American Psychologist, 45*, 252–261.

Ivancevich, J. M., Matteson, M. T., & Richards, E. P., III. (1985). Who's liable for stress on the job? *Harvard Business Review, 64*, 60–72.

Jacobson, M. (1988). Employers zero in on future health. *Business and Health*, October, 36–39.

Jones, K. R., & Vischi, R. R. (1979). Impact of alcohol, drug abuse, and mental health treatment on medical care utilization: A review of the research literature. *Supplement to Medical Care, 17*, iii–82.

Kryder, S. (1988). Organizational development in worksite health promotion programming. *Fitness in Business*, August, 3–9.

Levi, L. (1979). Psychosocial factors in preventive medicine. In D. A. Hamburg, E. O. Nightengale, & V. Kalmar (Eds.), *Healthy people: The Surgeon General's Report on Health Promotion and Disease Prevention* (pp. 207–252). Washington, DC: U.S. Department of Health, Education, and Welfare.

Maloney, S. (1990). *Community-based health promotion programs for employees and their families.* Washington, DC: Washington Business Group on Health.

Matarazzo, J. D., Weiss, S. M., Herd, J. A., Miller, N. E., & Weiss, S. M. (1984). *Behavioral health: A handbook of health enhancement and disease prevention.* New York: Wiley.

Matteson, M. T., & Ivancevich, J. M. (1990). Merger and acquisition stress: Fear and uncertainty at mid-career. *Prevention in Human Services, 8,* 138–158.

McLeroy, K. R., Green, L. W., Mullen, K. D., & Foshee, V. (1984). Assessing the effects of health promotion in worksites: A review of the stress program evaluations. *Health Education Quarterly, 11,* 379–401.

Moss, L. (1981). *Management stress.* Reading, MA: Addison-Wesley.

Mullen, P. D. (1988). Health promotion and patient education benefits for employees. *Annual Review of Public Health, 9,* 305–332.

Mumford, E., Schlesinger, H. J., Glass, G. V., Patrick, C., & Cuerdon, T. (1984). A new look at evidence about reduced cost of medical utilization following mental health treatment. *American Journal of Psychiatry, 141,* 1145–1158.

Nathan, P. (1984a). The worksite as a setting for health promotion and positive lifestyle change. In J. D. Matarazzo, S. M. Weiss, J. A. Herd, N. E. Miller, & S. M. Weiss (Eds.), *Behavioral health: A handbook of healthy enhancement and disease prevention* (pp. 1061–1063). New York: Wiley.

Nathan, P. (1984b). Johnson & Johnson's Live for Life: A comprehensive positive lifestyle change program. In J. D. Matarazzo, S. M. Weiss, J. A. Herd, N. E. Miller, & S. M. Weiss (Eds.), *Behavioral health: A handbook of health enhancement and disease prevention* (pp. 1064–1070). New York: Wiley.

Nathan, R. G., Nixon, F. E., Robinson, L. A., Bairnsfather, L., Allen, J. H., & Hack, M. (1987). Effects of stress management course on grades and health of first-year medical students. *Journal of Medical Education, 62,* 514–517.

Neal, M. S., Singer, J. A., Schwartz, J. L., & Schwartz, G. E. (1983). *Yale-NIOSH occupational stress project.* New Haven: Yale Press.

Nelson, D. L., Quick, J. C., & Hitt, M. A. (1989). Men and women of the personnel profession: Some differences and similarities in their stress. *Stress Medicine, 5,* 145–152.

O'Donnell, M. P., & Ainsworth, T. H. (Eds.). (1984). *Health promotion in the workplace.* New York: Wiley.

Pelletier, K. R. (1977). *Mind as healer, mind as slayer: A holistic approach to preventing stress disorders.* New York: Delcorte Press.

Pelletier, K. R., Klehr, N. L., & McPhee, S. J. (1988a). Town and gown: A lesson in collaboration. *Business & Health, February,* 34–38.

Pelletier, K. R., Klehr, N. L., & McPhee, S. J. (1988b). Developing workplace health promotion programs through university and corporate collaboration: A review of the corporate health promotion research program. *American Journal of Health Promotion, 2,* 75–81.

Pelletier, K. R., & Lutz, R. (1988). Healthy people—healthy business: A critical review of stress management programs in the workplace. *American Journal of Health Promotion, 2,* 5-12, 19.

Pilisuk, M., Parks, S. H., Kelly, J., & Turner, E. (1982). The helping network approach: Community promotion of mental health. *Journal of Primary Prevention, 3,* 116–132.

Quick, J. C. (1988, January). *Health Objectives for the Nation, Year 2000.* Testimony for the American Psychological Association before the U.S. Public Health Service and the Institute of Medicine, National Academy of Sciences. U. T. Health Science Center at Houston, School of Public Health, Houston, TX.

Quick, J. C. (1989). An ounce of prevention is worth a pound of cure. *Stress Medicine, 5,* 207–210.

Quick, J. C. (1990). Development of program standards. In A. D. Mangelsdorff (Ed.), *Proceedings of the 7th Combat Stress Conference: Training for psychic trauma* (pp. 116–120). San Antonio: U.S. Army Health Services Command.

Quick, J. C., & Quick, J. D. (1984). *Organizational stress and preventive management.* New York: McGraw-Hill.

Raymond, J. S., Wood, D. W., & Patrick, W. K. (1990). Psychology doctoral training in work and health. *American Psychologist, 45,* 1159–1161.

Sauter, S. L., Murphy, L. R., & Hurrell, J. J. (1990). Prevention of work related psychological distress: A national strategy proposed by the National Institute of Occupational Safety and Health. *American Psychologist, 45,* 1146–1158.

Shostak, A. B. (1980). *Blue-collar stress*. Reading, MA: Addison-Wesley.

Stoto, M. A., Behrens, R., & Rosemont, C. (Eds.). (1990). *Health people 2000: Citizens chart the course*. Washington, DC: National Academy Press.

Stern, L. (1990). Why EAPs are worth the investment. *Business & Health, May*, 14–19.

U.S. Government. (1988a). *Vital Statistics of the United States. 1985. Life Tables*, Vol. II, Section 6. (DHHS Publication No. PHS 88-1104). January.

U.S. Government. (1988b). *Information about D/ART and depressive disorders: Depression/Awareness, recognition, and treatment program*. U.S. Department of Health and Human Services. Rockville, MD: National Institute of Mental Health.

U.S. Government. (1989). *Disease prevention and health promotion: The facts: Office of Disease Prevention and Health Promotion Prevention Report, December 1–5*. Washington, DC: U.S. Government Printing Office.

University of Houston. (1990). *Graduate and Professional Studies 1990-1992*. 83.

University of Texas at Arlington. (1990, June). *Graduate Catalog 1990–1992, LXXIII* (3), 167, 208.

Verbrugge, L. (1989a). Recent, present, and future health of American adults. *Annual Review of Public Health, 10*, 333–361.

Verbrugge, L. (1989b). Gender, aging, and health. In: Markides, K. S. (Ed.). *Aging and health: Perspectives on gender, race, ethnicity, and class* (pp. 23–78). Newbury Park, CA: Sage Publishers, Inc.

Warner, K. E., Wickizer, T. M., Wolfe, R. A., Schildroth, J. E., & Samuelson, M. H. (1988). *Journal of Occupational Medicine, 30*, 106–112.

Wegman, D. H., & Fine, L. J. (1990). Occupational health in the 1990s. *Annual Review of Public Health, 11*, 89–103.

Weiss, S. M., Fielding, J. E., & Baun, W. B. (1990). *Health at Work*. Hillsdale, NJ: Lawrence Erlbaum Associates.

Winpisinger, W. W. (1987). A labor view of stress management. In: Quick, J. C., Bhagat, R. S., Dalton, J. E., & Quick, J. D, (Eds.) *Work Stress: Health care systems in the workplace* (pp. 210–216). New York: Praeger.

Summary of Panel Comments

James Campbell Quick

The Health Promotion Panel's position paper should be treated as a developmental, not a finished, product. Dave Mangelsdorff's series of well founded, practical questions in a position letter highlighted this fact. The panel members' letters reflected professional positions in relationship to the collective work. In particular, five key points emerged from the letters which I will emphasize here. In addition, one final point from breakout session, ably moderated by Jonathan Fielding, should be highlighted.

First, health promotion should not be a substitute for primary prevention. While mentioned in the paper, the comments of Jordan Barab, Jack Ivancevich, and Veronica Vaccaro suggest an insufficient emphasis on primary (i.e., organizational) prevention. The work of the Health Promotion Panel cannot be taken out of the larger context of the *Work and Well-Being Conference*'s larger structure of work design, surveillance, and health promotion. As Barab stated, health promotion is typically directed at symptoms, not causes. Yet, it is the causes of distress in the workplace which must receive priority and are the purview of primary prevention. Ivancevich challenged the philosophy and procedures of many organizations who do not attend to working out their own stress kinks. We need to, according to Ivancevich, scold corporate inaction, where it exists, and scrutinize corporate activities better. Vaccaro called our attention to corporate policies and procedures which have a detrimental effect on employee mental health and ability to manage stress. So, the first order of business in addressing the larger issues of work and well-being must be the systemic issues of concern to the Work Design Panel and which fall under the responsibility of management. This means addressing the organizational causes of distress and the structural barriers to the health and well-being of workers.

Second, we need positive examples for modeling and emulation. On the positive side, we should not lose sight of the fact that there are enlightened, exemplary organizations and managements who create healthy, safe, and growthful work environments. In this regard, Mangelsdorff emphasized that top level management must play an important role in demonstrating by example. This is particularly important given the hierarchical nature of the vast majority of work organizations, be they large corporations or smaller enterprises. We can also extend his point to the issue of systemic models and examples. Ivancevich made an excellent point concerning the need to find program models beyond the large corporate ones which have drawn much attention during the 1980s. While referring to health promotion programs in particular, Ivancevich stressed that the point should be generalized to entire organizational systems. That is, organizations with healthy corporate policies, philosophies, procedures, and/or practices should be identified and held up as examples to the nation.

Third, mental health promotion and preventive stress management must be placed in a comprehensive context. Steve Weiss addressed the problem of a false dualism created if we separate "mental health" from "overall health." According to Ken Pelletier, we must focus on stress management and/or psychological care in the CONTEXT of "comprehensive" disease prevention and health promotion programs. Joe Hurrell's work deals with the issue from an evaluation research perspective, attending to the psychological impacts of comprehensive health promotion programs. The conclusion is that we *can* address occupational mental health and stress management through a comprehensive health promotion framework. We do not want to disconnect our efforts from the broader efforts at advancing the health and well-being of the nation, efforts which have been very successful during the twentieth century.

Fourth, we must have trust and confidentiality with regard to health records. Both Vaccaro and Mangelsdorff had the panel address the issue of the stigma associated with mental health and stress management in the workplace. Ivancevich and Barab contended that the paper did not take the issue far enough and that, because of the stigma issue, we must be more concerned with confidentiality. Barab was concerned that the typical workplace does not have adequate trust and confidentiality guarantees for the worker to feel secure. And, Ivancevich was concerned that executive resistance to health promotion is grounded in the legal aspects of the confidentiality issue. So, it is more than a labor-management trust issue, it is related to the larger stigma issue within most workplace cultures and the larger society's culture.

Fifth, we must attend to the issue of human capital for the foreseeable future. Dan Smith drew our attention to the critical issue which American business is facing concerning the physical, educational, and psychological capacity of our pool of human capital to sustain itself in the workplace. Hence, a powerful motivational force for the national agenda for which the *Work and Well-Being Conference* argued. Vaccaro pointed out that we need not sing to the choir in this regard. We need to identify target populations for specific interventions *based on risks and symptoms* and this becomes an important way of investing in or nurturing our human capital. The work of the Surveillance Panel becomes critical here.

Finally, national leadership is vital to advancing a work and well-being agenda through the 1990s. During our breakout session, part of what I heard was a plea from those on front lines. These professionals are battling distress in the workplace daily. They have trials, tribulations, and struggles which require strong leadership at the national level. The real foes in this struggle are humanity's eternal enemies, clearly identified by Walter B. Cannon 60 years ago as pain, disease, poverty, and sin. Work is not the foe: It has the powerful potential to elevate the human spirit, a point embodied in the thinking of the Work Design Panel. Thus, there is an army of professionals out there in need of national leadership which can, should, and must be provided if we are to be successful in advancing occupational mental health and preventive stress management during this decade.

Summary of Audience Comments

Steven Weiss and Jonathan Fielding

In the conceptualization of stress and determination of the appropriateness of alternative stress management strategies, attention should be accorded to the differing worksite demographic characteristics. Critical variables include gender, race, culture, and age. The experience of stress, reactions, and attractiveness and efficacy of stress management programs is likely to be different among a work force that is primarily older White women than among a work force of primarily young Black and Hispanic men. Assessments of worksite populations should include queries about how valuable different health attributes are, including low levels of stress and confidence in ability to manage stresses that emanate from the worksite and other relationships and settings.

Educational programming should include primary prevention. For example, top and middle management should be educated on the organizational characteristics of the work environment and leadership styles that tend to promote (and reduce stress), and the potential benefits of an environment that controls the amount of stress routinely experienced by workers. Primary prevention should include education for the entire work force, not just those who self-identify or are identified through other mechanisms as suffering from high stress levels or who appear to have an inadequate inventory of coping skills.

Employers, worker's compensation carriers, and health insurers have a community of interest in finding ways to reduce the incidence and size of stress related claims. Employers and insurers should undertake needs assessments to identify patterns of stress among different employed populations and their dependents. Employees should also be queried about their sources of stress, both inside and outside the work setting, and their needs for changes in the working environment and for programs to help reduce and better manage their stress. Analysis of stress related claims for workers' compensation could indicate patterns suggesting intervention opportunities. For example, high incidence of claims might be associated with a particular type of job, job level, or component of the organization. In addition, the size of claims might be examined for patterns, with longer periods of disability and higher aggregate costs considered indicators of severity.

Union representation is particularly important in establishing effective partnerships between management, labor, and health promotion personnel. Unions often see such programs as management efforts to "paper over" what they consider serious environmental safety and health hazards in the workplace which are not corrected by management because of cost, fear of admitting liability, and so forth. The willingness to consider the structure of the work environment as a potential stressor and health hazard as well as attempting to enhance the coping capabilities of the individual will certainly facilitate cooperation among the various groups noted here.

Practitioners with experience in developing and implementing stress programming at the worksite should be systematically queried to obtain their perspective on what works and what does not. Their experience can also be helpful in determining optimal matches between programs and work settings. Additionally, more effort should be exerted to translate the results of scientific studies into the language and perspectives of business. The best way to "sell" that stress is important and that its adverse effects can be reduced is to identify the priority issues for the organization (e.g., cost control, declining productivity, high turnover) and to show how stress may be an important but somewhat reducible contributor. Assessment of intervention effectiveness should preferentially address those parameters considered most salient to the employer. It is not always possible, however, to justify stress management interventions based on clear-cut cost-benefit or cost-effectiveness analyses.

Reaching employees in smaller organizations—who account for the majority of all workers in the United States—will require innovative approaches. Coalitions of smaller employers and trade organizations (e.g., Chambers of Commerce) may be the most efficient vehicle to reach employees in these work settings. Such groups can develop common approaches to assessing stress and can contract with outside vendors to provide employer consultation and employee (and dependent) educational services. Alternatively, demonstration health promotion programs might be established to serve a specific geographical area, encouraging small businesses to enroll as "corporate" members. This could provide many of the advantages of an "in house" facility (social support of coworkers, etc.) at a cost commensurate to the size of the organization. This model could be tested for efficacy in serving the needs of organizations which (as noted previously) employ the majority of working Americans.

Public employers have needs for stress management programming as substantial as private employers. However, programmatic approaches need to address the unique environment of each public sector worksite. Such programs have been and are being conducted in many federal agencies on a regular basis. Unfortunately, there has been little published evaluation of the utilization, efficacy, impact on job satisfaction, staff retention and absenteeism rates, and so on that might encourage (or discourage) other agencies with respect to adopting such programs.

Responsibility for identifying and monitoring stress within the organization and accountability for assuring appropriate interventions should reside with a specific functional unit within the organization. Existing institutional mechanics should be harnessed to assure that all of the relevant units are involved, that responsibility for specific tasks is clear, and to avoid redundancy. In many cases, outside organizations with specific expertise should be sought by employers to assure appropriate assessment of the problem and relevant educational and behavioral change programming.

To maximize population effectiveness, stress management interventions should be directed at all employees, and marketing and promotional materials should position these interventions as valuable to all employees. Integration of worksite stress management programs into broad worksite health promotion programs is desirable and has the potential of increasing both management and employee acceptance and levels of program participation. Such multimodal programs—which also encourage environmental/job restructuring as a means of reducing stressors in the workplace—have repeatedly demonstrated efficacy over program efforts united to stress management, per se.

Many mental health professionals could benefit from training on how to approach employers about stress and stress management programming, and the specific types of interventions that are likely to be best received by employers and employees. Training should also include ways in which mental health professionals can market stress management services to employers.

There is a clear need for groups advocating organizational mechanisms (e.g., Washington Business Group on Health) to facilitate translation of research results into program interventions and broad dissemination of this information to interested businesses. These groups could also provide effective feedback to employers and insurers as to the cost-effectiveness and cost-benefit of such programs.

Stress management programs could also be helpful to individuals suffering job loss, reentry into the work force, or "out placement" which might involve dealing with the impact on families, as well as enhancing the coping skills of the individual. As companies "downsize," workers who remain employed are also affected by such restructuring in terms of job security, additional responsibilities, loss of social support/networks, and so forth.

In summary, discussion and recommendations focused on the necessity for interdisciplinary, multi-modal programs that involved employer, employee and union, health promotion expertise, and relevant representation from the community. Needs assessment should be conducted with both employers and employees and evaluation criteria designed to address specific concerns as well as more general health outcomes. A continuing partnership among all relevant parties will enhance credibility and cooperation among these groups, as well as allowing them to integrate their respective agendas. Programs must be designed to accommodate efforts to reduce environmental and job-related stressors as well as enhancing the coping skills of the individual.

Finally, there is a common denominator of health improvement/maintenance among all parties in supporting "wellness at the worksite" which must be supported and amplified by all concerned. Through such a collective will, such programs, unquestionably, will be given ample opportunity to demonstrate their worth to all concerned constituencies.

Surveillance of Psychological Disorders in the Workplace Panel

Panel Members

Stanislav V. Kasl, Chairperson, *Yale University School of Medicine, New Haven, CT*

Edward Bernacki, *Tenneco Incorporated, Houston, TX*

Evelyn Bromet, *State University of New York at Stony Brook, Stony Brook, NY*

E. Carroll Curtis, *Westinghouse Corporation, Pittsburgh, PA*

William W. Eaton, *Johns Hopkins University, Baltimore, MD*

Lawrence J. Fine, *National Institute for Occupational Safety and Health, Cincinnati, OH*

Robin Mary Gillespie, *Service Employees International Union, New York, NY*

Ronald W. Manderschied, *National Institutes of Health, Rockville, MD*

Lawrence Murphy, *National Institute for Occupational Safety and Health, Cincinnati, OH*

David Parkinson, *State University of New York at Stony Brook, Stony Brook, NY*

Dianne K. Wagener, *National Center for Health Statistics, Hyattsville, MD*

Stanislav V. Kasl

Surveillance of Psychological Disorders in the Workplace

Identifying and Defining the Issues

Diverse indicators of psychological health and functioning have been suggestively linked to the work setting. The purpose of the APA/NIOSH conference was to explore prevention strategies which focus on the work setting and which are designed to improve psychological health and functioning of the employed population. The overall task of the conference was divided into three areas: (a) job design (redesign) to improve working conditions; (b) surveillance of work-linked risk factors and of psychological disorders; and (c) health promotion, including education, training and health services. These three areas are, naturally, interlinked. Specifically, the proposed surveillance should include all of the work dimensions that are also selected for attention by the Job Design and Stress Panel. Similarly, indicators of psychological health and functioning selected for attention by the Health Promotion, Education, and Treatment Panel need to be included in the proposed surveillance as well. However, it is likely that surveillance (when defined broadly) should also include work dimensions and psychological/behavioral outcomes that are not included in the other two panels. This would be because it appears unfeasible and/or inappropriate to suggest redesign or health promotion activities regarding certain dimensions or outcomes even though such dimensions are still relevant for surveillance efforts because they are part of an established link between the work setting and psychological health and functioning.

The APA/NIOSH conference was not without inherent ambiguities of boundaries, scope, and purpose. These are not easily resolved; however, they need to be at least brought to the surface so that during the course of the conference we do not keep rediscovering them and keep being surprised by their perverse persistence. They are offered here from the perspective of the Surveillance Panel though the issues are germane for all three panels.

Perhaps the most important issue concerns the set of criteria, on the basis of which the work dimensions (risk factors) and psychological health and functioning (outcomes) shall be selected are recommended as relevant for the proposed surveillance. These criteria are partly a priori conceptual ones since we need explicit principles and guidelines. However, they are also empirical in the sense that research evidence may need to be brought in in order to see if the proposed dimensions or outcomes satisfy the criteria. The a priori criteria for relevance can be stated very broadly and ambitiously or very narrowly and cautiously. Of course, by attempting to select and elucidate the criteria, we are once more defining and rede-fining the scope and objectives of the APA/NIOSH conference.

A broad, ambitious approach would adopt a public health perspective in which the work role is seen as a crucial human activity uniquely influencing psychological health and well-being, and the work setting is seen as an important and special arena for diverse health promotion and disease prevention activities; and the target individuals are not just those in the labor force but also their spouses and immediate family (if not themselves in the labor force). In this broad approach, we would be *blurring a number of distinctions which might be otherwise utilized to define the limits of some narrower approach.*

Some of the blurred or erased distinctions are: (a) between psychological and physical health (a potentially difficult distinction in any case); (b) between specific dimensions of work and work setting and broad corporate policies (e.g., paid leaves of absence or health insurance coverage); (c) between outcomes that are etiologically linked (directly or indirectly) to the work setting and outcomes that have no estab-lished etiological linkage; (d) between influences of work on health and well-being that are detrimental (e.g., as indexed by symptoms of dysphoria) and those that are health-enhancing (e.g., as indexed by humanistic concepts of "positive mental health," such as self-actualization); and (e) between workers and their families, and, possibly as well, between the work and the home settings.

A concrete example will illustrate some of the questions which can be raised by such a broad, ambitious approach. Health promotion activities in the work setting include, among others, smoking cessation which appears to be the most frequently offered program (Fielding & Piserchia, 1989). However, there is no decent evidence that the onset of smoking or that temporal fluctuations in level of consumption have any etiological linkages to aspects of the work setting. Furthermore, smoking while admittedly a behavioral variable, has its primary implications for purely physical health outcomes (cancers, heart disease). Should smoking behavior be mon-itored as part of the proposed surveillance for outcomes? Is it a relevant domain of functioning in the APA/NIOSH conference? High rates of smoking in a particular work setting would very likely be due to self-selection into the job on preexisting stable characteristics (e.g., lower education), rather than revealing "risk factors" in the work environment. However, such high rates do suggest a higher potential for benefits derived from some intervention, and smoking cessation success does seem to be, in part, embedded in a rich organizational and psychosocial matrix (e.g., Sorenson, Pechacek, & Pallonen, 1986). In thinking through the relevance of smok-ing behavior for surveillance, it is instructive to realize that, in fact, the vast majority of health promotion activities at the work site target outcomes without presuming (or even wondering about) an etiological linkage of such outcomes to aspects of work (Kasl & Serxner, in press). This observation seems to apply to some extent even to "stress" (i.e., distress) reduction programs, which seems distinctly odd. In any case, it might be viewed as inappropriate for the APA/NIOSH conference to restrict itself to a narrow set of outcomes for surveillance when the large domain of health promotion at the worksite activities is so much more inclusive.

There are many difficulties attendant upon the adoption of a broad and am-bitious approach in which, in addition, a number of boundaries and distinctions are blurred. Two of the more obvious ones are: First, it implies an *expensive* agenda against a political reality, characterized by brinkmanship over reducing budget deficits and by a peace dividend whose half life is measured in mere seconds. Second, it implies an *unrealistic* agenda, given that corporate America is used to creating, altering, and abolishing jobs from the perspective of shareholders rather than workers; furthermore, corporate America cannot be expected to welcome an extension of compensable and/or insurable conditions in the direction of psychological disorders. Thus a broad agenda is best viewed as an ideal which demands an explicit accounting for offering various narrower, less ambitious alternatives, and from which the distance of such lesser goals can be measured.

It is possible to enumerate separate components of an agenda, which then can be put together in various combinations to form alternative composites. I shall try to characterize the different components in causal or etiological language.

First, an objectively assessed risk factor in the work environment ("work hazard") represents a direct effect (in path analysis sense) on some indicator of workers' health, well-being, or functioning. This would appear to be the clearest and simplest case, which then calls for surveillance of that risk factor and that outcome.

It needs to be noted, however, that such a barebone statement of an etiological linkage by itself does not settle *the question of what hazards and/or what outcomes are to be excluded or ignored.* Presumably, we still need to attempt to differentiate between: (a) work hazards that are social/psychological (i.e., relevant) versus those that are physical/chemical/biological (i.e., not relevant) and (b) outcomes that are psychological/behavioral (i.e., relevant) versus those that reflect health/functioning defined along biomedical parameters (i.e., not relevant). And should we succeed in such a differentiation, we would still need to decide if the criterial conditions for surveillance require the joint presence of both a relevant hazard and relevant outcome, or only one or the other. Or, we could decide that distinguishing among hazards is unnecessary since the critical requirement is the impact on psychological/ behavioral outcomes. In any case, distinguishing among relevant and irrelevant hazards and outcomes will not be easy. For example,

- industrial noise can be seen both as a physical and a psychological stimulus (e.g., Evans, 1982; Jones & Chapman, 1984; Kryter, 1972);
- ergonomic issues are not easily separated into physical and psychological (e.g., Corlett & Richardson, 1981; Shephard, 1974);
- exposure to carcinogens and toxic materials may have a psychological impact, depending upon information and awareness (e.g., Houts & McDougall, 1988; Schottenfeld & Cullen, 1985);
- symptom checklists pose particular difficulties for separating physical and psychological disorder (e.g., the increased reporting of eye strain among female telephone office workers who are video display terminal [VDT] users; Haynes, LaCroix, & Lippin, 1987).

Second, an objectively assessed work hazard is etiologically linked to a particular outcome, but only among a subgroup of those exposed; the defining criteria of the subgroup, in effect, represent a "vulnerability factor." Such vulnerability factors can fall into different classes:

1. sociodemographic characteristics such as age or education;
2. aspects of the social environment, such as living alone;
3. personality traits, such as Type A behavior;
4. skills and abilities;
5. health status, such as a previous heart attack or a history of alcohol problems; and
6. ongoing life stresses that are not part of the work role.

The issue here is whether or not surveillance needs to include such vulnerability factors or, more precisely, specific work hazard by vulnerability combinations. Clearly, failure to monitor such vulnerability factors leads to detecting only weaker effects (on the total group); when the vulnerability factor is relatively uncommon, then the general effect on the total group will be particularly weak. Vulnerability factors are, of course, a particular class of moderator variables. When another kind of a moderator variable is involved in determining which subgroups experience a positive impact and others a negative one, then failing to include such a moderator in surveillance will miss the etiological dynamics altogether (rather than detecting only a weak effect, as in the case of a vulnerability factor). The Person-Environment Fit (P-E fit) formulation (e.g., French, Caplan, & Van Harrison, 1982) is the most likely source of such a class of moderator variables where, on the average, there may be no detectable impact.

Third, an objectively assessed work hazard is etiologically linked to a particular outcome, but it is mediated by subjective appraisals or perceptions of the work setting and/or by specific behavioral reactions. The implications of this situation for surveillance are not clear. If, on the one hand, the effects of the work hazard are all indirect, in the path analysis sense (i.e., the effects are completely mediated by the appraisals or behaviors), and if appropriate interventions with the appraisals or behaviors can interrupt the causal sequence, then the surveillance might well focus on the mediating processes and ignore the work hazard itself. If, on the other hand, there are both direct and indirect effects, and if interventions are easier at the level of the work environment, or if work redesign efforts cannot be targeted only to a subgroup of individuals, then we may not have to worry about such mediating processes. And if the applicable situation is somewhere in-between these two possibilities, then the mediating processes are analogous to vulnerability factors and previous comments apply.

The aforementioned three types of etiological dynamics all implied an effect from exposure to incidence (onset) of new conditions. Additional possibilities exist if one is dealing with prevalent (pre-existing) conditions and the impact is on course or recurrence of such conditions.

Fourth, an objectively assessed work hazard is etiologically linked to one or another aspect of course and outcome of a pre-existing condition: (a) frequency of recurrences; (b) length of recurrent episodes, or other indicators of severity; (c) compliance with treatment regimen (e.g., mediations, abstinence in alcoholism programs); and (d) effectiveness of treatment, apart from compliance.

These four categories of etiological relationships involving work hazards and psychological/behavioral outcomes should help us define some of the main issues in developing prevention strategies and thus identifying the necessary surveillance efforts. Even though the four classes of relationships collectively represent an ambitious agenda, the categorization is not necessarily complete. One may briefly note here some of the additional categories which could be subsumed under a truly broad public health agenda:

1. The impact of work hazards on members of the employee's family and the whole issue of work-nonwork interface (e.g., Barling, 1990; Gutek, Repetti, & Silver, 1988; Repetti, 1987); presumably, the effects on other family members are mediated by effects on the employee.
2. The impact of the absence of a work role, both in the sense of becoming unemployed as well as failing to enter the labor force after the end of formal education; presumably, such effects (e.g., Dooley & Catalano, 1988) are beyond the mission of NIOSH, but certainly not of APA.
3. The therapeutic role work may play, particularly among severely disturbed psychiatric patients (e.g., Strauss, Harding, & Silverman, 1988); and
4. Psychological distress secondary to occupational diseases and injuries, such as occupational cancers or loss of limb.

It was noted earlier that in addition to trying to establish a priori or conceptual criteria for defining the scope of the APA/NIOSH conference, we also need to be concerned with *research evidence* and examine the extent to which it supports a particular claimed or suspected etiological association. Here again we need to recognize—without being able to resolve—the possible quagmire this issue represents. First, we need to keep clear the distinction between two different types of meaning in the assertion that "there is no evidence that . . . ": (a) the evidence is pretty consistently negative, that is, showing no association; and (b) the evidence is not there because the issue has not been studied or studied well. Since the proposed APA/NIOSH conference wishes, in part, to alert a number of audiences—the scientific community, national and state legislators, the general voting public—to the importance of psychological disorders in the workplace and to the need to have a better documentation of the etiological dynamics, then it seems appropriate, if not necessary, to go beyond the bounds of available evidence. However, it is still desirable to develop broad guidelines for being concerned with undocumented or poorly documented etiological associations. For example, it might be argued that work settings which are associated with nontrivial injuries and/or certain disease conditions (awkwardly labeled "psychosomatic" in the past, such as heart disease or peptic ulcer) should be considered relevant for surveillance by our panel. Similarly, it might be proposed that even if job dissatisfaction is not considered a psychological disorder or outcome of interest, that, nevertheless, work conditions linked to high levels of job dissatisfaction are promissory of other types of impact, there are of interest, and thus surveillance is again indicated.

Second, the issue of research evidence is far from straightforward since investigators and scholars are likely to view the evidence from different perspectives and thus arrive at different conclusions about soundness of evidence. For example, the support for Karasek's demand/control model is variously assessed by a NIOSH conference panel (Sauter, Hurrell, & Cooper, 1989) and by Karasek himself (Karasek & Theorell, 1990). In general, some reviews are primarily descriptive and informative, explaining what work is being conducted and what independent-intervening-dependent variables are typically chosen for study (e.g., Holt, 1982). Others are quite selective, choosing to teach from a few illustrative studies' generalizable principles and findings (e.g., Kahn, 1981). One common reason for different evaluations of evidence is that some authors wish to paint the "big picture" or to argue for the viability of some overarching concept or hypothesis and thus they cite evidence only from a partial list of studies supporting the point; other authors wish to assess the complete evidence for and against a particular hypothesis or association, and they are more diligent in citing the nonsupporting studies as well. Another reason for high variation in the evaluations of evidence is due to the variety of ways in which methodological-design issues are handled. Fundamentally, methodological criticism of quasi-experimental field research concerns probable and possible flaws, as well as probable and possible alternative explanations. Certainty about presence of spurious effects and confounding and reverse causation may be as difficult to achieve as certainty about a desired cause-and-effect relationship; thus reviewers have considerable latitude in raising methodological issues and in dismissing particular evidence as unsound. I personally have been considerably bothered by the extent to which our accumulated evidence is based on studies which are cross-sectional and in which the "independent variable" (work hazard), which is being linked to psychological outcomes, is based on subjective appraisals only (e.g., Kasl, 1978, 1986). This issue has recently been examined in some detail by Frese and Zapf (1988).

In the remainder of this paper, I will devote myself to three topics which collectively define the task of surveillance of psychological disorders in the workplace: (a) the aspects or dimensions of the work setting which might be included, (b) the psychological and behavioral outcomes which might be targeted, and (c) the issues which pertain to surveillance and assessment activities and methodologies.

In approaching this task I believe we need to be quite sensitive to the *difference in issues and problems* we face, as opposed to issues and problems faced by those in traditional occupational epidemiology, dealing with work-related injuries and illnesses. Basically, the bread and butter paradigm in occupational epidemiology is still the approach of establishing (observing, noting, detecting) disease differences by occupations or job titles and then tracing them to exposure to some environmental agent or hazard. However, this approach may be, in most instances, too simple a guide for strategies linking psychosocial aspects of the work environment to psychological disorders. Consider the following contrast. Angiosarcoma of the liver is so extremely rare that just three or four cases were enough to alert health officials and start a search for agents (Creech & Johnson, 1974). The disease and its natural history are such that many traditional problems are minimized: (a) differential diagnosis, pinning down its occupational origin; (b) relatively short latency between exposure and diagnosis (and/or death); (c) absence of multiple risk factors; (d) not confusing treatment-seeking with the disease itself; and (e) unavailability of effective treatment, thus making it easier to track cases in retrospective cohort designs. Moreover, the search for agents produced a quick convergence on polyvinyl chloride as the probable cause. Corroborating information came in quickly from many manufacturing places around the world. Finally—and this is something not available to the social scientists examining work stress and mental health—short term laboratory studies on animals provided further confirmatory evidence. In short, a tight little package and a scientific success story. Now let us contrast this with the results obtained when the occupational epidemiology paradigm is applied to studying psychosocial aspects of work and psychological disorders. This is a study, entitled, "Job Stress and Psychiatric Illness in the U.S. Navy" (Schuckit & Gunderson, 1973). The authors identified, through case files, all Navy men hospitalized with a psychiatric diagnosis in the years 1966–1968, and then computed rates of 'first' (in the Navy) psychiatric hospitalization by occupation. Jobs which had high and low rates were designated as high and low 'risk' jobs, respectively. Independent assessments of 'severity of working conditions' failed to show any association with high-low risk classification. Job satisfaction data on a separate sample produced some ambiguous results, showing both more boredom and more overall job satisfaction on the high risk jobs. In general, the jobs with higher hospitalization rates tended to be more routine and those with lower rates, more technical. Data on characteristics of individuals revealed men in high risk jobs to be older, of lower education, of lower social class of origin, more likely to be divorced or single, and so on. Since these are all characteristics the men brought with them to the jobs, and since these characteristics have been found in innumerable studies to be associated with higher rates of treated (and untreated) mental illness, the conclusion is quite compelling that this approach failed to reveal anything about job stresses—in fact, possibly, it failed to be a study of job stresses at all.

Psychosocial Work Hazards

In this section, I wish to suggest a number of aspects or dimensions of the work environment which might be included in surveillance efforts. The list and the discussion are somewhat more detailed, compared to the next section on psychological disorders. This reflects the general presumption in surveillance of occupational illness and injury (e.g., Baker, Melius, & Millar, 1988) that in targeting prevention programs, the surveillance of responsible workplace exposures or hazards may be *more useful* than health effects surveillance, if the latter are complex, multifactorial (both work-related and nonwork-related) outcomes. The following material is based on a more detailed discussion of these issues (Kasl, 1990).

It is clear that no one has attempted to systematically and comprehensively dimensionalize the work environment, to develop an adequate taxonomy. In the absence of such a taxonomy, it is difficult to know for the present purpose if one has identified an adequately complete subset of dimensions, those relevant for surveillance of work-related disorders. The listing which follows represents the amalgamated influence of examining various sources:

1. Diverse reviews, overviews, and edited volumes, mostly on stress: Baker, 1985; Beehr and Bhagat, 1985; Beehr and Newman, 1978; Burke, 1984; Cataldo and Coates, 1984; Cohen and Syme, 1985; Cooper and Marshall, 1980; Cooper and Payne, 1978, 1980, 1988; Cooper and Smith, 1985; Corlett and Richardson, 1981; Elliott and Eisdorfer, 1982; Gardell, 1976, 1982; Holt, 1982; House, 1980, 1981; House and Cottington, 1986; Hurrell and Colligan,

1982; Kahn, 1981, 1987; Kahn, Hein, House, Kasl, and McLean, 1982; Karasek and Theorell, 1990; Kasl, 1978, 1984, 1986; Kasl and Cobb, 1983; McGrath, 1976; McLean, 1979; Payne and Firth-Cozens, 1987; Quick, Bhagat, Dalton, and Quick, 1987; Salvendy and Smith, 1981; Sauter, Hurrell, and Cooper, 1989; Sethi and Schuler, 1984; Sharit and Salvendy, 1982; Shostak, 1980; Steptoe and Mathews, 1984; Tasto, Colligan, Skjei, and Polly, 1978.

2. Individual studies which have had a great influence on the field, particularly because they generated measures later used by others: Caplan, Cobb, French, Harrison, and Pinneau, 1975; Kahn, Wolfe, Quinn, Snoek, and Rosenthal, 1964; Quinn, Seashore et al., 1971; Quinn and Shepard, 1974.

3. Various instruments for measuring dimensions of work environment, including those based on job satisfaction measures such as: Minnesota Satisfaction Questionnaire (Weiss, Davis, England, & Lofquist, 1967); Job Descriptive Index (Smith, Kendall, & Hulin, 1969); Job Diagnostic Survey (Hackman & Oldham, 1975); Job Content Questionnaire (Karasek, 1985); Index of Organizational Reactions (Smith, 1976); dimensions based on standardized descriptions by "expert" observers (e.g., House, 1980; Jenkins, Nadler, Lawler, & Cammann, 1975). The job satisfaction measures are easily accessible through various reviews and compilations (e.g., Jenkins, DeFrank, & Speers, 1984; Locke, 1976; Robinson, Athanasiou, & Head, 1969).

4. Instruments developed to measure the work environment in specific jobs, such as policemen (Cooper, Davidson, & Robinson, 1982), air traffic controllers (Crump, 1979; Rose, Jenkins, & Hurst, 1978), nurses (Gentry & Parkes, 1982; Gray-Toft & Anderson, 1981) medical technologists (Matteson & Ivancevich, 1982), teachers (Fimian, 1984; Phillips & Lee, 1980), and scientists in organizations (Pelz & Andrews, 1966).

It is proposed that the following dimensions of the work setting be provisionally considered as having an impact on psychological health.

1. *Physical (hygienic) conditions at work*: (a) those related to comfort, such as heat, cold, humidity; (b) hazardous exposures to radiation, chemicals, pollutants; (c) other exposures which relate to symptoms or annoyance, such as dust and fumes; (d) noise; and (e) dangerous machinery. The presumption with this list is that aside from "direct" effects (which presumably bypass cognitive or emotional processing, such as the radiation-to-cancer association), indirect effects are likely, either because awareness of exposure to hazards may have its own consequences (e.g., Kasl, Chisholm, & Eskenazi, 1981) or the physical conditions interact with psychosocial variables.

2. *Physical aspects of work*: (a) bad ergonomic or man-machine design; (b) physical constraints on movement; (c) comfort; (d) vibrations; (e) physically demanding (e.g., lifting); and (f) pacing by machinery, including breakdown of machinery. Clearly it is somewhat arbitrary to list these separately from the previous category above.

3. *Temporal aspects of work day and work itself*: (a) shift work, particularly rotating shift; (b) overtime, unwanted or "excessive" hours; (c) two jobs; (d) piecework vs. hourly pay (pay mechanism influencing pace); (e) fast pace of work, particularly in the presence of high vigilance demands; (f) not enough time to complete work, deadlines; (g) scheduling of work and rest cycles; (h) variation in work load; and (i) interruptions.

4. *Work content* (other than temporal aspects): (a) fractionated, repetitive, monotonous work, low task/skill variety; (b) autonomy, independence, influence, control; (c) utilization of existing skills; (d) opportunity to learn new skills; (e) mental alertness and concentration; (f) unclear tasks or demands; (g) conflicting tasks or demands; and (h) insufficient resources, given work demands or responsibilities (e.g., skills, machinery, organizational structure).

5. *Interpersonal—work group*: (a) opportunity to interact with coworkers (during work, during breaks, after work); (b) size, cohesiveness of primary work group; (c) recognition for work performance; (d) social support; (e) instrumental support; and (f) equitable work load.

6. *Interpersonal—supervision*: (a) participation in decision making; (b) receiving feedback and recognition from supervisor; (c) providing supervisor with feedback; (d) closeness of supervision; (e) social support; (f) instrumental support; and (g) unclear, conflicting demands.

7. *Financial and economic aspects*: (a) pay, basic wages; (b) additional compensation (overtime, shiftwork, bonuses); (c) retirement benefits; (d) other benefits (e.g., health care); and (e) equity, predictability of compensation.

8. *Organizational aspects*: (a) size; (b) structure (e.g., "flat" structure with relatively few levels in the organization); (c) having a staff position (vs. line position); (d) working on the boundary of the organization; (e) relative prestige of the job; (f) unclear organizational structure (lines of responsibility, organizational basis for role conflict and ambiguity); (g) organizational (administrative) red tape and cumbersome (irrational) procedures; and (h) discriminatory policies (e.g., hiring, promotion).

9. *Community and societal aspects*: This is not a category which is frequently considered and thus it is much less clear what might turn out to be important. At minimum, we need to consider occupational status/prestige, since there are many studies showing an association (however opaque!) between status and health outcomes. Other considerations include community perceptions of certain jobs (e.g., policemen) and their visibility (e.g., uniforms) and community–company relations.

10. *Changes (or threatened changes) in the work setting*: Many of the dimensions listed above can undergo change and such changes may also be worthy of our attention because of their possible impact on health. The kinds of changes which are likely to be important are often more global than dimensional: promotion, demotion, loss of job, full-time to part-time transition, increased job insecurity, various organizational changes, and so on. The following cautions should be noted with respect to the study of change in the work setting: (a) In spite of the widespread presumption in the stress field that change per se is stressful, the evidence favors the

stance that we should emphasize "negative" changes only (i.e., an aggravation along an already adverse or pathogenic work dimension, or global changes perceived as unwanted and undesirable). (b) Many changes in the work setting represent self-selection and are desired or sought; this makes it more difficult to determine the independent effects of such a change. (c) When change takes place from a less pathogenic environment to a more pathogenic one, then adverse impact of change per se is difficult to disentangle from the chronic effect of exposure to the latter environment. (d) We need to also pay attention to "nonchanges" (above all, a promotion or desired transfer which fails to take place), since these may represent important stressors; detecting such nonchanges is, of course, difficult.

In addition to the above listing of the dimensions of the work setting, it is important to consider, however tentatively, the *work-nonwork interface*. This has usually meant a consideration of the family roles of spouse and parent (e.g., Gutek et al., 1988; Repetti, 1987) and of the family setting with its own stress process and dynamics (e.g., Pearlin & Turner, 1987), but some investigators have also examined such issues as the impact of difficult rush hour commuting to and from work (Lundberg, 1976; Stokols & Novaco, 1981), recency of a vacation (Johansson, 1976), and the impact of work on political behavior and participation (Gardell, 1987; Levi, Frankenhaeuser, & Gardell, 1982) and leisure activities (Frankenhaeuser, 1977).

Finally, we need to remind ourselves that the pathogenic process which links up the work environment to psychological disorder is likely to involve (specific) interactive dynamics, rather than just a series of "main effects" of the various dimensions, which presumably become additive in impact. Elsewhere (Kasl, 1981), I have tried to outline broadly the possible interactive dynamics of such a pathogenic process: (a) the work condition tends to be chronic rather than intermittent or self-limiting; (b) habituation or adaptation to the chronic situation is difficult and, instead, some form of vigilance or arousal must be maintained; (c) failure to meet the demands of the work setting has serious consequences (e.g., high level of responsibility for various outcomes such as the lives of others or equipment or profits); and (d) there is a "spillover" of the effects of the work role on other areas of functioning (e.g., family, leisure) so that the daily impact of the demanding job situation becomes cumulative and health-threatening, rather than being daily defused or erased, thereby having little long-term impact on health. The lay concepts of "spillover" effects and "unwinding" appear important, on the one hand, and neglected, on the other. The Scandinavian work is highly relevant here, such as recovering from high arousal levels among female workers with unwanted overtime (Frankenhaeuser, 1979; Rissler, 1977), or among sawmill workers whose work is highly repetitive, machine paced, and highly constricting (Gardell, 1976; Johansson, Aronson, & Lindstrom, 1978).

Indicators of Psychological Health and Functioning

In the previous section we have identified dimensions of work environment which might be considered appropriate for surveillance. The total list is formidable, is based on a liberal reading of the research evidence, and needs to be pruned. When we now turn to a consideration of the impact indicators, psychological health, and functioning, we face again the issue of research evidence. In a general way, the same body of research considered relevant for identifying the dimensions of work is also relevant for this task. However, it is possible to argue that the role of evidence is somewhat less important, in the sense that we may have certain outcomes in mind which are so important to us (e.g., depression) that we would propose them for surveillance no matter what the accumulated state of evidence is.

It is somewhat difficult to think through the issues which can guide us in selecting relevant indicators of psychological health and functioning. For example, can we follow the strategy of developing a list of Sentinel Health Events (SHE) (Rutstein et al., 1983)? The SHE represents a disease/disability/untimely death, which is occupationally related and the occurrence of which signals the need for epidemiological and/or industrial hygiene studies, and/or preventive interventions. The actual list of occupational diseases proposed by the authors includes predominantly conditions which are not intrinsically "occupational," (e.g., malignant neoplasm of the bladder) but rather, such conditions become occupational as a result of a diagnostic work-up in which the industry/occupation and the agent need to be considered as well. Such a reconstruction of etiology is relatively easy, say, for injuries on the job, but is next to impossible for indicators of psychological health. We simply do not have a way of taking the paradigm for occupational bladder cancer and applying it to "occupational depression" or "occupational low self-esteem." Possibly, the issue can be finessed through measurement approaches, but this raises the danger that in attempting to measure, say occupational depression, we would be asking the respondent not only to describe affect and symptoms, but also to provide causal attribution or explanation for such symptoms. This is highly suspect. Alternately, to try to ask about affect and symptoms only for the times when they are in their work environment is probably a totally unwarranted and artificial strategy. And trying to pick some sentinel health events from among the psychological disorders, such as suicide (Sauter, Murphy, & Hurrell, 1990) seems rather arbitrary, since there is little evidence that suicides are sufficiently often work-related (with the possible exception of unemployment), and very difficult psychological autopsies would be needed to pin down a work-related etiology.

A strategy which is an alternative to selecting specific psychological disorders or outcomes (because of well-documented work-related etiology) which can be placed on a list of sentinel health events, is to develop a two-stage procedure for case identification (e.g., Dohrenwend & Shrout, 1981). The point, however, is that one would be using a screening instrument which would have a dual purpose: (a) allow for an identification of cases and (b) allow for an identification of "problem" jobs in which probable cases are concentrated. What outcomes might be assessed in such a screening strategy? Let us consider briefly four types of outcomes, two general ones and two work-related ones.

Among the general ones, one could certainly use Langner's 22-Item Screening Score (Langner, 1986) or the Dohrenwend Demoralization Scale (Dohrenwend, Levav, & Shrout, 1986). Such scales are broad screening instruments, but they correlate highly with measures of more specific constructs, such as depression, so that scales such as the Center for Epidemiologic Studies Depression scale (CES-D) (Radloff & Locke, 1986) could also be used for screening purposes. An alternative to general symptom-based screening instruments would be to use measures which are intended to reflect a direct appraisal of stress, such as the Perceived Stress Scale (Cohen, 1986; Cohen, Kamarck, & Mermelstein, 1983). Items in this scale are intended to reflect how unpredictable, uncontrollable, and overloading respondents find their lives. Even though such a scale appears to assess appraisals of one's circumstances—which apparently makes it suitable to identify individuals vulnerable to diverse work hazards—the correlations with symptom-based screening instruments are so high, and the unique variance so small, that in the present context it can be viewed as interchangeable with the symptom-based screening scales.

Within the domain of work-related concepts and measures, one type of a screening approach could be based on *job satisfaction* measures. The primary advantage here is that they have a built-in relevance to the work setting and we have available to us a plethora of measures with a reasonably well-documented construct validity. One disadvantage is that job satisfaction (and its various components) does not link up that strongly with outcomes of probable greater interest (Kasl, 1978). Moderately strong associations are found for other measures of (life) satisfaction, but correlations with symptom-based checklists are weaker, typically in the .20's. Correlations of job satisfaction with psychiatric diagnoses have generally not been established. Thus unless we are interested in job dissatisfaction per se, they may represent rather inefficient screening instruments. Another possibility might be to develop screening procedures on the basis of data on *absences*. The hope here is that absences operationalize a partial withdrawal from the work setting which is indicative of the presence of some work hazard and/or of an impact on the individual worker. However, the convenience and easy availability of such data would have to compensate strongly for their limitations. There are many "local" influences on absences (e.g., company policy, record keeping, hourly vs. salaried, etc.) so that meaningful comparisons across industries and companies—possibly even across jobs within the same company—may be difficult. In addition, various constraints on absences, such as the local labor situation or personal finances, would further tend to undermine the interpretability of high and low rates.

I shall now offer a reasonably comprehensive grouping of types of outcomes, or indicators, from which one could make a selection for surveillance of work-related psychological disorders.

1. *Psychiatric diagnoses*: At first blush, these appear to be the most obvious and compelling outcomes to be included in surveillance. However, such a first impression need not be correct; for example, an NIMH conference on risk factor research completely ignored the work environment and made only a passing reference to employment (vs. unemployment) (NIMH, 1983). It is possible that assessing major psychiatric diagnoses does not represent a sensitive method for detecting the impact of work environments. Thus it would seem that we need to start with an accepted classification system— inevitably the *DSM-III-R* Axis I disorders (American Psychiatric Association, 1987)—and consider for deletion selected categories: those with a relatively early onset (e.g., schizophrenia), those with a likely strong genetic involvement (e.g., bipolar disorder), those which are likely to be quite rare

(e.g., dissociative disorders), or those which can be rejected on a combination of grounds, including pragmatic ones (e.g., psychosexual disorders). A pruned list might thus include: affective disorders, anxiety disorders, and substance use disorders.

2. *Indices based on treatment and care seeking*: Since seeking treatment and receiving care for psychological disorders is such a highly discretionary behavior (both from the perspective of the individual and of the social/health care system), it is difficult to determine if this class of indicators should have any place in surveillance. Certainly, some kinds of institutional records could be highly convenient and accessible (at least as rates of use on groups), but without some attempts to estimate biases, such information could be quite misleading (e.g., Colligan, Smith, & Hurrell, 1977).

3. *Symptom checklists*: There is a plethora of indices which have been developed to measure general dimensions of "psychiatric impairment" or "distress" or "psychophysiological symptoms," as well as more specific dimensions, such as depression, anxiety, hopelessness-helplessness, (low) self-esteem, and specific kinds of dysphoria. These checklists can be used to estimate "caseness," to identify those individuals in need of further assessment, or to simply measure the level of symptomatology with respect to the construct they are intended to represent. Obviously, such uses are not mutually exclusive. If there are state and trait versions of these constructs, then presumably the former is the more appropriate one. It might be also noted that even though in general, cross-sectional community surveys the various indicators are substantially intercorrelated, this does not rule out the possibility that specific aspects of the work setting will have specific and differential effects, such as on self-esteem but not on anxiety.

4. *Indices of functional effectiveness*: Conceptually, the intent here is to measure the extent to which the person is able or unable to perform usual duties and activities, especially those connected with the primary social roles the person is expected to fulfill. In practice, the measures turn out to be difficult to develop in accordance with the broad conceptualization and end up being either indicators of subjective satisfaction in the various roles (e.g., Weissman & Bothwell, 1976) or specific and narrow indicators which only partially get at the construct (e.g., absence from work, quitting a job, poor performance on the job).

5. *Indices derived from notions of "positive mental health"*: The variables included in this grouping are presumably relevant for detecting the positive benefits (rather than just negative impact) of aspects of the work environment: growth and self-actualization, adequacy of coping, attainment of valued goals, and so on. Clausen (1969), for example, has proposed the following components: (a) ability to interact closely with others in a mutually satisfying and enduring relationship; (b) ability to mobilize one's personal resources to meet the demands of unexpected or difficult circumstances; and (c) adequate autonomy or ability to regulate one's life. The primary problem with this domain is that we lack adequate assessment tools. Given that so much effort in the last 10–15 years has gone into assessment of psychiatric diagnoses, the concepts in this grouping look like a throwback

to the 1950s and 1960s—however important they may be for the full under-standing of the impact of work.

6. *Indicators of quality of life*: Developments in the field of social indicators and the considerable emphasis given to perceived quality of life and broad self-assessments of well-being (e.g., Campbell, 1981; Campbell, Converse, & Rodgers, 1976), suggest that this is another class of potential indicators of impact. The different domains covered typically include: (a) various mea-sures of satisfaction (life in general, with job, with housing, with neigh-borhood, etc.); (b) global measures of happiness and well-being; (c) worries about future; (d) anomia, alienation, sense of efficacy; and (e) mistrust of authorities.

7. *Activities and behaviors*: This is admittedly an open-ended category and the inclusion of these variables is tied to how broadly one defines the scope of the APA/NIOSH conference. Some potential variables are: (a) life style habits with health implications, such as cigarette smoking, alcohol con-sumption, and level of physical activity; (b) participation in recreational and leisure activities; (c) social interaction with friends and kin; and (d) volunteer activities and involvement in the political process.

Surveillance and Measurement Issues

It is crucial to recognize that virtually all scientific, administrative, and regulatory written material available to us on occupational surveillance deals with physical/chemical/biological hazards, and with injuries and (physical) illnesses. For example, the recent NIOSH/CDC statement on surveillance (Baker, 1989) excludes any con-sideration of psychosocial hazards and of psychological disorders. Historically, ideas in occupational surveillance appear to derive from surveillance of infectious diseases (Baker et al., 1988). Thus there is little a priori promise that current occupational surveillance ideas and practices will be readily applicable to the surveillance of work-related psychological disorders. Given that the current system for collecting and using occupational health and safety statistics has received considerable crit-icism (e.g., Pollack & Keimig, 1987), it is easy to predict that proposing viable methods for surveillance of psychological disorders will be difficult.

Surveillance is typically defined very broadly—for example, "the systematic collection, analysis, and dissemination of disease data on groups or populations" (Levy & Wegman, 1983). In the discussion which follows I would like to distinguish between: (a) classical epidemiological or social science surveys designed to reveal some etiological dynamics; typically, the researcher-investigator has considerable control over the design, and data on both risk factors and outcomes are collected; and (b) all other systems of accessing and compiling data; typically, this represents some departure (compromise, short cut) from the classical survey approach, such as in the use of "available" institutional data, the way the disease is recognized and/or reported, or the splitting apart of surveillance of hazards from surveillance of outcomes. The conclusion can be anticipated that in proposing surveillance strat-egies for work-related psychological disorders, we will become more dependent on the classical surveys because the various shortcuts in other surveillance strategies are likely to compromise the value of the data too much.

It is useful to list some of the components and/or strategies which are part of occupational surveillance and attempt some preliminary judgments regarding their suitability for psychological surveillance.

1. *Using occupational health clinics* (e.g., Welch, 1989): It is difficult to see how problems of self-selection (who presents), of reconstructing the etiological dynamics in order to make the "occupational" diagnosis, and of identifying a work hazard that is not idiosyncratic to the presenting case, could be overcome to make this a useful approach. Of course, at present occupational clinics are not set up to deal with psychological disorders.

2. *Reporting based on emergency room visits*: This appears suitable for occupational injuries only. Substance abuse medical emergencies could also be reported by this system but their link to the work setting would be quite unclear.

3. *Law-mandated physician reporting*: In the United States, the system does not seem to work even for well-defined instances of work-related injuries or diseases.

4. *Registries*: Even in optimal circumstances (e.g., statewide tumor registry), the occupational data are generally inadequate and further data collection is needed. Psychiatric registries are rare and represent only treated cases.

5. *Sentinel health events*: The difficulty of selecting a particular psychological disorder as such a sentinel event was discussed already. In addition, even after targeting an event (e.g., suicide attempt), we would still need to set up a viable and comprehensive reporting system.

6. *Employer records*: Employers must record all work-related injuries and illnesses on OSHA 200 logs. These logs have been criticized as inadequate for injuries and just about worthless for illness (Pollack & Keimig, 1987). Thus adding the reporting of specific psychological disorders seems hardly promising. Other employer records might be used, such as information on EAP programs designed for employees with alcohol problems. But such additional records are set up by the companies themselves; they are not standardized and may not be comparable across companies. In addition, they are treatment-based indicators with hard-to-determine self-selection.

7. *Union records*: This is a theoretical possibility, but the promise of setting up a reporting system in this fashion is difficult to evaluate.

8. *Bureau of Labor Statistics (BLS) Annual Survey*: The usefulness of the occupational disease data reported by this mechanism appears limited. By implication, the inclusion of psychological disorders would produce additional data of even more limited usefulness. However, the National Research Council (NRC) panel (Pollack & Keimig, 1987) felt that modifications of the BLS survey mechanism were feasible and would improve the usefulness of information. However, the NRC panel was not addressing issues of psychological health.

9. *Workers' Compensation Data*: Again, this source has many built-in problems and limitations, such as: (a) state-by-state variations, (b) workers have to

file, (c) most chronic work-related diseases are excluded, and (d) adjudication procedures distort the picture. In addition, there appears to be a built-in tautology due to the political nature of decisions about compensable conditions. Thus since in Connecticut hypertension is a compensable disability for policemen and firemen, analysis of such data would "reveal" that these jobs increase the risk for hypertension. So, if burnout becomes compensable among teachers, being a teacher would automatically produce a hazard condition for burnout.

The above is a listing of various components and strategies of a surveillance system for occupational injuries and diseases. None of these was seen (in a quick judgment) as promising for the surveillance of work-related psychological disorder. In a scenario which repeated itself over and over, a particular approach was seen as pretty reasonable for surveillance of injuries, somewhat useful for a narrow band of work-related diseases but inadequate for the intended broader spectrum of such diseases, and by implication inestimably useless for surveillance of psychological disorders.

It appears that no adequate surveillance procedures for psychological disorders can be set up which depart too far from investigator-designed epidemiological surveys of hazards and outcomes. This is an expensive solution and even then, to the extent that they may be no more than cross-sectional surveys, they may not yield associations with a convincing causal interpretation (e.g., Eaton, Anthony, Mandell, & Garrison, 1990). At this point I wish to discuss briefly possible partial strategies which are more focussed, somewhat less ambitious, and thus less-expensive.

1. *Environmental monitoring*: When a specific agent (e.g., a chemical carcinogen) is a known hazard, and when there is an adequate list of manufacturing processes (and thus jobs) which use the agent, then the first two steps in environmental monitoring have been accomplished. In the case of psychosocial hazards, more of the background work needs to be accomplished first. A specific strategy would be to take the list of psychosocial hazards offered earlier and prune and modify it, and develop a survey instrument. Then surveys are carried out in a variety of selected jobs which offer the promise of adequate contrast on various hazards, as well as different combinations of hazards. In this way, we would wish to build up adequate hazard information about specific jobs so that future investigators would not need to collect the same information and the job title itself would stand for the specific mixture of hazards present. Part of this strategy is to identify a few crucial or central "linking" variables which would be available on all jobs and which would allow extrapolation of hazard data from jobs which were studied to those which were not on the basis of the association of the hazards with such linking variables.

2. *Surveillance of disorders*: The strategy here is to accumulate information on prevalence rates of specific outcomes (disorders) for a selected set of job titles, where only the linking variables (see previous entry) represent the extent of data collected on the hazard side. Since one of the major problems with analyzing national data sets such as NHIS or ECA is that there are

relatively few people in each job title (and aggregation is undesirable), this strategy perforce means larger numbers and fewer different jobs. Here again, then, a thoughtful selection of "contrasting" jobs is needed. If the goal is to estimate rates for relatively rare disorders and/or if the definitive assessment strategy is too cumbersome, a first stage screening step would be in order. Such a screening instrument might well include both a symptom checklist and a job satisfaction measure. Basic sociodemographic data would be needed to adjust for nonjob factors such as gender.

3. *Hazard-disorder linkages examined in a few carefully selected jobs*: It would seem that the section on psychosocial hazards contains enough information for us to be able to select some high risk jobs which could then be studied longitudinally and in greater depth. For example, the following conditions at work would indicate a setting in need of study: highly repetitive, short-cycle, high vigilance, machine controlled (e.g., electronically monitored), high cost of mistakes, and piece rate pay. The strategy of studying a few jobs intensively is not just to learn more about a few jobs but to provide information (e.g., on mediating mechanisms and processes, on confounding or moderating influences) which would feed back and inform better the studies done under the previous two strategies.

The above strategies obviously need to be fleshed out. Furthermore, all of the various issues and problems raised in the first 13 pages or so are still applicable. It is also worth noting that the strategies discussed presuppose an orderly program of research in which later steps build upon earlier steps, and some core methodology remains common to most or all. This does not seem feasible under the usual investigator-initiated federal research funding mechanism, some kind of a collaborative contract arrangement between investigators and the granting agency needs to be envisioned.

A collaborative arrangement among investigators should include tackling the issue of better *assessment* of work environmental dimensions. Several areas of need for better measures could be cited. I will offer one which I find important, and that is the question of: When do we need job-specific measures and when are generic measures (usable in all settings) appropriate? Consider two examples. One concerns the measure of role ambiguity (Caplan et al., 1975), a major concept in occupational stress research. It contains four items dealing with clarity of job responsibilities and of work objectives, and with clarity and predictability of the expectations others have about the worker (respondent). The curious fact is that administrators—a group for whom the concept was practically invented—are quite a bit lower ($M = 2.06$, $SD = 0.88$) than such uncomplicated blue collar occupations as fork lift driver ($M = 2.74$, $SD = 1.29$) and machine tender ($M = 2.83$, $SD = 1.17$). Perhaps, there are several culprits involved. Developing scales usable for "all" occupations makes the items rather vague and general. The anchoring in specific and concrete work conditions becomes intentionally obscure and the items drift toward dealing with the respondents' cognitive processing and with reactions rather than simple description of environmental conditions. The respondents end up anchoring the items to various expectations and "levels of adaptation" which are based perhaps on personal experience and their judgments of how their jobs ought to be. Since respondents cannot be asked to judge their jobs in relation to other jobs (very few are that well informed), they should be asked to provide descriptive information in specific concrete terms.

As another example, consider the item "Is your job hectic?" When asked of blue-collar workers in various assembly-line and machine-paced jobs it could reflect a specific aspect of pacing, plus some elements of quality control, and allowances for taking breaks. However, when the occupations also include managers, teachers, farmers, doctors, and so forth, then high–low scores on the total study population are very difficult to interpret. In fact, it is not implausible to suggest that those scoring high, but coming from a wide spectrum of jobs, are more likely to share common personal characteristics than common work setting characteristics.

Some Concluding Cautionary Remarks

In a review of the literature on job satisfaction, Locke (1976) characterized desirable conditions at work as follows:

1. work represents mental challenge (with which the worker can cope successfully) and leads to involvement and personal interest;
2. work is not physically too tiring;
3. rewards for performance are just, informative, and in line with aspirations;
4. working conditions are compatible with physical needs and they facilitate work goals;
5. work leads to high self-esteem; and
6. agents in the work place help with the attainment of job values.

This represents an admirable summary which in a creative and responsible fashion goes beyond the immediate evidence to paint a "conservatively ideal" picture of desirable work conditions. This could also represent the target work conditions for the APA/NIOSH conference.

However, we must also consider the contemporary United States reality with respect to "meaning of work." There is much evidence (reviewed in Kasl, 1978) that for large segments of United States adults, work may not be a very meaningful human activity, and that the work role is not as important to them as our sociological and social-psychological theories indicate. But we need to understand that this is part of a process of impoverishment, of giving up, of withdrawal, as the worker is trying to adapt to an unsatisfactory job. The work role becomes less salient in the maintenance of self concept (self-identity) and less important in self-evaluation. For example, Quinn and Shepard (1974) found that, in response to the question "How much do you think you can tell about a person just from knowing what he or she does for a living?" some 48% of the national sample chose *nothing* or *a little* as their answers. Shepard (1971) found that blue collar workers in mechanized production were the lowest on *self evaluative involvement*, that is, the degree to which work (versus nonwork) activity was most important for self-evaluation. Strauss (1974) has suggested that workers "can adjust to nonchallenging work, usually by lowering their expectations, changing their need structure, making the most of social opportunities on and off the job" (p. 78). Kornhauser (1965) offers a similar interpretation, but with a more pessimistic emphasis: "The unsatisfactory mental health of working people consists in no small measure of their dwarfed desires and deadened initiative, reduction of their goals, and restriction of their efforts to a point where life is relatively empty and only half meaningful" (p. 270). Kornhauser goes on to discuss the two dead-end options for the car worker: maintain high expectations from work, which leads to constant frustration, or limit one's expectations, which leads to a drab existence.

The challenge for the APA/NIOSH conference is to develop prevention and health promotion strategies which recognize the delicate dynamics of lowered aspirations and withdrawal, and which raise expectations about work becoming a more meaningful human activity only conservatively, that is to the extent that true job redesign and job enlargement changes can be implemented.

References

American Psychiatric Association. (1987). *Diagnostic and statistical manual of mental disorders* (3rd ed. rev.). Washington, DC: Author.

Baker, D. B. (1985). The study of stress at work. *Annual Review of Public Health, 6,* 367–381.

Baker, E. L. (Ed.). (1989). Surveillance in occupational safety and health. *American Journal of Public Health, 79,* Supplement, 1–63.

Baker, E. L., Melius, J. M., & Millar, J. D. (1988). Surveillance of occupational illness and injury in the United States: Current perspectives and future directions. *Journal of Public Health Policy, 9,* 198–221.

Barling, J. (Ed.). (1990). *Employment, stress, and family functioning.* Chichester, England: Wiley.

Beehr, T. A., & Bhagat, R. S. (Eds.). (1985). *Human stress and cognition in organizations; An integrated perspective.* New York: Wiley.

Beehr, T. A., & Newman, J. E. (1978). Job stress, employee health, and organizational effectiveness: A facet analysis, model, and literature review. *Personnel Psychology, 31,* 665–699.

Burke, R. J. (Ed.). (1984). *Current issues in occupational stress: Research and intervention.* Downsview, Ontario: Faculty of Administrative Studies, York University.

Campbell, A. (1981). *The sense of well-being in America: Recent patterns and trends.* New York: McGraw-Hill.

Campbell, A., Converse, P. E., & Rodgers, W. L. (1976). *The Quality of American Life.* New York: Russell Sage Foundation.

Caplan, R. D., Cobb, S., French, F. R. P., Jr., Harrison, R. V., & Pinneau, S. R., Jr. (1975). *Job demands and worker health* (HEW Publication No. NIOSH 75-160). Washington, DC: U.S. Government Printing Office.

Cataldo, M. F., & Coates, T. J. (Eds.). (1986). *Health and industry: A behavioral medicine perspective.* New York: Wiley.

Clausen, J. A. (1969). Methodological issues in the measurement of mental health in the aged. In M. F. Lowenthal & A. Zilli (Eds.), *Colloquium on health and aging of the population* (pp. 111–127). Basel: S. Karger.

Cohen, S. (1986). Contrasting the Hassles Scale and the Perceived Stress Scale: Who's really measuring appraised stress. *American Psychologist, 41,* 717–718.

Cohen, S., Kamarek, T., & Mermelstein, R. (1983). A global measure of perceived stress. *Journal of Health and Social Behavior, 24,* 385–396.

Cohen, S., & Syme, S. L. (Eds.). (1985). *Social support and health.* Orlando, FL: Academic Press.

Colligan, M. J., Smith, M. J., & Hurrell, J. J., Jr. (1977). Occupational incidence rates of mental health disorders. *Journal of Human Stress, 3,* 34–39.

Cooper, C. L., Davidson, M. J., & Robinson, P. (1982). Stress in the police service. *Journal of Occupational Medicine, 24,* 31–36.

Cooper, C. L., & Marshall, J. (Eds.). (1980). *White collar and professional stress.* Chichester, England: Wiley.

Cooper, C. L., & Payne, R. (Eds.). (1978). *Stress at work.* Chichester, England: Wiley.

Cooper, C. L., & Payne, R. (Eds.). (1980). *Current concerns in occupational stress.* Chichester, England: Wiley.

Cooper, C. L., & Payne, R. (Eds.). (1988). *Causes, coping and consequences of stress at work.* Chichester, England: Wiley.

Cooper, C. L., & Smith, M. J. (Eds.). (1985). *Job stress and blue collar work.* Chichester, England: Wiley.

Corlett, E. N., & Richardson, J. (Eds.). (1981). *Stress, work design, and productivity.* Chichester, England: Wiley.

Creech, L., & Johnson, M. (1974). Angiosarcoma of liver in the manufacturer of polyvinyl chloride. *Journal of Occupational Medicine, 16,* 150–151.

Crump, J. H. (1979). Review of stress in air traffic control: Its measurement and effects. *Aviation, Space, and Environmental Medicine, 50,* 243–248.

Davidson, M. J., & Veno, A. (1980). Stress and the policeman. In C. L. Cooper & J. Marshall (Eds.), *White collar and professional stress* (pp. 131–166). Chichester, England: Wiley.

Dohrenwend, B. P., Levav, I., & Shrout, P. E. (1986). Screening scales from the Psychiatric Epidemiology Research Interview (PERI). In M. M. Weissman, J. K. Myers, & C. E. Ross (Eds.), *Community surveys of psychiatric disorders* (pp. 349–375). New Brunswick, NJ: Rutgers University Press.

Dohrenwend, B. P., & Shrout, P. E. (1981). Toward the development of a two-stage procedure for case identification and classification in psychiatric epidemiology. In R. G. Simmons (Ed.), *Research in community and mental health* (Vol. 2, pp. 292–323). Greenwich, CN: JAI Press.

Dooley, D., & Catalano, R. (Eds.). (1988). Psychological effects of unemployment. *Journal of Social Issues, 44*(4), 1–191.

Eaton, W. W., Anthony, J. C., Mandel, W., & Garrison, R. (1990). Occupations and the prevalence of major depressive disorder. *Journal of Occupational Medicine, 32,* 1079–1087.

Elliot, G. R., & Eisdorfer, C. (Eds.). (1982). *Stress and human health.* New York: Springer.

Evans, G. W. (Ed.). (1982). *Environmental stress.* New York: Cambridge University Press.

Fielding, J. E., & Pischeria, P. V. (1989). Frequency of worksite health promotion activities. *American Journal of Public Health, 79,* 16–20.

Fimian, M. J. (1984). The development of an instrument to measure occupational stress in teachers: The Teacher Stress Inventory. *Journal of Occupational Psychology, 57,* 277–293.

Frankenhaeuser, M. (1977). Job demands, health, and well-being. *Journal of Psychosomatic Research, 21,* 313–321.

Frankenhaeuser, M. (1979). Psychoneuroendocrine approaches to the study of emotion as related to stress and coping. In H. E. Howe, & R. A. Dienstbier (Eds.), *Nebraska Symposium on Motivation* (pp. 123–161). Lincoln, NE: University of Nebraska Press.

French, J. R. P., Jr., Caplan, R. D., & Van Harrison, R. (1982). *The mechanisms of job stress and strain.* Chichester, England: Wiley.

Frese, M., & Zapf, D. (1988). Methodological issues in the study of work stress: Objective vs subjective measurement of work stress and the question of longitudinal studies. In C. L. Cooper & R. Payne (Eds.), *Causes, coping, and consequences of stress at work* (pp. 375–411). Chichester, England: Wiley.

Gardell, B. (1976). *Job content and quality of life.* Stockholm: Prisma.

Gardell, B. (1982). Scandinavian research on stress in working life. *International Journal of Health Services, 12,* 31–41.

Gardell, B. (1987). Efficiency and health hazards in mechanized work. In J. C. Quick, R. S. Bhagat, J. E. Dalton, & J. D. Quick (Eds.), *Work stress: Health care systems in the workplace* (pp. 50–71). New York: Praeger.

Gentry, W. D., & Parkes, K. R. (1982). Psychological stress in intensive care unit and non-intensive care nursing: A review of the past decade. *Heart & Lung, 11,* 43–47.

Gray-Toft, P., & Anderson, J. G. (1981). The nursing stress scales: Development of an instrument. *Journal of Behavioral Assessment, 3,* 11–23.

Gutek, B. A., Repetti, R. L., & Silver, D. L. (1988). Nonwork roles and stress at work. In C. L. Cooper & R. Payne (Eds.), *Causes, coping and consequences of stress at work* (pp. 141–174). Chichester, England: Wiley.

Hackman, J. R., & Oldham, G. R. (1975). Development of the job diagnostic survey. *Journal of Applied Psychology, 60,* 159–170.

Haynes, S. G., LaCroix, A. Z., & Lippin, T. (1987). The effect of high job demands and low control on the health of employed women. In J. C. Quick, R. S. Bhagat, J. E. Dalton, & J. D. Quick (Eds.), *Work stress* (pp. 93–110). New York: Praeger.

Holt, R. R. (1982). Occupational stress. In L. Goldberger, & S. Breznitz (Eds.), *Handbook of stress* (pp. 419–444). New York: The Free Press.

House, J. S. (1980). *Occupational stress and mental and physical health of factory workers.* Ann Arbor, MI: ISR Research Report.

House, J. S. (1981). *Work stress and social support.* Reading, MA: Addison-Wesley.

House, J. S., & Cottington, E. M. (1986). Health and the workplace. In L. H. Aiken & D. Mechanic (Eds.), *Applications of social science to clinical medicine and health policy* (pp. 392–416). New Brunswick, NJ: Rutgers University Press.

Houts, P. S., & McDougall, V. (1988). Effects of informing workers of their health risks from exposure to toxic materials. *American Journal of Industrial Medicine, 13,* 271–279.

Hurrell, J. J., & Colligan, M. J. (1982). Psychological job stress. In W. N. Rom (Ed.), *Environmental and occupational medicine* (pp. 425–430). Boston: Little, Brown, & Co.

Jenkins, C. D., DeFrank, R. S., & Speers, M. A. (1984). *Evaluation of psychometric methodologies used to assess occupational stress and strain.* Galveston, Texas: Department of Preventive Medicine and Community Health, University of Texas Medical Branch.

Jenkins, G. D., Nadler, D. A., Lawler, E. E., III, & Cammann, C. (1975). Standardized observation: An approach to measuring the nature of jobs. *Journal of Applied Psychology, 60,* 171–181.

Johansson, G. (1976). Subjective well-being and temporal patterns of sympathetic adrenal medullary activity. *Biological Psychology, 4,* 157–172.

Johansson, G., Aronsson, G., & Lindstrom, B. P. (1978). Social psychological and neuroendocrine stress reactions in highly mechanized work. *Ergonomics, 21,* 583–599.

Jones, D. M., & Chapman, A. J. (Eds.). (1984). *Noise and society.* Chichester, England: Wiley.

Kahn, R. L. (1981). *Work and health.* New York: Wiley.

Kahn, R. L. (1987). Work stress in the 1980s: Research and practice. In J. C. Quick (Eds.), *Work stress: Health care systems in the workplace* (pp. 311–320). New York: Praeger.

Kahn, R. L., Hein, K., House, J., Kasl, S. V., & McLean, A. A. (1982). Report on stress in organizational settings. In G. R. Elliot & C. Eisdorfer (Eds.), *Stress and human health* (pp. 81–117). New York: Springer.

Kahn, R. L., Wolfe, D. M., Quinn, R. P., Snoek, J. D., & Rosenthal, R. A. (1964). *Organizational stress: Studies in role conflict and ambiguity.* New York: Wiley.

Karasek, R. A. (1985). *Job content questionnaire.* Los Angeles: Department of Industrial and Systems Engineering, University of Southern California.

Karasek, R., & Theorell, T. (1990). *Healthy work: Stress, productivity and the reconstruction of working life.* New York: Basic Books.

Kasl, S. V. (1978). Epidemiological contributions to the study of work stress. In C. L. Cooper & R. Payne (Eds.), *Stress at work* (pp. 3–48). Chichester, England: Wiley.

Kasl, S. V. (1981). The challenge of studying the disease effects of stressful work conditions. *American Journal of Public Health, 71,* 682–684.

Kasl, S. V. (1984). Stress and health. *Annual Review of Public Health, 5,* 319–341.

Kasl, S. V. (1986). Stress and disease in the workplace: A methodological commentary on the accumulated evidence. In M. F. Cataldo & T. J. Coates (Eds.), *Health and industry: A behavioral medicine perspective* (pp. 52–85). New York: Wiley.

Kasl, S. V. (1990). Assessing health risks in the work setting. In S. Hobfoll (Ed.), *New directions in health psychology assessment* (pp. 95–125). Washington, DC: Hemisphere.

Kasl, S. V., Chisholm, R. F., & Eskenazi, B. (1981). The impact of the accident at the Three Mile Island on the behavior and well-being of nuclear workers. *American Journal of Public Health, 71,* 472–483, 484–495.

Kasl, S. V., & Cobb, S. (1983). Psychological and social stresses in the workplace. In B. S. Levy & D. H. Wegman (Eds.), *Occupational health* (pp. 251–263). Boston: Little, Brown, & Co.

Kasl, S. V., & Serxner, S. (in press). Health promotion in the workplace. *International Review of Health Psychology.*

Kornhauser, A. (1965). *Mental health of the industrial worker.* New York: Wiley.

Kryter, K. D. (1972). Nonauditory effects of environmental noise. *American Journal of Public Health, 62,* 389–398.

Langner, T. S. (1986). What do instruments like the 22-Item Screening Score measure? In M. M. Weissman, J. K. Myers, & C. E. Ross (Eds.), *Community surveys of psychiatric disorders* (pp. 317–347). New Brunswick, NJ: Rutgers University Press.

Levi, L., Frankenhaeuser, M., & Gardell, B. (1982). Report on work stress related to social structures and processes. In G. R. Elliott & C. Eisdorfer (Eds.), *Stress and human health* (pp. 119–146). New York: Springer.

Levy, B. S., & Wegman, D. H. (1983). Recognizing occupational disease. In B. S. Levy & D. H. Wegman (Eds.), *Occupational health* (pp. 29–39). Boston: Little, Brown.

Locke, E. A. (1976). The nature and causes of job satisfaction. In M. D. Dunnette (Ed.), *Handbook of industrial and organizational psychology* (pp. 1297–1349). Chicago: Rand McNally.

Lundberg, U. (1976). Urban commuting: Crowdedness and catecholamine excretion. *Journal of Human Stress, 2,* 26–32.

Matteson, M. T., & Ivancevich, J. M. (1982). Stress and the medical technologist: I. A general overview. *American Journal of Medical Technology, 48,* 163–168.

McGrath, J. E. (1976). Stress and behavior in organizations. In M. D. Dunnette (Ed.), *Handbook of industrial and organizational psychology,* (pp. 1351–1395). Chicago: Rand McNally.

McLean, A. A. (1970). *Work stress.* Reading, MA: Addison-Wesley.

National Institute of Mental Health. (1983). *Risk factor research in the major mental disorders* (DHHS Publication No. ADM 83-1068). Rockville, MD: The Institute.

Payne, R., & Firth-Cozens, J. (Eds.). (1987). *Stress in health professionals.* Chichester, England: Wiley.

Pearlin, L. I., & Turner, H. A. (1987). The family as a context of the stress process. In S. V. Kasl & C. L. Cooper (Eds.), *Stress and health: Issues in research methodology* (pp. 143–165). Chichester, England: Wiley.

Pelz, D., & Andrews, F. (1966). *Scientists in organization.* New York: Wiley.

Phillips, B. N., & Lee, M. (1980). The changing role of the American teacher: Current and future sources of stress. In C. L. Cooper & J. Marshall (Eds.), *White collar and professional stress* (pp. 93–111). Chichester, England: Wiley.

Pollack, E. S., & Keiming, D. G. (Eds.). (1987). *Counting injuries and illnesses in the workplace: Proposals for a better system.* Washington, DC: National Academy Press.

Quick, J. C., Bhagat, R. S., Dalton, J. E., & Quick, J. D. (Eds.). (1987). *Work stress: Health care systems in the workplace.* New York: Praeger.

Quinn, R., Seashore, S., Kahn, R., Mangione, T., Campbell, D., Staines, G., & McCullough, M. (1971). *Survey of working conditions* (Document No. 2916-0001). Washington, DC: U.S. Government Printing Office.

Quinn, R. P., & Shepard, L. J. (1974). *The 1972–1973 quality of employment survey.* Ann Arbor, MI: Institute for Social Research.

Radloff, L. S., & Locke, B. Z. (1986). The community mental health assessment survey and the CES-D scale. In M. M. Weissman, J. K. Myers, & C. E. Ross (Eds.), *Community surveys of psychiatric disorders* (pp. 177–189). New Brunswick, NJ: Rutgers University Press.

Repetti, R. L. (1987). Linkages between work and family roles. In S. Oskamp (Ed.), *Applied social psychology annual: Vol. 7. Family processes and problems* (pp. 98–127). Beverly Hills: Sage Publishers, Inc.

Rissler, A. (1977). Stress reactions at work and after work during a period of quantitative overload. *Ergonomics, 20,* 13–16.

Robinson, J. P., Athanasiou, R., & Head, K. B. (Eds.). *Measures of occupational attitudes and occupational characteristics.* Ann Arbor, MI: Institute for Social Research.

Rose, R. M., Jenkins, C. D., & Hurst, M. W. (1978). *Air traffic controller health change study.* Boston: Boston University School of Medicine. (A report to the FAA, Contract No. DOT-FA72WA-3211)

Rutsein, D., Mullan, R. J., Frazier, T. M., Halperin, W. E., Melius, J. M., & Sestito, J. P. (1983). Sentinel health events (occupational): A basis for physician recognition and public health surveillance. *American Journal of Public Health, 73,* 1054–1062.

Salvendy, G., & Smith, M. J. (Eds.). (1981). *Machine pacing and occupational stress.* London: Taylor & Francis.

Sauter, S. L., Hurrell, J. J., Jr., & Cooper, C. L. (Eds.). (1989). *Job control and worker health.* Chichester, England: Wiley.

Sauter, S. L., Murphy, L. R., & Hurrell, J. J., Jr. (1990). Prevention of work-related psychological disorders. *American Psychologist, 45,* 1146–1158.

Schottenfeld, R. S., & Cullen, M. R. (1985). Occupation-induced posttraumatic stress disorders. *American Journal of Psychiatry, 142*, 198–202.

Schuckit, M. A., & Gunderson, E. K. E. (1973). Job stress and psychiatric illness in the U.S. Navy. *Journal of Occupational Medicine, 15*, 884–887.

Sethi, A. S., & Schuler, R. S. (Eds.). (1984). *Handbook of organizational stress coping strategies.* Cambridge, MA: Ballinger.

Sharit, J., & Salvendy, G. (1982). Occupational stress: Review and appraisal. *Human Factors, 24*, 129–162.

Shepard, J. M. (1971). *Automation and alienation.* Cambridge: The MIT Press.

Shephard, R. J. (1974). *Men at work.* Springfield, IL: C. C. Thomas.

Shostak, A. B. (1980). *Blue-collar stress.* Reading, MA: Addison-Wesley.

Smith, F. J. (1976). Index of organizational reactions (IOR). *JSAS of Selected Documents in Psychology, 6*, (1265), 54.

Smith, P. C., Kendall, L. M., & Hulin, C. L. (1969). *The measurement of satisfaction in work and retirement.* Chicago: Rand McNally.

Sorensen, G., Pechacek, T., & Pallonen, V. (1986). Occupational and worksite norms and attitudes about smoking cessation. *American Journal of Public Health, 76*, 544–549.

Steptoe, A., & Mathews, A. (Eds.). (1984). *Health care and human behaviour.* London: Academic Press.

Stokols, D., & Novaco, R. W. (1981). Transportation and well-being: An ecological perspective. In I. Altman, J. Wohlwill, and P. Everett (Eds.), *Transportation environments.* New York: Plenum Press.

Strauss, G. (1974). Workers: attitudes and adjustments. In the American Assembly, Columbia University, *The worker and the job: Coping with change* (pp. 73–98). Englewood Cliffs, NJ: Prentice-Hall.

Strauss, J. S., Harding, C. M., & Silverman, M. (1988). Work as treatment for psychiatric disorder: A puzzle in pieces—Report of a conference. In J. Ciardello & M. Bell (Eds.), *Vocational rehabilitation of persons with prolonged psychiatric disorders.* Baltimore, MD: Johns Hopkins University Press.

Tasto, D., Colligan, M. J., Skjei, E. W., & Polly, S. J. (1978). *Health consequences of shiftwork* (DHEW NIOSH Publication No. 78-154). Washington, DC: U.S. Government Printing Office.

Weiss, D. S., Davis, R. V., England, G. W., & Lofquist, L. H. (1967). *Manual for the Minnesota Satisfaction Questionnaire.* Minneapolis, MN: University of Minnesota Industrial Relations Center.

Weissman, M. M., & Bothwell, S. (1976). Assessment of social adjustment by patient self-report. *Archives of General Psychiatry, 33*, 1111–1115.

Welch, L. (1989). XI. The role of occupational health clinics in surveillance of occupational disease. *American Journal of Public Health, 79*, Supplement, 58–60.

Panel Comments

E. Carroll Curtis

I shall approach this topic on a good-news, bad-news basis. The good news is that the majority of United States workers are psychologically sound and are coping relatively well with work and with life in general. This is true in part because of the healthy worker effect, whereby the less mentally healthy and less adequate copers tend to be either initially precluded or eventually excluded from the workforce. Work and the socialization and self esteem it provides are, in effect, therapeutic for many; while being unable to work, whether due to disability or to unemployment, is in itself a serious detractor from good health in a psychosocial sense. In addition, the relatively high degree of mental wellness we see among workers testifies to the fact that humans are adaptable to life's sometimes heavy and constantly changing demands.

The bad news is that a substantial number of workers are afflicted by the troubled worker syndrome. Some of them are struggling with personal or family problems unrelated to work. At the same time, many are experiencing mental and emotional disorders to which work is a contributor. Thus far, too few of these troubled workers are being recognized and/or helped and all too little is being done in most workplaces to identify and modify the causal factors.

The good news is that at last the mental health community and some governmental agencies have developed heightened interest in work and mental health issues. The APA/NIOSH conference on work and well-being is evidence of that fact. The concerned observer dares to hope that it represents the opening gun in a meaningful initiative on this front. Certainly such a conference, per se, can do little more than delineate major components at issue and point at potential strategies for follow up, but that is an important first step.

The bad news, however, is that most of the available study paradigms are inadequate or they are largely irrelevant. This is because they were designed with physical ills in mind. Also, when one seeks to focus on the interactions of work and psychological disorders, he or she finds that even baseline data are scarce, while longitudinal information is almost nonexistent. Since surveillance (alert watchfulness) has to do primarily with following trends over time, the present prospects in that realm are poor.

However (the good news), demographic and sociologic methods are becoming more sophisticated and are being selectively adapted to workplace settings. For example, the recently reported Westinghouse study addressed many of the psychosocial variables which are assumed to have an impact on psychological health.[1] It

---

[1] Bromet, E. J., Parkinson, D. K., Curtis, E. C., Schulberg, H. C., Blane, H., Dunn, L. O., Phelan, J., Dew, M. A., & Schwartz, E. (1990). Epidemiology of depression and alcohol abuse/dependence in a managerial and professional workforce. *Journal of Occupational Medicine, 32*, 989–995.

looked for prevalence rates of specific major mental and emotional disorders in a population of 1,870 workers. Semi-structured questionnaires and validated instruments (e.g., symptom checklists and job satisfaction measures) were used in addition to extensive sociodemographic, historical, and other data collection.

The study focused intensively on individuals in a relatively narrow spectrum of white-collar jobs, taking into account such factors as exacerbating and ameliorating events and influences in both work and home environments concurrently. It revealed levels of major depression among this group of well-educated, stably employed managers and professionals which far exceed those suggested as likely by general community studies such as the ECA and despite the assumption made by an early proposal review committee that "nothing much" would be found. It also confirmed many findings of earlier studies, but went beyond them, for example, by demonstrating a previously unnoted, strong association between negative work events—particularly discordant relations with supervisors—and onset of serious depressive episodes. Thus, research is at least moving in the appropriate direction.

The bad news here is that well-designed and executed studies of this type are far too costly to allow for wide spread duplication. Parenthetically, many employers are reticent to open their doors to such studies as well. Therefore, we must find and try out alternative approaches to surveillance of mental and emotional needs and opportunities in the workplace. In effect, we are being challenged to come up with a variety of supplementary approaches. Clearly, this is not an either/or need. We still must have research along classical lines; but our efforts can also be furthered by creative thinking and innovative methods. As I see it, that is a major part of the task we face today.

The following suggestions are in no sense definitive, instead, they are put forth in the hope that they may stimulate us to look in new directions which both complement and go beyond traditional research efforts.

1. Perhaps we can influence the revision of *position descriptions* to make them more realistic and functional. Among other things, this would include inserting a section on psychosocial demands of the job and on the job's potential effects vis à vis worker mental health. Such position descriptions would:
    *   provide examiners with information they need to assess how well a worker matches the proposed work,
    *   remind managers that certain jobs impose an emotional toll on workers, and
    *   inform workers of the nonphysical stressors they are likely to experience in a particular job.

    They would also aid surveillance, assuming concurrent efforts to assess job conditions and to document subjectively experienced effects, which can then be compared against mental health outcomes identified by survey methods.
2. We could also recommend the inclusion in *medical examinations* of workers of at least a modicum of inquiries regarding mental health/chemical dependency factors. For instance, in the chemical dependency area we cur-

rently use the four CAGE[2] questions in voluntary exams. The answers given help alert examiners to persons who might benefit from counsel or referral. If such information were sought in a standardized way on occasion of every periodic health assessment, and collected in a systematic fashion, it might prove to be quite useful for surveillance purposes.

3. We might also advocate a requirement that *management credentialing* be initiated relative to health and safety competence. This would, *inter alia*, call for:

    - a knowledge of relevant facts about mental health and chemical dependency,
    - an understanding of managers' potential to influence workers' well-being, as well as
    - a recognition of managers' responsibility to recognize workers in need of referral.

    I am *not* proposing that managers or supervisors collect surveillance data. I am suggesting that simple studies could be done which measure mental health conditions before, and outcomes after, instituting such training for managers and supervisors.

4. In addition, we might well encourage the provision of *incentive arrangements* to help move employers toward greater involvement in provision of employee assistance programs and in mental health/chemical dependency education. The nature of the incentives need not be addressed here.

Relatively uncomplicated surveillance instruments can then be designed to measure how employees working for such employers fare mentally and emotionally as compared with employees working for nonparticipating employers. I have no doubt that brainstorming sessions among groups of occupational and mental health professionals would come up with still other suggestions. Consideration of such ideas and suggestions might well point out some new and exciting approaches to surveillance of worker mental health.

But meanwhile, let me go back to my original scheme and theme. A commanding officer in Saudi Arabia, having called his troops together, told them he had some good news and some bad news. When he asked which they wanted to hear first, they requested the latter. "The bad news is that we must fill all these sand bags before morning." "Then what's the good news?" "The good news is that there's plenty of sand." Similarly, the bad news regarding surveillance of mental and emotional disorders related to work is that the task before us is a large one and will require great effort and persistence. The good news is that there is no shortage of opportunities.

The need for such surveillance is unquestionably real. Indeed, as the Westinghouse study implies, it may be greater than we have thought. Let us all resolve to work hard and long to meet the challenge that need poses.

---

[2] Mayfield, D., McLeod, G., & Hall, P. (1974). The CAGE questionnaire: Validation of a new alcoholism screening instrument. *American Journal of Psychiatry, 131*, 1121–1123.

Panel Comments

William W. Eaton

Dr. Kasl has prepared a thoughtful document which has as its goal a comprehensive framework for the issue of surveillance—"the systematic collection, analysis, and dissemination of disease data on groups or populations" (Kasl, this volume, pages 73–95). In general I concur with that framework and with the most important broad conclusion he makes: that "there is little a priori promise that current occupational surveillance ideas and practices will be readily applicable to the surveillance of work-related psychological disorders" (Kasl, this volume, page 86). I agree that the "partial strategies" he discusses, following that conclusion, are the most likely to be fruitful.

The comprehensive quality of the document produced by Dr. Kasl lays out the conceptual map well, but, as he frequently suggests, needs "pruning." I offer the following suggestions for pruning.

First, concentrate on disorders for which the need for treatment is not controversial. The *DSM-III* can be used as a general guide (American Psychiatric Association, 1980). As Dr. Kasl recommends, the affective disorders, anxiety disorders, and substance use disorders, should be included. It also should include schizophrenia, in view of recent research linking it to workplace conditions (Link, 1986). The possibility that episodes of bipolar disorder could be triggered by workplace conditions is also important to consider. Data on treatment seeking will not be informative because of help seeking biases, indices of functional effectiveness have too many causes to be useful, and positive mental health and quality of life are not public health priorities when we have accomplished so little regarding bad disorders such as those listed here.

Second, for general surveillance activities, do not consider the question of the interaction of work with nonwork factors and vulnerability groups. This is too large a job and leads inevitably to ethical problems—for example, the obvious choice for a vulnerability factor is a family history of disorder; but inquiring about family history of psychological disorders will not be a useful aspect of occupational surveillance.

Third, consider as target populations specific occupations with known high prevalence or incidence of a given disorder. Unfortunately we have little data comparing occupations as to the prevalence of specific disorders. However, large-scale surveys, such as the Health Interview Survey (NCHS, 1975), the Health and Nutrition Examination Survey (NCHS, McDowell, Engle, Massey, & Maurer, 1981), and the NIMH Epidemiologic Catchment Area Surveys (Eaton, Regier, Locke, & Taube, 1981), do exist, and they produce large enough samples in specific occupations to be interesting, even for disorders with relatively low prevalence. But they have not been analyzed in the simple informative way I am suggesting. Table 1, an excerpt from a larger table of 105 occupations, gives examples of DIS/*DSM-III* major depressive disorder. The prevalence varies from above 10% in a few occupations, to nearly 0% in some others (Eaton, Anthony, Mandell, & Garrison, 1990). Many of these differences continue to exist after control of socio-demographic differences between occupations. Dr. Kasl has concentrated on etiological forces in the workplace and I agree with that focus over the long term. But if these results are replicated in another data set, as I think they will be, it may be worthwhile setting up some sort of surveillance mechanisms, in specific occupations, to screen for individuals who have major depressive disorder. A program to increase the public awareness of depression, called D/ART (Depression/Awareness, Recognition, Treatment) is underway now at the NIMH—why shouldn't it be started in an occupation like data-entry keyers, where the prevalence appears to be high? This recommendation is made without knowledge of whether workplace conditions endured by data-entry keyers actually cause depression, or whether individuals who are likely to be depressed for other reasons end up keying in data: That is, the public's health can be served simply by locating individuals likely to be depressed (if a good treatment exists). It is also true that intensive longitudinal research is recommended for these occupations with high prevalence, to suggest more clearly the causal order.

We have produced similar analyses for anxiety and substance use disorders, and there are strong differences in prevalence of these disorders by occupations, also, but the occupations with high prevalence are different than for major depressive disorder.

Table 1. Prevalence of DIS/*DSM-III* Major Depressive Disorder with Crude Odds Ratio From Case-Control Sample for 105 Occupations and Occupational Groups

Occupation title (census code)	N	Prevalence	Odds ratio	Confidence interval
Data-Entry Keyers (385)	63	13	3.303	(1.470, 7.424)
Computer Equipment Operators (308)*	56	13	2.764	(1.185, 6.447)
Other Teachers and Counselors/Not College (155)*	98	10	2.208	(1.103, 4.421)
Typists (315)	112	10	3.178	(1.596, 6.328)
Lawyers (178)	52	10	2.362	(0.882, 6.319)
⋮				
Construction Laborers (869)	75	5	1.254	(0.440, 3.575)
Teachers/Elementary (156)	161	5	1.123	(0.536, 2.352)
⋮				
Computer Programmers (229)	50	0	0.001	(. , .)
Auto Mechanics (505)	68	0	0.001	(. , .)
Electrical/Electronic Equipment Repairer (523)*	69	0	0.001	(. , .)
Miscellaneous Mechanics and Repairers (535)*	57	0	0.001	(. , .)
Precision Textile Occupations (666)*	53	0	0.001	(. , .)
Total	11,789	4		

*indicates grouped occupation.
Note. Numbers in parentheses indicate census codes.

Fourth, consider as target populations occupations and jobs with high levels of exposures. Dr. Kasl provided a list of dimensions which is quite useful. I offer as a less-inclusive alternative the following factors which were produced in a partially successful attempt to replicate work by Cain and Treiman (1981).

Factor 1: Substantive complexity
Factor 2: Motor skills
Factor 3: Physical demands and hazards
Factor 4: Expressive work
Factor 5: Interpersonal stress
Factor 6: Steam

The input correlation matrix for the factors used the average scores of 44 dimensions of work included in the *Dictionary of Occupational Titles* (U.S. Department of Labor, 1977) as variables, and the 502 specific occupations in the Census Detailed Classification (U.S. Bureau of the Census, 1980) as observations. The data are available in a public use tape created by England and Kilbourne (1988). Any of 12,099 occupations in the *Dictionary of Occupational Titles* can be described as to its placement on these dimensions. Since this classification scheme already exists, I suggest we take advantage of it in attempting to locate pockets of high prevalence.

In conclusion, I believe we need another round of epidemiologic research which is designed to locate target populations by specific occupational categories and dimensions of work. Only then can we choose occupations and workplaces for more intensive etiologic studies, intervention studies, and continuing surveillance.

References

American Psychiatric Association. (1980). *Diagnostic and statistical manual of mental disorders* (3rd ed.). Washington, DC: Author.

Cain, P., & Treiman, D. (1981). The dictionary of occupational titles as a source of occupational data. *Am. Sociol. Rev.*, 253–278.

Eaton, W. W., Anthony, J. C., Mandell, W., & Garrison, R. (1990). Occupations and the prevalence of major depressive disorder. *J. Occup. Med. 32*, 1079–1087.

Eaton, W. W., Keyl, P. M., Garrison, R., Anthony, J. C., & Mandell, W. (1991). *Occupations, job characteristics, and the occurrence of panic attacks.* Manuscript submitted for publication.

Eaton, W. W., Regier, D. A., Locke, B. Z., & Taube, C. A. (1981). The NIMH Epidemiologic Catchment Area Program. *Public Health Report, 96*, 319–325.

England, P., & Kilbourne, B. (1988). *Occupational measures from the dictionary of occupational titles for 1980 census detailed occupations.* Ann Arbor, MI: Inter-University Consortium for Political and Social Research.

Link, B., Dohrenwend, B., & Skodol, A. E. (1986). Socioeconomic status and schizophrenia. *American Sociological Review, 51*.

National Center for Health Statistics. (1975, April). *Health Interview Survey procedure, 1957–74: Vital and Health Statistics. Series 1, No. 11* (DHEW Publication No. HRA 75-1311). Washington, DC: U.S. Government Printing Office.

National Center for Health Statistics, McDowell, A., Engel, A., Massey, J. T., & Maurer, K. (1981, July). *Plan and operation of the Second National Health and Nutrition Examination Survey, 1976–80: Vital and Health Statistics. Series 1, No. 15.* (DHHS Publication No. PHS 81-1317. Washington, DC: U.S. Government Printing Office.

U.S. Bureau of the Census. (1980). *Alphabetical index of industries and occupations.* Washington, DC: U.S. Government Printing Office.

U.S. Department of Labor. (1977). Dictionary of occupational titles (4th ed.). Washington, DC: U.S. Government Printing Office.

Panel Comments

Robin Mary Gillespie

I am a health and safety specialist for Service Employees International Union. SEIU represents 925,000 building service, health care, clerical, and social service workers in the United States, Canada, and Puerto Rico. As you might expect, our members score high on most indices of stressful working conditions. In commenting on Dr. Kasl's paper and contributing to the discussion I will be drawing on the experiences of SEIU members in all sectors, as well as a project run by the Utility Workers Union of America to identify and eliminate stressful working conditions in power plants and on power lines.

To start, I want to consider the function of surveillance. NIOSH proposes that it should "detect and react to emerging problems and . . . evaluate interventions." How problems, solutions, and surveillance methods are defined derives from the program's goals. For unions like SEIU, the primary goal is to increase the chance for working people to lead satisfying and healthy lives, at work and away from it. As Karen Nussbaum, director of 9 to 5, the National Association of Working Women, and president of SEIU District 925, puts it, "The point is not simply to contain the problem [but] to improve the working life of working Americans. This may result in other benefits, but this goal is the precondition."

The goal you pursue most actively will influence what you look for. If it is research, you will probably look at extreme cases of disorder, and try to control for as many factors as possible. If it is work output, you will relate productivity and psychological disorders. If it is cost, you might use a method of surveillance that provides early identification of symptoms amenable to treatment, or you might choose pre-employment testing to avoid hiring workers with presumed tendencies to psychological disorders. But if the goal is a real change in how work affects people, you will need to engage in an active kind of research that addresses problems as it explores them. It is not enough to figure out what causes distress and psychological disorder, we must use this research and surveillance to identify what conditions can be changed, and what changes make a difference.

Some small changes may have far-reaching effects. For example, during the utility union project, most participants complained that management waited until a few minutes before the end of the shift to announce that overtime was required. By that time workers had showered, set their minds on dinner, and made last minute arrangements. This minor issue confirmed workers' feelings that management had no respect for them, it contributed to family conflict, and it even divided workers among themselves. When the union took this issue, along with many others, to the bargaining table, management agreed to give several hours' notice in all except emergency situations. As a result, workers were a lot more willing to volunteer because they could do it conveniently, with time to plan, and even emergency overtime was more equitably distributed. This project succeeded because through the union, affected workers identified the sources and the appropriate corrections of the stressors they experienced.

This is a reminder that we also need to examine who does the surveillance. The employer, the government, the health system, and the workers themselves all have different goals in this program, as well as different knowledge and skills. Workers and their unions must be involved in the definition of the problems and in directing surveillance and corrections. Scientists may find it "highly suspect" to ask workers to identify causes as well as symptoms of work-related disorder, but when it comes to what happens on the shop floor, workers are the experts. If you rigidly adhere to the controlled model of research directed by the scientist you will lose your best source of data about cause, effects, and solutions.

In addition, local or shop-level surveillance can be used to screen for severe distress, as for any other disease related to work. This kind of screening, like that for more physical disorders, can lead to discrimination and loss of work. As a research method, it is likely to identify differences between workers rather than work conditions. The union approach has been to understand how groups of workers are affected by stressful conditions in order to identify solutions that protect everyone.

In any case, a policy of waiting until workers become clinically disturbed or ill before eliminating the hazards does not make sense. Gross symptoms show up too late for prevention. Tools for measuring less quantifiable outcomes, such as effectiveness or quality of life, are not well developed. What goes into these indices is political as well as psychological and cultural. Even what constitutes a symptom is debatable.

In addition to formal evaluations, informal surveys and field experience have made local unions aware of how stress affects their members. Every day I hear, from workers, of symptoms not usually linked with specific aspects of work, such as divorce or other personal troubles. Though not clinically depressed, health care workers are deeply saddened by the increasing difficulty of providing quality care while understaffed. Still able to function, service workers are anxious about their children while on night shift. While maintaining some self-esteem, people in every sector feel humiliated and angry when their grievances are not fairly addressed. These outcomes affect many more workers than do diagnosable illnesses, and they must be monitored if anything is.

SEIU agrees with Dr. Kasl's position that "in targeting prevention programs, the surveillance of responsible workplace exposures or hazards may be more useful than health effects surveillance." We would say that it is, because looking at concrete working conditions gives us a chance to improve conditions for the collective, not just moderate stressors for a few. Again, the conditions must be analyzed for their effects on groups, not just individuals.

However, one suggested goal of environmental monitoring is to "build up adequate hazard information about specific jobs so that . . . the job title itself would stand for the specific mixture of hazards present." Jobs should not be equated with their nonintrinsic stressors. In secretarial work, the worst stressors, such as electronic monitoring, are actively created by the employer in a misguided attempt to increase productivity (which they do not) and maintain control (which they might).

Of course low pay and job security are only intrinsic to jobs as long as they are allowed to be. All of these things can be changed. The fact is, many workers expect their work to be demanding. Clients have problems. Patients die. Storms bring down power lines, and somebody has to bring them up. But avoidable hazards make these unavoidable stressors even more destructive.

Sylvia Tesh summarizes our position on the surveillance of work-related psychological disorders:

> Terrible job conditions are terrible regardless of their ability to cause disease. Even if people could work at them in perfect health they should, in a just society, be changed. . . . [Only] the people who work at jobs day after day really know what about them is demanding, tense, and unpleasant. Outsiders can merely guess, at best.

A host of surveys and studies have already illuminated a large number of serious stressors in health care and service work. Union members point out more to us every day. We hope that this project can join unions, and all workers in this country, in rooting out and eliminating the problems workers know they face: lack of control, lack of recognition, demand that exceeds the power to effect change, conflicts with family or social roles, physically hazardous or unpleasant working conditions, discrimination, lack of security, and low pay. Let's survey workplaces for these hazards, help groups of people change these conditions, and then see what results.

Panel Comments

Ronald W. Manderscheid

Dr. Kasl has done a fine job at an exceptionally difficult task. His paper clearly analyzes and clarifies the questions being asked, proposes a hazard-effect model, discusses a range of measures for each key variable, and proposes a measurement approach for consideration. His paper represents an excellent forum for initiating discussion and for developing a concrete approach to the problem. Several of my comments are for Dr. Kasl, and several go beyond the scope of his presentation.

First, I would like to make explicit three tensions that need to be considered in amplifying Dr. Kasl's presentation. These are:

1. *etiology versus prevalence design.* Clearly, our approach will be different if we are trying to establish the causative role of jobs in mental distress or disorder versus just examining the prevalence of distress or disorder among job holders. Both issues need attention, but required approaches will vary.
2. *objective versus subjective measurement.* Mental health consequences of jobs are generally mediated by the characteristics of job holders, including their perceptions. Thus, the hazard–effect measurement model needs to be expanded to a hazard–person–effect model.
3. *research versus routine surveillance.* Dr. Kasl proposes a series of epidemiological studies. However, even if initiated in the laboratory of epidemiological surveys, surveillance needs, ultimately, to become a routinized process in work settings.

Now, I would like to go beyond the scope of Dr. Kasl's presentation and provide a few further thoughts.

Although a hazard–person–effect model is essential, I would question whether even it goes far enough. For example, should we be measuring behavioral consequences in addition to mental distress or disorder? In the determination of disability, the Social Security Administration currently uses a four dimensional model to assess work behavior for persons with mental disorders. These factors include capacity to perform instrumental activities of daily living, social functioning in the workplace, concentration and task persistence, and decompensation under work stress. We may need to develop less intensive versions of these dimensions to examine the effects of jobs on typical job holders.

Job redesign will be essential not only to prevent adverse consequences for typical entrants, but also for disabled populations who suffer from a preexisting mental disorder. A likely change during the 1990s will be the mainstreaming of mentally ill persons into the occupational world. This change is likely to be facilitated by the Americans with Disabilities Act. The requirements of these disabled populations need to be considered in job redesign.

Although job redesign will be essential for many occupations, I question whether we ought not also do better in matching persons to jobs. Some jobs are inherently stressful and dangerous. This implies that more care ought to be exercised in selecting entrants.

Clearly, the topic of job surveillance is extremely important. I trust that we are ready and committed to meet the challenges posed by the complexities of this undertaking.

Panel Comments

Diane Wagener

I certainly cannot add to the discussion of the assessment issues or research needs that Dr. Kasl has outlined in his presentation. However, I want to look more broadly at the needs of the Public Health Service and discuss the possibilities of using existing data systems to obtain greater information regarding psychological well-being of the work force. First, let me note the following comments are my own and do not represent any discussions of these issues by the National Center for Health Statistics. Our Center has not been asked to consider any of these issues.

As you will see, my bottom line is that there is more than one objective of surveillance and that the implementation of any strategy to achieve the objectives will depend on setting relative priorities. However, it is clear that whatever the strategy, there will be a need for greater integration of the data systems relevant to achieving better surveillance of psychological status of the work force.

Surveillance, broadly defined, is the systematic collection, analysis, and dissemination of disease data on groups or populations. I propose that this encompasses five objectives:

1. research on etiologic relationships of mental illness or stress to various risk factors;
2. identification of high-risk jobs;
3. identification of work-hazards;
4. identification of affected individuals; and
5. evaluation of work-environment modifications or treatment programs.

Research on Etiologic Relationships

Research is an *essential* component in any strategy to prevent and treat work-related psychological disorders. My colleagues have spoken of the needs. However, research is only one of three basic types of data that are needed for comprehensive strategy to improve psychological well-being in the work force. The three basic types of data are research data (from studies of targeted populations or targeted risk factors), descriptive data (from studies of the well-being of the work force), and programmatic or monitoring data (from evaluations of programs and identification of "outbreaks").

Because of the targeted feature of research studies, these data cannot be obtained from data systems that have broad-based objectives or have broad sampling schemes. I have heard disparaging remarks at the APA/NIOSH conference that national data systems cannot address this or that particular research issue. I find that to be an oxymoron, not a complaint. The national data systems were not designed to serve as a source that would provide complete information needed for targeted research studies. National data systems, or state-based data systems, are designed to provide descriptive data that may suggest directions for research, but they were not designed to substitute for targeted research studies. The collection of data for the research objective of a strategy to improve psychological well-being of the work force will need to be conducted by federal, academic, and state investigators through specially designed studies.

Identification of High-Risk Jobs

The purpose of this objective is to identify those jobs in which workers have higher rates of psychologic disorders than like individuals employed in other jobs. This objective might be achieved through a case study approach, but I am going to assume that our intent is to achieve this in a more systematic approach.

This is the easiest objective to address with existing data systems, which is not to say that the objective can *be* achieved. First, we need a case definition of what psychological disorders should be assessed. Second, we need to determine how these psychological disorders can be assessed. Given these difficult prerequisites, the data can be collected through judicious sampling of job types, establishment types, or the population. This objective cannot be achieved by sampling medical establishments, such as the SENSOR program, that are more appropriate for addressing the following objectives. The reason the medical surveillance model is inappropriate for this objective is that there is no information on the sampling frame. Relying on physicians or hospitals to identify affected individuals provides no information on the employment characteristics of the populations that might seek such help. Medical access and health care utilization differ greatly by sex, cultural groups, and socioeconomic status. Hence, using the clinician (even an industry-based clinician) to identify individuals with psychological distress is a biased method of ascertainment.

Establishment-based record systems are also a biased method of ascertainment. Given the complex, multifactorial etiology of psychologic disorders, the management of an establishment is not eager to label any particular case as work-related. So underascertainment obviously exists in the OSHA logs. But equally so, the worker is concerned with privacy issues. Given the impact of nonwork-related social settings on psychological well-being of the worker, the worker often does not want the management of the establishment to have knowledge of family or other problems. Hence, there is another source of underascertainment if employer records are used as a data source.

Therefore, my personal evaluation is that interviews with individuals selected according to a prescribed sampling scheme is the only way to achieve this objective. Furthermore, if this is to be conducted on a large scale and on anything other than a onetime basis, the interviews will have to be conducted by interviewers with minimal psychological training. A model for this is the NHIS of the NCHS. Because of respondent burden in a survey of this scale, any single topic can only be addressed in a short time frame, up to 20 minutes of interview time. In general the instruments are structured, although semi-structured formats are used for a few items on the NHIS to gather information on medical conditions. Therefore, it is important that researchers imbed short, structured interviews within their more complex research protocols to assess the sensitivity and specificity of these instruments. With this information, the results from the larger data systems can be interpreted in meaningful ways.

Identification of Work Hazards

Preliminary information on relevant work hazards is needed before this objective can be adequately addressed. Dr. Kasl has given us a long list of possible characteristics that might be addressed. The problem I see with this list of physical conditions at work, physical aspects of work, temporal aspects of the work day and work itself, work content, interpersonal-work group, interpersonal-supervision, financial and economic aspects, and organizational aspects is that the assessment of all these aspects requires information from several different sources. For instance, personal interviews with the worker cannot provide information on exposures other than the perception of exposure by the worker. Evaluation of the ergonomic design of machines must be done by an expert. Size and structure of the organization requires information from management. Utilization of worker skills and sufficiency of resources are additional items that require information from several sources. It will not be possible to assess all of these items on a large, diffuse work force. Therefore, to achieve this objective, the first step must be the narrowing of possible work hazards to be assessed. Only after these have been more closely defined, can any evaluation be performed on the data system design and relevance of existing data systems.

Identification of Morbidity in Individuals

The medical establishment is the primary source of information for this objective. The SENSOR program being developed and expanded by NIOSH and several states will be successful in identifying methods for capturing information on morbidity for a variety of medical diseases and disorders. I hope that psychologic disorders become the focus of some of these cooperative agreements.

Other data systems are not appropriate to achieve this objective. The surveys are only probability samples of the population, hence, many affected individuals are missed. Further screening instruments that might be used are inadequate for attribution of cause in the individual. For instance, at the NCHS we have used the CES-D and a special supplement designed by the NIMH in the 1989 NHIS. These can be used to note associations of psychological distress and various risk factors on a population-wide basis. However, in the case of any particular individual, the attribution of a morbid state to work-related stress can only be done through the extended evaluation of health professionals. Another problem with the survey mechanism, is that psychological distress is an episodic state. This means that one time assessments are generally inadequate due to biased recall. Therefore, an ongoing system that continually reassesses the population or has continual access to the population is required.

Evaluation of Treatment Programs

The evaluation of work-environment modification or treatment programs must be conducted on the same scale as the program being performed. That is, if the purpose is to evaluate an establishment-based treatment program, the evaluation must be conducted at the establishment level. If the purpose is to evaluate a national program in work-environment improvement, the evaluation must be conducted at the national level. Evaluation must be an integral part of any program plan.

Conclusions

The successful strategy to achieve improved work-related psychological health must be multifaceted. There is no single surveillance mechanism that can adequately address all these objectives. It is also unlikely that, in the short term, all objectives can be achieved for the entire work force. Therefore, priorities must be set. Once priorities are set, the existing data systems and research protocols can be evaluated. I am optimistic that when that is done, we will identify ways to use existing data systems to begin to provide information relevant to many objectives. However, I am equally pessimistic that these objectives cannot be fully met. That is, because of the extraordinary assessment issues discussed by the other panelists, identification of all risk factors or all cases of work-related psychological disorders is probably unrealistic. We can, however, improve the current state of affairs.

Work Design and Stress Panel

Panel Members

Frank J. Landy, Chairperson, *Pennsylvania State University, University Park, PA*

Harold Davis, *Prudential Insurance, Newark, NJ*
Mirian Graddick, *AT&T International Communications Services, Morristown, NJ*
Barbara A. Gutek, *University of Arizona, Tucson, AZ*
Susan Jackson, *New York University, New York, NY*
Robert Kahn, *University of Michigan, Ann Arbor, MI*
David LeGrande, *Communications Workers of America, Washington, DC*
Gavriel Salvendy, *Purdue University, West Lafayette, IN*
Lawrence Schleifer, *National Institute for Occupational Safety and Health, Cincinnati, OH*
Fred Schott, *Aetna Life and Casualty, Hartford, CN*
Michael Smith, *University of Wisconsin, Madison, WI*
Leon Warshaw, *New York Business Group on Health, New York, NY*

Frank J. Landy

Work Design and Stress

In October of 1986, a symposium on the prevention of work related diseases was held in Cincinnati, Ohio. The symposium was jointly sponsored by the Association of Schools of Public Health, the National Institute of Occupational Safety and Health, and the Association of University Programs in Occupational Health and Safety (Association of Schools of Public Health [ASPH], 1988). One of the themes of that symposium was the prevention of work related psychological disorders. A number of topics were identified within that theme; among them was the issue of job design and working conditions. The *Work and Well-Being: An Agenda for the 1990s* conference takes that theme as a point of departure and examines three different facets of the issue: work design and job stress, surveillance of psychological disorders at the work place, and health promotion at the workplace. The latter two topics will be covered by the other two panels. In this paper, we will consider the issues raised by the first facet, work design and stress.

In developing the outline for this paper, it was clear that in order to be complete, one should cast a wide net and consider not only traditional issues of job design as "independent variables," but also issues related to the broad environmental context in which work occurs, individual differences that might act as moderator variables, methodological and analytic issues, and anticipated changes in the nature of work. In fact, we will mention all or almost all of these topics in this paper. Nevertheless, for purposes of the conference, we must exercise some discipline in the amount of coverage that we give to each. Thus, for the most part, we will allocate most of our attention to the issues of work and job design and the implications of such design for the construct of stress. In our treatment of work design and stress, we will adopt a convention intended to distinguish between the objective events, conditions, work characteristics, and so forth that are contributors to or antecedents of worker reactions and the reactions themselves. We will refer to the antecedent or contributory variables as *stressors* and the consequent worker reactions as *strains*. The term *stress* will simply be used to refer to the broad domain of research and intervention that is the topic of *Work and Well-Being* conference.

A consideration of stress in the workplace is an enormously complex undertaking. This is best illustrated by a recent review of the construct of work stress by Kahn and Byosiere (in press). Figure 1 is taken from that review and presents an excellent structural view and theoretical framework. It would be wonderful if we had firm conclusions about the implications of each of the boxes in that figure. Unfortunately, that is not the case. We know more about some topics than about others. In this paper we will attempt to identify what we know with some confidence and what we do not know. This will lead to recommendations regarding future

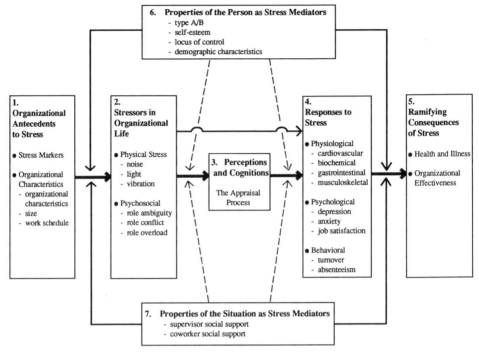

Figure 1. A Theoretical Framework for the Study of Stress in Organizations.

Note. From "Stress in Organization" by R. L. Kahn and M. Byosiere, in M. Dunnette (Ed.), *Handbook of Industrial and Organizational Psychology*, (Vol. 3, 2nd ed.), 1991. Copyright 1991 by Consulting Psychologists Press. Reprinted by permission.

research and application initiatives. The central focus, however, will be on implementation and we will end our paper on that note. We will attempt to illustrate how what we currently know can become part of a broad intervention strategy. Furthermore, we will illustrate how what we *do not know* currently limits intervention efficacy. In the earlier symposium identified previously (ASPH, 1988), a series of intervention proposals were suggested. We will revisit and extend those proposals in our presentation.

Part of the difficulty in dealing with the topic of stress in the workplace is that it will not stand still long enough to give us a good look. The nature of work is changing rapidly. No one can ignore the revolution in work that is represented by computer technology. Everyone from the teenager operating the french fry machine at McDonald's to the psychiatrist diagnosing affective disorders has been affected by the introduction of the computer into the workplace (Garson, 1988; Oskamp & Spacapan, 1990; Zuboff, 1988). In some senses, the nature of work has been in a state of flux for a decade or more. This has created a particular challenge for research efforts in work design and its consequences. It has become abundantly clear that the introduction of a video display terminal at the worksite is not simply placing a screen on a desk. The correlative changes in work methods, social interaction patterns, patterns of supervision, and productivity goals (not to mention the obvious correlative changes) are extensive (Gutek, Bikson, & Mankin, 1984; Landy, Rastegary, & Motowidlo, 1987; Majchrzak & Davis, 1990; Nieva, Newman, & Bottlik,

1990). This makes the evaluation of any intervention particularly challenging. Coupled with such technological changes, there are also dramatic changes occurring in the work force (Greller, 1990). Work groups are becoming older. Additionally, new members of the working population are more demographically diverse and possess skill sets and value systems that are not identical to those possessed by earlier generations. These changing skills and values also have implications for understanding stress in the workplace. It is becoming increasingly clear that the gap between skills demanded in new technological environments and skills possessed by the work force is growing (Herold, 1990). This gap is bound to make itself felt in increased worker strain resulting from performance problems that represent increased demands coupled with diminished resources. This is likely to be just as true of existing workers whose skills are becoming obsolete as it is with new workers whose skills are deficient.

Two additional changes in the environment of work organizations must be considered as sources of stress: the intensification of international competition and the restructuring of American corporations. The increase in competition has been studied most intensively in the case of Japan and the manufacture of automobiles, but the phenomenon involves many other countries and industries (Bennis & Nanus, 1985; Lawrence & Dyer, 1983; Ouchi, 1981; Walton, 1987). The phenomenon of corporate structuring—voluntary mergers, corporate takeovers, white-knight rescues, and the like—has generated a continuing narrative in newspapers and magazines. For workers, both of these developments, however remote their origins, are experienced as sources of uncertainty and demands for change.

In the context of introducing the concept of work design, a caveat is in order. For purposes of this paper, we will treat "productive work" in an orthodox manner, that is "paid" work. It is clear that this is a limited (and arbitrary) definition. Consider housework and care giving. Both could easily be included in the broader concept of productive effort (Kahn & Byosiere, in press) and in fact we will consider the interaction of paid and nonpaid work in a later section of the paper. Nevertheless, in the service of our current charge, we will consider only the issue of paid work in our direct treatment of work design.

Finally, a complete understanding of the phenomenon of work stress and work design will depend on the enthusiastic interactions of several distinct scientific disciplines. To mention but a few, industrial engineering and ergonomics, industrial and organizational psychology, sociology, cognitive science, applied physiology, medicine, and epidemiology all have insights to offer that inform the discussion. In this paper, we will deal with the more narrow issue of work and job design, but the implications for and from these other fields will be obvious.

It is axiomatic that we will know more tomorrow than we do today, and even more the day after that. We know a great deal about stress in the workplace as well as methods for ameliorating worker strain. It is our hope that by virtue of the present treatment, we will be able to identify the parameters of interest for tracking the scientific progress as well as those findings robust enough to imply efficacious interventions in the rapidly changing work environment.

In the paper to follow, we will consider a diverse array of variables that could be considered stressors in the workplace, with a particular emphasis on the design of work. There will be six major sections in this paper. The first four sections will deal with stressors, beginning with a broad view and gradually narrowing. Section one will deal with the "architecture" of work. This will be followed by a more specific treatment of the social aspects of that architecture. We will then consider the issue of control in the workplace, a construct receiving increasing attention in the stress literature (Sauter, Hurrell, & Cooper, 1989). Finally, we will consider the nature of work and task demands, one of the enduring foci for stress research. This will be followed by a consideration of potential endogenous moderators of or contributors to strain. A recurring "question" in stress research and theorizing has been the extent to which stress is a product of the environment (e.g., a search for stressors) and the extent to which stressors are defined within an individual (e.g., the vulnerability of the Type A behavior pattern [TABP] individual). Endogenous factors represent the latter approach. Our position will be that exogenous variables (e.g., work design) and endogenous variables (e.g., TABP) interact to produce strain. The last section will include a synthesis of the conclusions and recommendations imbedded in and implied by the body of the paper. The recommendations will comprise two categories: recommendations for action and recommendations for research.

The Psychological Architecture of Work

In this section, we will consider some structural characteristics of work and, in particular, the behavioral implications of these components. This is meant to present broad representative components. In a later section, titled "Social Fabric of Work," we will examine the pieces of architecture that have particularly social implications. As such, this later section will represent more of a magnification than of a change in perspective.

Tasks, Jobs, and Work

In considering issues of stress in the workplace, one must inevitably deal with issues of the level of aggregation (Schuler & Jackson, 1986). This is not simply an issue of analytic strategy. It is a fundamental question that relates to the nature of the phenomenon under consideration. To return to Figure 1 briefly, one can imagine at least three levels of aggregation imbedded in that model. The first is at the task level. Thus, in component 2, one might consider not only conflict among individuals filling different roles (e.g., job titles) but also conflict *within* a single role between or among tasks that compete for attention (Jackson & Schuler, 1985). Similarly, component 1 in Figure 1 implies a level of aggregation (and influence) that transcends both the task and the role level. The organization is seen to have influences independent of and interacting with those that characterize the task and the job. In considering the consequences of work design for strain, we must remain open to the widest interpretation of the phrase "work design." The concept will include not only the individual tasks that collectively define a job title, but also the job title in interaction with other job titles. In addition, the design of work will include not only the formal duties and responsibilities of the incumbent but also the administrative and organizational environment in which those duties and responsibilities are carried out. From this perspective, work schedules become part of work design as do methods of payment, performance monitoring, and work group composition. It has become clear that in order to understand the impact that work has on people, we must consider the phenomenon from the sociotechnical perspective (Landy, 1989). Considering the psychosocial aspects of work at the exclusion of the technological parameters (or vice versa) will provide a superficial and ultimately misleading avenue for intervention. It seems clear that after decades of awareness of the importance of the sociotechnical perspective, those responsible for the design of work continue to ignore that broader perspective. It is essential that the social and behavioral scientists demonstrate the practical importance of this concept to those who design work. Just as the Tavistock researchers illustrated the sociotechnical perspective through the study of the transformation of longwall mining, careful case studies representative of other forms of technological change in the workplace should be conducted in order to sensitize designers to these psychosocial issues. A case in point is the introduction of information technology to the workplace (Zuboff, 1982, 1985, 1988). The "simple" introduction of personal computers to the clerical environment has enormous consequences for all types of variables and outcomes. Nevertheless, these consequences are often considered one at a time (if at all) by the individual responsible for the actual technological change. This is the equivalent of changing the backswing in a golf stroke without making any adjustments to grip or stance—disaster is likely to occur! As another example of the importance of the sociotechnical perspective in work design, one might consider the introduction of robots (and, more generally, automation), to the workplace (e.g., Argote, Goodman, & Schkade, 1983; Nieva et al., 1990). Researchers have failed to adequately demonstrate the importance of the sociotechnical perspective to practitioners of work design. This shortcoming can be most effectively and quickly addressed through the publication and dissemination of carefully done, representative case studies. A first, albeit broad, intervention in reducing strain through work design is the sensitization of the designers to the importance of sociotechnical design.

Work Design and Motivation

The earliest (modern) discussions of work design occurred in the context of satisfaction and productivity (e.g., Herzberg, Mausner, & Snyderman, 1957; Herzberg, Mausner, Peterson, & Capwell, 1959; Porter & Lawler, 1968; Vroom, 1964). The notion was that by designing tasks and task groups in a particular way, individuals could be motivated to productive effort and, through this effort, could be rewarded in a way that would result in a positive emotional state known as job satisfaction. Herzberg championed a process known as "job enrichment" that would optimize productivity and satisfaction. Similarly, the downside of the motivational curve was considered to result in low levels of productivity and high levels of dissatisfaction. The dissatisfaction, in turn, was expected to lead to tardiness, absence, turnover, and accidents. There was less discussion of the impact of "demotivating" jobs on psychological well-being. More recent treatments of the topic of job enrichment (e.g., Hackman & Oldham, 1975) have broadened the consequent side of the equation somewhat but there is still a tendency to concentrate on the productive effort and worker satisfaction rather than the more direct indicators of well-being such as physical and mental health.

The concept of job satisfaction as introduced in that early literature had little or no physiological or health-related dimension to it. It was thought of primarily as an attitude that might act as an influence on behavioral choice. Furthermore, it was thought to be a predictor of performance. The concept of strain is considerably more physiological in tone. It implies consequences for physical and emotional well-being. In some respects, the earlier conceptions of satisfaction implied that the state of being satisfied was *itself* the reward that one received from a benevolent work environment. Conversely, dissatisfaction was a recognition that some environments and conditions were less desirable than others. There was little clear recognition, however, of the direct implications of job design and conditions for physical and emotional well-being.

The fact is that the nature of work can have a substantial impact on the psychological and physical well-being of workers. For example, the nursing profession is approaching a point of crisis because so many experienced and effective incumbents are leaving the nursing profession (Colligan, Smith, & Hurrell, 1977; Curran, Minnick, & Moss, 1987; Humphrey, 1988; Maslach & Jackson, 1984). Warr (1987) clearly illustrated the close relations between the nature of work and mental health. The public at large has been shown the powerful impact of work on well-being in popular books such as "Working" by Studs Terkel, "All the Livelong Day" by Barbara Garson (1975), and "Not Working" by Maurer. The point is that work is not just something that one engages in, it is a force that has dramatic consequences on the well-being of workers. For many people, work is the essential and defining characteristic of their existence. This is not simply because work provides for one's livelihood. Schlenker and Gutek (1987) found that social service professionals who were assigned clerical tasks at no reduction in pay (rather than being laid off) exhibited lower self-esteem. Thus, social and behavioral scientists must be as concerned about the design of work as nuclear engineers are about the design of a nuclear reactor.

The Concept of Uncertainty

McGrath (1976) has suggested that the concept of perceived uncertainty may represent a unifying theme for stress research. Jackson (1989) defines uncertainty from an organizational perspective as inadequate knowledge about an event that requires action or resolution. As a simple illustration of the strain that might result from uncertainty, consider the last time you were confronted with a flight delay at an airport. What you wanted was information. Was the problem weather, equipment, or personnel? Would the flight be canceled? If is was not canceled, how late would it depart? If it was canceled, were there any contingency plans in place for alternative means of transportation? The longer this information was withheld, the more strain you experienced. The culprit in this situation was uncertainty. Workers and managers complain of uncertainty in their work environments. The difference between them and you is that their "flights" may have been delayed for years not hours. The issue of uncertainty is central in any discussion of the architecture of work.

It is clear that uncertainty can occur at several levels in the organization (Schuler & Jackson, 1986). At the individual level, uncertainty may appear as a problem of prioritizing—what should be done first? At the group level, it may be manifest in unpredictable interactions with a leader. At the unit or department level, uncertainty may characterize the flow of work, particularly when one unit or department must depend on another department in accomplishing its mission. Finally, uncertainty might exist at the organizational level in something as basic as whether or not the organization can survive for another quarter or another year.

It has been widely proposed that uncertainty is a stressor and that there are inevitable consequences of this uncertainty (e.g., Schuler & Jackson, 1986). Table 1 presents a taxonomy of these types of uncertainty as well as the potential consequences. To be sure, this is not (nor was it intended to be) an exhaustive list of all elements of uncertainty in the workplace, nor does it include nonwork sources of uncertainty that interact with stressors at the workplace (e.g., uncertain reliability of child care services). Nevertheless, it does provide a broad conceptual avenue for the consideration of strain and work design.

There are several working hypotheses one might pursue in consideration of perceived uncertainty. The first is that perceived uncertainty is always a stressor. Alternatively, one might propose that only certain aspects or parameters of uncertainty are important, such as the speed of information flow in the situation or the number of variables involved. Several suggested parameters appear in Table 1. It is also possible that uncertainty is only a problem for a subset of individuals. Thus, we might consider the potential moderators of uncertainty. Some suggested moderators also appear in Table 1. Finally, it may not be necessary to assume that uncertainty inevitably leads to strain. Instead, one might simply propose that when strain is present, uncertainty is often the "active ingredient."

Potential uncertainty must be considered in the design of work. It is hard to imagine what the advantages of uncertainty might be. As a result, a prescriptive statement seems warranted. In the design of work, a specific design parameter should be uncertainty and values on this parameter should be minimized. There are many avenues for the reduction of uncertainty. These avenues include clear and unequivocal policy statements from organizations to workers and consistent applications of these policy statements. The new information technology of the modern workplace permits the widespread use of electronic bulletin boards in the dissemination of important information to workers. These may serve the important function of reducing uncertainty by providing employees with useful information. Alternatively, they may greatly exacerbate feelings of uncertainty by spreading rumors. From the research perspective, we need to know a great deal more about what sources of uncertainty are most closely associated with worker strain. It is likely that the strain that results from uncertainty about possible layoffs or labor contract negotiations is equivalent to the strain that results from not knowing who a new supervisor will be or if vendor orders will arrive by Friday.

The reality of the work environment is that in some jobs and in some environments, uncertainty is a fact of life. Uncertainty is endemic to the work of the stock broker or the police officer in a large urban department. Nevertheless, a line of earlier experimental personality research (e.g., Kahn, Wolfe, Quinn, Snoek, & Rosenthal, 1964) suggests that individuals may differ in their tolerance for ambiguity or uncertainty and that strain might be reduced by judicious selection or placement of personnel such that those with the least tolerance for uncertainty are placed in

Table 1. Components of a Model of Uncertainty

Levels of Analysis	Origins of Uncertainty	Responses to Uncertainty
Organization	Environment (e.g., suppliers, clients, competitors, creditors, government agencies, unions)	Strategy (e.g., marketing, personnel, financial production, public relations) Interorganizational structure (e.g., mergers interlocking directorates, joint ventures) Intraorganization design
Unit	Technology (e.g., operations workflow, input, characteristics, knowledge) Organizational politics	Strategy (e.g., bargaining, competition, coalition information) Organizational design (e.g., allocation of authority, coordinating mechanisms, rules)
Group	Interaction patterns (e.g., roles, norms, status, hierarchy, leader behavior)	Cohesiveness Rule of enforcement Influence attempts
Individual	Tasks Rewards Roles Job qualities Individual qualities	Psychological states (e.g., satisfaction, perceived threat, anxiety, tension) Physiological symptoms (e.g., heart rate, blood pressure, gastrointestinal disorders) Behavioral reactions (e.g., avoidance, attack) Cognitive information processing (e.g., use of heuristics, biases)

Dimensions of Uncertainty[1]
Number of elements
Rate of change
Heterogeneity of elements
Clarity of elements
Relationship among elements
Predictability of change

Moderators of the Experience
and Reactions to Uncertainty

Relative power	Ambiguity tolerance
Time pressure	Field dependence
Importance of issue	Availability of feedback
Individual ability	Task interdependence
Locus of control	Group cohesiveness

[1]The dimensions of uncertainty are common to all levels of analysis (i.e., organization, unit, group, individual).

Note. From "Managing Stress Through PHRM Practices: An Uncertainty Interpretation; by R. S. Schuler and S. E. Jackson, 1986, *Research in Personnel and Human Resource Management, 4,* pp. 183–224. Copyright 1986 by JAI Press, Inc. Reprinted by permission.

environments that would be characterized by low uncertainty. Recent work by Moses and Lyness (1988) supports the proposition that managers may vary in their ability to cope with uncertainty and ambiguity. This begs the question of a possible dynamic mechanism by which individuals adapt to uncertainty by increasing their tolerance for such ambiguity. It also begs the question of the extent to which people seek out ambiguous or uncertain environments as a form of stimulation (e.g., Zuckerman, Bone, Neary, Mangelsdorff, & Brustman, 1972; Zuckerman, 1979). Nevertheless, from the perspective of strain, one must allow for the possibility that the uncertainty in some environments or jobs can be reduced only minimally.

The Changing Nature of Work

A great deal of the variability that results in uncertainty comes from the fact that the nature of work is changing on many dimensions and at many different rates.

The technological context of change. As mentioned earlier, one of the most substantial technological changes that has occurred has been the introduction of computer technology into the workplace. It has radically altered skills sets, patterns of social interaction, information availability, mechanisms of control, and so on. While not as widespread as earlier, there are still workers who resist the introduction of computer technology at their workplace. In addition, there are those who currently use computers as a tool of work who experience substantial frustration because of system problems (Smith & Salvendy, 1989).

The role of computers in the workplace is really a symptom of a much broader shift to an information-based workplace (Galegher, Kraut, & Egido, 1990). As part of this shift, one can see a shift in which expectations regarding speed of information transmission has changed as well. This can be seen most clearly in the emerging instruments of communication: express mail has replaced regular mail and if you miss the express mail pickup, an airline will ship a package or letter on the next available flight; voice mail permits 24 hour voice-to-voice communication; and cellular phones permit one to communicate from briefcases and automobiles at any time. BITNET and FAX machines allow real time hard-copy communication of complex issues at any hour of the day or night. The introduction of these technological innovations has also changed *where* and *when* work is done (Davis, 1987). They permit work to be anywhere and at anytime. It is increasingly common to see cellular phones on the beach or telephone conversations on the freeway. Information and communication technology has altered the landscape of work and the alterations are not over yet. Little is known about the extent to which this rather simple "speed" parameter has contributed to strain in the workplace. We know a great deal about the systems in which speed is imbedded, but we know little about the speed parameter itself. For example, many managers report that the introduction of FAX and express mail has exacerbated deadline problems, not reduced them. One no longer waits until the last minute to get moving on a project; one now waits until the last second. Research must be undertaken that will illuminate the issue of time urgency as it appears in the infrastructure of work and in particular as it appears in the instruments of communication.

New operational concepts are appearing as companions to the enhanced information flow technology. These concepts are associated with the issue of time just described. For example, consider the concept of "just in time" manufacturing (or as some cynical workers refer to it, "just in case" manufacturing). The implication of this system is not only that high quality information can flow quickly but that those who receive that information will respond immediately. Through such speed, organizations anticipate increased profitability by reducing inventory and storage costs. Nevertheless, the uncertainty of the manufacturer has simply been transferred to the vendor or supplier. Transitions from traditional to just-in-time manufacturing processes continue to occur. These transitions lend themselves nicely to the pre- and postresearch designs seen in the work of Majchrzak and Davis (1990). It is reasonable to hypothesize that just-in-time manufacturing may reduce strain on those responsible for inventory control while increasing strain on those responsible for production. Other predictions based on such a transition in manufacturing process are possible. Careful attention should be given to these "naturally occurring" experiments in the workplace. Nieva et al. (1990) provides an illustration of just such a naturally occurring experiment.

Another substantial change that will continue for the next several decades is a shift from manufacturing jobs to service jobs. It is clear that more workers will come into direct contact with clients and that performance will be measured in terms of the quality and quantity of service provided rather than the quality and quantity of manufactured output. There will be more work with people and less work with things. In contrast, training programs emphasize technical rather than interpersonal skills. As a result, the gap between job demands and requisite knowledge, skills, and abilities should grow as we approach the year 2000. It is likely that this mismatch will result in increased strain for workers in this new service-based economy. In certain human service occupations, burnout seems to be common. The phenomenon is cumulative suggesting some threshold value for the most serious consequences. It is not clear, however, exactly what all of the active ingredients of burnout may be. In order to understand the implications of the shift to a service-based economy for worker strain, we need to know a great deal more about exactly what aspects of dealing with people tend to produce the greatest strain. Is it simply being exposed to the problems of others? Is it the inability to solve their problems? Is it the fact that the interaction is often emotional and involves autonomic response systems? Is it the sheer volume of work? Is it that people represent a greater source of uncertainty and unreliability than things or machines? There are other parameters that might be similarly explored (see Bowen & Schneider, 1988) but the point is that we must know a great deal more about the critical elements of service jobs than we do now if we hope to enter gently into this new service based economy, at least from the perspective of work stress. The pessimist might predict that the burnout currently affecting particular subgroups (e.g., human service workers) will become more widespread as this shift to a service economy accelerates in the next decade.

Along with change has come an increase in awareness of potential illness and injury associated with the workplace. The debate about the impact of long term video display terminal (VDT) use continues. Workers at plants producing nuclear power or nuclear weapons are concerned about physiological damage. Health care workers face the danger of contracting AIDS. Recent concern has been expressed about the harmful effects on humans of high power transmission lines and electric power substations. The current Supreme Court case on the rights of female workers of child-bearing age at the Johnson Control Company to work in environments that might result in damage to a fetus is a case in point. Regardless of the outcome of that case, it is likely that there is increased strain on all workers in that environment (and in particular, female workers) as a result of increased sensitivity to the effect of toxic substances (e.g., lead) on health and well-being. A similar issue arose at the Bunker Hill mine in Kellogg, Idaho and a good description is provided by Randall (1985). Should the Supreme Court rule in favor of the female plaintiffs, organizations will likely have the responsibility to provide safe working environment for *all* workers (including women able to bear children).[1] A serious issue from the perspective of worker strain will be to convince the workers that this level of safety has been achieved.

Workers are a great deal more concerned today than they were 20 years ago about the physical and physiological consequences of where they work and what they do. It is of no consequence that study after study demonstrates that there is no harmful radiation coming from VDT screens if the VDT operator does not believe those studies. The strain resulting from the *belief* of the worker is an issue that behavioral scientists must deal with independent of the objective stress represented by the antecedent variable or condition under examination. Similarly, if electric utility workers *believe* that exposure to low cycle current results in brain cancer, this *belief* is a circumstance of interest for the behavioral scientist. This belief may add to or neutralize the strain that might result from the objective conditions. Emergency medical technicians who believe that the autoimmune deficiency syndrome (AIDS) virus is airborne experience strain in treating homosexuals or drug users whether or not that belief is justified. Psychosomatic illness is defined, in part, by real symptoms. There is a broad and emerging literature on mass psychogenic illness at the workplace (Caldwell, personal communication, September, 1990; Hall & Johnson, 1989; Stahl & Lebedun, 1974) that provides dramatic illustrations of the importance of perceptions vis à vis reality. We do not mean to imply that actual or objective stressors (such as work design) are of no concern to the behavioral scientist and that only *beliefs* are important. Rather, the point to be made is that perception can *also* play an exaggerating or ameliorating role in strain.

Although the direct effect of various toxic substances and working conditions on worker health is the material for other NIOSH conferences, the strain that results from worker perception of these circumstances is appropriate for current consideration. This issue is a legitimate part of work design as broadly defined. Thus, a recommendation can be made that organizations be more sensitive to the apprehensions of workers regarding the technology that defines their work. These apprehensions should be recognized and addressed through programs of research and education. A simple message telling workers that they need not worry, that working conditions are safe, that the organization will monitor possible hazards falls on deaf ears in light of the increasing national embarrassment represented by the shame of toxic waste treatment. From the research perspective, it would be useful if epidemiologists began to catalogue those occupations where such concerns were the

---

[1] The particular issues of women's occupational health from the legal perspective are covered by Bertin and Henefin (1987).

greatest. This would permit an assessment of the relative strain in those occupational environments.

The organizational context of change. Just as the technological and operational framework of work has changed, so has the organizational framework. There are many new concepts that have altered the nature of work. Many companies are experimenting with autonomous or semi-autonomous work groups in which traditional methods of supervision are abandoned in favor of matrix management or self-direction. Dray (1988) has characterized this shift from traditional forms of hierarchical supervision to work teams and matrix groups as a shift form "tier" to "peer." Additionally, workers are given opportunities to influence the nature of their work through quality circles. These enhanced opportunities for control, however, are balanced by other, less desirable, changes. The ownership patterns of organizations has changed. As implied by the earlier discussion of uncertainty, mergers and take-overs (often hostile) have added substantially to the uncertainty of organizational life. Foreign ownership often injects substantially different value systems into the workplace. Domestic and foreign competition in basic industries has become more intense. The defense industry has become less predictable as a result of funding battles between the pro- and antimilitary representatives in Congress. This uncertainty among the government contractors and subcontractors, like the pressure from competition mentioned above, has resulted in rapid workforce changes in the form of downsizing (including changes at the top of organizations). Other similar perturbations appear in the organization unexpectedly. Consider the uncertainty and discomfort of government workers during the recent congressional budget negotiations. At one point, workers were forced to guess whether they would lose their jobs completely (if the government was forced to shut down) or if they would simply be asked to forgo payment for several days each month (if Gramm-Rudman automatic cuts were invoked).

One final and substantial change that is occurring in the organizational landscape relates to the diversity of the workforce (Jackson & Schuler, 1990; Morrison & von Glinow, 1990). Demographics point to a radical transformation of the American workforce from a White, male, middle-aged cadre to a heterogeneous mixture of the young and the older worker with the younger work group made up of more women, Blacks, Hispanics, and Asians than previously encountered. This will place pressures on both supervisors and the workers themselves to learn patterns of accommodation that will prevent the negative consequences of clashes of values or behavior patterns. It is likely to be a time of some confusion while cultural learning goes on. Again, to take just one recent example, football players, managers, and team owners are being asked to increase their sensitivity to the plight of the female sports writer seeking access to the locker room.

The Social Fabric of Work

The social context in which work occurs is a complex combination of dyadic relations, small group dynamics, large group dynamics, and cultural influences. In this section, we will examine some of these social variables that have implications for strain at the workplace. As we indicated earlier, we consider such variables as appropriate for a discussion of work design broadly defined.

Coworkers

There are few jobs that do not involve coworker interactions in some fundamental way. These interactions may represent either obstacles to well-being at the workplace or enhancers. As obstacles, consider the issues of output level. Coworkers may produce more or less than an expected standard. If they produce more than expected, this may present increased pressure on individuals in terms of both quantity and quality of production. Producing less than expected presents different problems, particularly if the productivity of the individual is linked to that of the coworker through interdependent or dependent task sequences.

There is also the issue of equity. A broad literature base suggests (e.g., Goodman, 1974) that individuals use a comparative mechanism for determining satisfaction with various aspects of work. Individuals compare personal input and outcomes to the input and outcomes of coworkers to determine their satisfaction with those personal outcomes. Thus one might expect that environments in which there are substantial discrepancies among outcomes for individuals with essentially identical inputs would lead to increased strain. Recent work in the area of comparable worth and equitable reward systems (Birnbaum, 1983; Mellers, 1982) suggests that there are broad expectations on the part of workers regarding effort and performance, on the one hand, and rewards, on the other. Schuler and Jackson (1986) propose that workers be involved in determining at least the broad outlines of their reward systems. This is seen as a way of reducing uncertainty and the strain resulting from that uncertainty. The critical issue, however, is the level and type of worker involvement. Vroom and Yetton (1973) have suggested that if the goals of the worker diverge from the goals of the organization, involvement should be limited to an expression of preference but not an active role in decisionmaking. The point is that it may be as important for workers to know that their views have been heard as it is for them to have a "vote" or a more active role in the decision to be made.

There is increasing evidence (e.g., Kahn & Byosiere, in press) that social support can help to reduce the experience of strain in the workplace. To the extent that coworkers are willing and able to provide such support, they enhance the work experience and help maintain some level of emotional well-being. This suggests that work designs that prevent interaction among coworkers may be problematic from the strain perspective. When VDT technology was introduced into the workplace, little attention was given to the psychosocial implications of the new technology. Desks became "work stations" and these stations were isolated from each other to keep the noise levels from the printers under control. This meant that there were obstacles to conversation among coworkers. Before, clerical workers simply talked across a desk or a work space. This was no longer possible. Similarly, prior to the VDT/personal computer revolution, a file was a folder in a cabinet. Filing and retrieving information in this format provided additional opportunities among coworkers. Then, a file became an electronic document that was retrieved at the work station with a key stroke. Again, the technology represented an obstacle to interaction. It should not have been surprising that complaints about VDT work emerged (and are still prevalent). The sociotechnical system had been changed (Landy et al., 1987). As another example, prior to the VDT revolution, clerical and secretarial workers would often check the accuracy of each other's work. That is no longer necessary as a result of the technological change in the nature of word processing. Now there are subroutines to check the spelling of documents (although these systems still permit grotesque errors as long as the offending word is spelled correctly and is recognized as a real word). Another opportunity for interaction has been lost. Theories of human motivation invariably identify social interaction as a positive circumstance. An equally universal conclusion can be drawn from 60 years of research on job satisfaction. Coworkers represent a valuable resource for the feeling of well-being at the workplace. Similarly, coworkers represent a useful source of support in environments with many stressors. As a result, the recommendation can be made that the design of work should facilitate interaction among coworkers rather than inhibit such interaction. Good examples of such design and redesign can be found in the Volvo and Saab experiments of the last several decades. Particular attention should be paid to the changes introduced with new information technologies. It is not clear if "nominal" teams can serve the same purpose as "real" teams in satisfying needs for social interaction. For example, it is possible to be a member of a team through e-mail yet never meet your other fellow team members. At one level, interaction has been enhanced but at another level, it has been inhibited. The work of Bandura in social learning theory (1986) suggests that electronic teams would not be ready substitutes for real teams but little is known at this point. In the computer environment, the value of a "local expert" (i.e., a real person who can troubleshoot hardware and software problems) is becoming more widely recognized (Landy et al., 1987).

A final issue in the consideration of coworkers relates to the earlier discussion of the increasing diversity of the work force. Konrad and Gutek (1987) have suggested that the ambient strain on minority group members and women in organizational settings is reduced in proportion to how many fellow subgroup members are in that organization. The implications for employers are fairly direct. If one wants to reduce strain on a woman in a nontraditional work setting, hire more women. The same would hold true for ethnic minorities, older employees, or handicapped employees. Case studies document the incredible strain experienced by the "pioneer."

Supervisors/Managers

Just as coworkers play an integral role in the social fabric of work, so do supervisors and managers. There is a 40-year research base indicating that the style of supervision can have a substantial impact on the emotional well-being of workers. The extent to which a supervisor uses a style of "consideration" (Fleishman & Harris, 1962) has been shown to be associated with the job satisfaction of his or her subordinates. In addition, Fiedler and Garcia (1987) have suggested that a poor interpersonal relationship between a supervisor and a subordinate represents a stressor that can inhibit the application of various cognitive abilities in problem solving at the workplace. This literature and theory suggests that strain is reduced in circumstances of good supervisor-subordinate interpersonal relations. The development and maintenance of such relations can be seen as an integral part of effective management. There are obvious implications for the selection and training of supervisors inherent in this recommendation. Nevertheless, the appreciation by supervisors for the importance of considerate and supportive interactions with subordinates is limited. This is, in part, the result of a concentration of productivity and output rather than worker well-being. It is clear that unhappy workers can still be productive and that happy workers can be unproductive. As a result, there is a tendency on the part of supervisors to see consideration and support as simply a reward or bonus that might be afforded workers. A more radical proposition would be that workers are ENTITLED to considerate and supportive leadership as a defining characteristic of a healthy work environment.

One particularly central issue in supervision and leadership is the issue of decision making. The question is the extent to which a leader will permit subordinates to share in the decision making process. Vroom and Yetton (1973) have developed a prescriptive model for assisting the supervisor in determining the "right" level and type of participation to provide to subordinates but, similar to the issue of supervisory support and consideration as discussed above, in this context, right is defined by the quality of the decision that is to be made not by the anticipated well-being of the subordinate. In the debates regarding participation in decision making, less attention has been paid to worker strain than to the correctness of a decision from the business perspective. There are, however, clear indications that worker participation in decision making can help to reduce worker strain. As an example, Karasek (1990) has studied the levels of strain among Swedish workers who experienced job changes through a process of reorganization. Those workers who were able to take part in the decision making process experienced significantly less strain than those who were not able to have input, in spite of the fact that both groups had jobs that were restructured as part of the reorganization process. It is not clear whether this reduced strain was the result of an enhanced feeling of control (as suggested by the authors) or of reduced uncertainty that resulted from being continuously involved in the deliberations. Psychologists have known for some time that signalled or predictable punishment (in animals and humans) is less aversive than unsignalled or unpredictable punishment. Similarly, Maslach and Jackson (1982) have reported that increasing participation in decision making among nurses can prevent the burnout that has become increasingly characteristic of the health care professions. Schuler and Jackson (1986) have also suggested that an increase in participation in decision making for employees can be built into the personnel and human resources management system. For example, employees can have a role in long term planning, in the performance appraisal system, and in the structure of the compensation system. In a sense, the notion seems to be that any involvement in the organizational decision making process can increase feelings of control and decrease strain. This, of course, is a hypothesis not a conclusion. If, as has been suggested earlier, uncertainty is the culprit in organizational strain, and if uncertainty accumulates over time and over regions of organizational life, then there would be reason to believe that any involvement in decision making would be of value. On the other hand, it is possible that one cannot substitute certainty in personnel and human resource areas for uncertainty related to task or role responsibilities. Nevertheless, it would seem that supervisors have control over a potentially critical work design element in the determination of levels of employee participation in decision making. From a research perspective, we need to know much more about the active ingredient of participation. Is it the reduction of uncertainty or the enhanced feeling of control or efficacy, or both? From a practical standpoint, participation in decision making would seem to be associated with reduced job strain and should become part of the overall design of work if a goal is the reduction of worker strain. This is a situation in which the needs of the researcher can be combined with the needs of the practitioner in the development of an action research paradigm similar to those suggested by Argyris (1980) and, more recently, Berlinguer (1990). In this paradigm, data are gathered while interventions occur rather than delaying intervention until all data are collected and analyzed.

In light of the earlier discussion of the changing technological nature of work, it seems likely that job design parameters may have an impact on the extent to which supervisors and subordinates interact in real time. As part of the shift to an information-based economy and the resultant computerization of work processes, the opportunity for electronic monitoring of work activity performed on the computer has been greatly enhanced (Schleifer & Amick 1989; Schleifer & Okogbaa, in press). This is particularly true in the service industries such as insurance or banking where the chief work "product" is actually information. Electronic work monitoring data can be used to provide more timely and accurate feedback to workers and can serve to reduce possible bias in subjective evaluations of worker performance. On the other hand, it is difficult to imagine how an electronic monitoring system, by itself, will provide appropriate amounts of consideration to the worker. This simply reinforces the earlier recommendation that work designs recognize the potential importance of face to face interaction between supervisors and subordinates. Guidelines for the proper use of electronic work monitoring should be developed so that this critical interpersonal bond between supervisor and subordinate is not diminished (Schott & Olson, 1988).

One final observation might be made of the supervisor in the "new" social environment illustrated by autonomous work groups. On the one hand, the supervisor is recast as an "advisor" to the work group with little line responsibility. On the other hand, the supervisor continues to be held accountable for the effectiveness of the work group activities by middle levels of management. This situation has all the ingredients for the classic case of role conflict (with the accompanying anticipation of supervisor strain).

Work Roles

The data related to work roles seem to be relatively clear with respect to work design and strain (Kahn & Byosiere, 1990). Ambiguous roles, conflicting roles, and overloaded roles all represent stressors and result in strain in the workplace. It is less clear if this effect is the result of uncertainty, excessive demand, or simply the type of mutually exclusive behavior demands that characterized the "learned helplessness" phenomenon popularized by Seligman.

The case for participation in decision making. Some evidence addressing particular methods for reducing conflict and ambiguity is provided by Jackson (1983).

She conducted a longitudinal study of nurses and demonstrated that participation in decision making (PDM) reduced role conflict and ambiguity. This suggests that excessive demand is not responsible for the reduction in conflict and ambiguity (at least not *directly*). This study is interesting for another reason as well. Data were collected in 3 month waves. After the first 3 months of PDM, there was a weak relationship between *actual* participation and conflict/ambiguity but a strong relationship between *perceived* PDM and conflict/ambiguity. After 6 months, there was a strong relationship between both actual and perceived PDM and conflict ambiguity. Thus, it would appear that the perception of participation may be as important as the participation itself. This can be interpreted several ways. One interpretation might be that individuals who have not had past PDM experiences tend to view any level of participation as salutary. Another interpretation would be that individuals are influenced by the potential to participate rather than the participation itself. Along with this new role, it is likely that the subjects received enhanced information and that there was an enhanced climate of openness. The Jackson study is as interesting for what it does not tell us as for what it does. It tells us that PDM reduces conflict and ambiguity, and by extension, strain. It does not tell us *why* this strain is reduced. The research implications are clear. We need a much more refined understanding of the dynamics of PDM. We need some careful studies of the effect of participation on feelings of efficacy (Bandura, 1986) and locus of control and uncertainty reduction. We also need to know more about the substance and results of participation in work and task design. Does the participation often (or ever) result in the reorganization of work in a more effective manner? For example, what are the implications for strain of a worker-initiated change in work process or task assignment that actually reduces efficiency? It is possible that both strain and productivity are reduced. On the other hand, if productivity is reduced and strain increases, we would come to very different conclusions regarding appropriate job and work design with respect to PDM.

There are even deeper and possibly more fruitful cognitive phenomena and structures to explore with PDM. One possibility is that PDM is effective because it is a vehicle for concept formation and organizational learning. It is likely that as part of the PDM process, workers get an enhanced view of the nature of their work. This would include the "significance" of their tasks and role; the interaction of what they do with what others do; feedback with respect to the effects of particular plans, strategies, and behaviors; and the capacity to conduct "mini-experiments" of their own with respect to altered methods or procedures. In contrast to the worker who is uninvolved in the decision making process, the PDM worker has a sophisticated blueprint of the work and the workers. It may be this enhanced blueprint that reduces the ambiguity and conflict. We need to know whether the facilitating effects of participation are simply the result of an increased sense of security or effectiveness on the part of the worker or the result of the inevitable increase in leader consideration (and decrease in supervisor-subordinate strain) that accompanies this process or the result of a more sophisticated and longer range view of the tasks and roles involved.

From the perspective of intervention, however, there seems to be a clear mandate for increasing participation. Regardless of how PDM effects its influence, the influence seems substantial. We can safely conclude that there is a nontrivial negative correlation between PDM and worker strain. The argument is often heard (from managers) that many workers "are not ready" for PDM or "do not want" PDM. Both of these arguments have a kernel of truth to them but the issue of readiness implies that some careful thought and preparation should precede the introduction of PDM and the issue of workers not wanting PDM is exaggerated. There will always be workers (and supervisors) who will resist change but they gradually adapt. It would appear that resistance on the part of management to introduce PDM is more likely founded on philosophical or sociopolitical grounds than on practical ones. Further, data like those presented by Jackson (1983) clearly contradict the management objections to PDM.

Role Conflict, Role Ambiguity, and Individual Differences

Jackson and Schuler (1985) have conducted a comprehensive meta-analysis of the effects of role conflict and role ambiguity. This review concluded that conflict and ambiguity are more likely to arise from organizational influences affecting the design of the roles than from individual characteristics of the incumbent. Thus, although it may be tempting to "blame" ambiguity and conflict on the worker, the larger problem remains that of work and role design.

Role overload. With respect to role overload, there also seems to be general agreement that some combination of quality and quantity demand within the context of a fixed time schedule results in strain (Kahn & Byosiere, in press). There is the strong possibility that such circumstances interact with other dispositional characteristics (e.g., locus of control, Type A Behavior Pattern, etc.) to exaggerate the negative consequences. Nevertheless, it seems clear that role overload is a property of the job and/or organization rather than of the person. As an exemplar of the phenomenon, research on stressors and strain in the nursing profession points to frustrations experienced by professional nurses trying to provide high quality health care to too many patients in too short a time span, with additional tasks being added throughout the shift in an unpredictable fashion. Time urgency and/or workload are commonly identified as the most substantial stressors in data gathered from professional nurses (Humphrey, 1988). Karasek (1979) developed a model to describe the negative consequences of environments characterized by high demands and low resources. One of the most important resources in the organizational environment is time. It is likely that effective workers plan their work day. It is also likely that some work is easier to plan and more predictable than other work. For example, the work of the emergency room nurse and the police officer is considerably less predictable, on a day to day basis, than the work of a college professor or a bus driver. To be sure, there are unpredictable events in every job but in some jobs, unpredictability is the norm rather than the exception. We need to know much more about the parameters of work load. Kahn and Byosiere (1990) have suggested that role load (and overload) are some function of quality, quantity, and time. These parameters need to be much more closely examined, particularly with respect to resultant strain. Does strain result from the perfection implied by professions with "standards" for judging quality (e.g., nursing) or from a daily work plan that is chronically destroyed, or from simply too much work? With respect to the last point, what little information exists seems to contradict the proposition that overload results from too much work. Alfredsson, Karasek, and Theorell (1982), in a study of Swedish workers, found that there was an increased risk of myocardial infarction from a combination of a hectic work pace and low decision latitude (i.e., low autonomy) but that the risk was unaffected by workload by itself. From an analytic perspective, we need to separate main effects from interactions as well as get some feel for the relative strength of these main effects. The Alfredsson et al. study is a good example of such a strategy. At this stage in our understanding of the concept of overload, any recommendation for action would be gratuitous.

Although we do not have the luxury in this paper of dealing with the interaction between work roles and nonwork roles, it is clear that strain can be increased or decreased by the nature of this interaction. On the one hand, several researchers (Frankenhauser et al., 1989; Gutek, Repetti, & Silver, 1988) have suggested that strain accumulates across settings such that women experience greater total strain in their lives than men because they often have the burdens of child care and housekeeping to add to their work burdens. Kahn and Byosiere (1990) also suggest that one needs to understand productive effort more broadly than is implied by the notion of paid work. But the issue must be more complex than just the number of distinct roles that an individual must fill (e.g., worker, mother, housekeeper, etc.). Warr (1987) has documented the fact that almost any type of work, regardless of how much of an underload or overload it represents, has the capacity to relieve depression in some people. Additionally, it has been reported that the family functions as a form of emotional support or buffer to stressors at the workplace, thus providing parents and spouses a seeming emotional *advantage* over nonparents and individuals living alone. What is abundantly clear is that strains experienced at work will carry over into nonwork environments (Jackson & Maslach, 1982) and vice versa (Barling & Rosenbaum, 1986). The implications for organizational policy would seem equally clear. Organizations should not demand levels of commitment that result in barriers between an individual and his or her nonwork emotional support systems. In every job, there are occasions when sacrifices must be made and work activities will replace family activities in one's schedule. Nevertheless, organizations (and professions) that communicate norms that imply total work commitment may be ultimately self-defeating. The emotional support of a family unit may be the most widely underutilized "treatment" for strain in the organizational environment.

Culture. An additional thread in the social fabric of work is represented by the broader cultural backdrop in which the work is accomplished. As was mentioned earlier, competition, both inside and outside of the organization represents one of those cultural parameters. In addition, many organizations are characterized by closed rather than open communications systems. All other things being equal, one might expect greater strain in environments that restrict communications. It is likely that these are the same environments that minimize the opportunity to participate in making decisions.

Commitment is also a strong cultural variable in the organizational environment (Jackson & Schuler, 1990; Kahn & Byosiere, 1990; Mathieu & Zajac, 1990). Organizations expect commitment from employees but are less willing to make this long term commitment (in terms of job security) to those same employees (Porter, 1990). This instability can be the source of considerable anxiety for employees in turbulent times (Kuhnert & Vance, 1990).

Other cultural influences at the workplace that might function as stressors include unethical behavior and practice by the organization and the extent to which employees are permitted to "blow the whistle" without committing professional suicide. A stylized version of this dilemma was presented in the case of Karen Silkwood and her attempt to expose the inefficiencies of the nuclear fuel and weapons industry. There have been similar incidents in the space shuttle program and defense department procurement operations. Although there has been little explicit treatment of the strain on the potential whistle blower, the implications are clear and implied in several interesting articles on the phenomenon of whistle blowing and the fear of retaliation (Miceli & Near, 1988; Near & Miceli, 1987; Parmalee, Near, & Jensen, 1982). The point is that one might reasonably expect strain to result when an individual is expected to ignore, or worse, engage in unethical or illegal behavior at the workplace. A more direct examination of this issue from the strain perspective would be useful. There is too little research in this area. A similar issue arises with respect to the strain imbedded in illegal or unethical acts perpetrated on the individual. An obvious example is sexual harassment at the workplace (Crull, 1982; Gutek, 1985).

A very different influence is the use of illegal substances (drugs and alcohol) at the workplace. Illegal substances create substantial problems in work settings, both with respect to productivity and with respect to safety. Nevertheless, supervisors are reluctant to intervene in such situations for fear of reprisals or legal action. This places an enormous burden on the coworkers who are often the victims of such behavior. This is particularly true in occupations where workers must depend on each other. For example, in some major cities, firefighters have expressed concern about the use of illegal substances by fellow firefighters. As the result of this circumstance, they express reluctance to take any chances or to fight fires aggressively since they feel that they cannot depend on a coworker to get them out of a jam if they get in trouble. For many experienced firefighters with a strong sense of dedication to saving lives and protecting property, this is a constant source of frustration.

Parameters of Control

Control is a major theme of stress and workplace design. Sauter, Hurrell, and Cooper (1989) have recently published a comprehensive treatment of the topic that concludes that lack of control at the workplace is one of the single greatest contributors to strain and the physiological concomitants of that strain. As an historical aside, it is interesting to note that one of the earliest theorists in work motivation, E. L. Thorndike, proposed that one of the primary "motives" operating in the workplace was the desire to submit to the "right man." He proposed that it was pleasurable to give up control to others, at least under certain facilitating conditions. Thorndike would have some difficulty defending his proposition today, even were he to change "right man" to "right person." His propositions represented the last gasp of instinct theory and were replaced within a decade by a contrary proposition—that is, individuals seek control rather than to be controlled.

Although all modern observers of organizational behavior might agree that the issue of control is central and that increased control may ultimately reduce the physiological consequences of strain, the meaning and dimensionality of control is not so obvious. An earlier NIOSH (ASPH, 1988) publication suggested that workers "should be given the opportunity to have input on decisions or actions that affect their jobs and the performance of their tasks" (p. 105). In contrast, the Swedish Work Environment Act, also aimed at increasing control for the worker, suggests that "work should be arranged so that the employee himself can influence his work situation" (Ministry of Labor, 1987, p. 3). This latter approach to control would seem considerably broader than the suggestion of input of NIOSH. It must also be recognized that the Swedish Work Environment Act is part of a much larger sociopolitical drama that has been playing itself out since the Social Democratic party achieved prominence in Sweden almost 50 years ago.

There are several issues that need to be examined with respect to the concept of control. The first is the level or type of control *experienced* by workers. The second is the level and type of control *exercised* by workers. The NIOSH and Swedish prescriptions address the issue of the exercise of control by workers. Nevertheless, in understanding strain, it might be best to begin by dimensionalizing the forms of control experienced by workers. As Sauter et al. (1989) point out, there are two different perspectives available for examining the issue of control. The first is broad and addresses the issue of the extent to which the worker has control of his or her job (defined as a collection of tasks) in some global sense and would include the methods and scheduling of that job. For example, Hackman & Oldham (1975) emphasize decision making related to work goals. Karasek (1979) also emphasizes the role of control in carrying out daily tasks. There is, however, a more delineated view that one might take. Frese (1989) has suggested that the parameters of control include control over work content, control over work pace, and control over the environment in which the work is done. This type of dimensionalization had been anticipated in some of the earlier work of Karasek, who had suggested that control over task organization and company policy are relevant parameters. Recently, Schuler and Jackson (1986) have provided a more elaborate set of propositions reinforcing this notion that control over company policy (at least personnel and human resource policy) can reduce worker strain. McClaney and Hurrell (1988) have suggested that relevant dimensions of control include task control, decision control, resource control, and environmental control. These preliminary "taxonomies" point out the need for some consensus on the dimensionality of control. Further, they make the point by default that was introduced above: It is important to distinguish between the *experience* of control and the *exercise* of control. The implications of such a distinction may be substantial. Consider two possibilities. One position might be that there is a complete compensatory relationship between the experience of control and the exercise of control such that the strain produced by control in one domain (e.g., task control) can be offset by the exercise of control in another domain (e.g., environment or schedule control). The contrasting position might be that there is no "trade off" in the calculus of strain—that strain introduced by externally imposed schedule control can only be reduced by transferring that control to the worker. In any event, basic taxonomic work needs to be done in both experience and the exercise sides of the control coin.

In this section, we will consider some possible parameters or elements of a control taxonomy. The parameters will be those of the experience side of the coin and, where appropriate, we will highlight some issues related to the exercise of control by the worker. Note that a good deal of the exercise discussion has already occurred in the earlier sections (e.g., PDM).

Technological and Administrative Control

Job definition. Hacker (1985) has suggested that the very design of work implies control to the worker. He proposes that job design only be taken so far and that aspects of jobs (e.g., task sequence or task procedure) be left for final modification by the workers who will hold those jobs. In essence, he is suggesting that the most basic of documents, the job description, is an element of technological and task control. This is a radical view of technological control and one that would seem at odds with the efficient conduct of work. Further, in many instances (at least in the United States), workers complain more about lack of control when job descriptions are broad and lacking detail than when they are clear and specific. Nevertheless, Hacker is suggesting the ultimate in worker control—allow the worker to be the sculptor of the work. Since Hacker's work was produced in the prerevolutionary environment of the German Democratic Republic of East Germany, it is hard to separate the Marxist perspective and the full employment guarantees of socialism (and the correlative absence of a legitimate profit motive as conceptualized in the West) from a legitimate statement about the desirable characteristics of work design. It is tempting to see quality circles as manifestations of the type of involvement contemplated by Hacker since these devices (in their grandest forms) are intended to provide a mechanism for the reorganization of any aspect of work. Since there is little good data available with respect to the effect of quality circles on worker strain or perceptions of control, no conclusions can be drawn. Nevertheless, the earlier section on PDM strongly suggested that the opportunity to take part in decisions addressing the fundamental aspects of work design represent opportunities for the exercise of control by the worker.

Workload and work pace. Technological and administrative control can be either prominent or subtle. There is the control represented by workload and associated work pace. Work pace is often under the control of those who design the equipment used by the workers. This is most obvious in the speed of machines in traditional manufacturing positions. This type of pace can be considered an enduring characteristic of the work. There are jobs, however, in which pace is considerably more variable. Consider the work of the firefighter who varies between sedentary activity which could best be described as boring and the time urgent behaviors associated with rescue and fire suppression. Similarly, nurses in an emergency or operating room may be faced with variable workload as a result of externally imposed events. It might be useful to consider a workload index based on the frequency, intensity, and duration of effort required. This might be best viewed at the task or task group level. Thus, jobs which have more tasks associated with frequent, intense, and long duration effort expenditure (mental or physical) might be considered high workload jobs and more likely to be associated with strain. As described earlier, Kahn and Byosiere (1990) have suggested that workload is associated with quality and quantity demands which conflict because of time demands. That definition is more conceptual and applies more to entire jobs than tasks. Nevertheless, jobs high on the workload index proposed above are also likely to be high on the Kahn index. We are simply suggesting a more sensitive continuum. More must be known about the dimensionality of the concept of workload, as suggested above. It is likely that jobs with the highest workload value are those in which the most frequent and important tasks have a high time urgency value.

Although workload is associated with work pace, the terms are not synonymous. Work pace is more closely associated with the cycle time of a traditional machine operation and the system response time of a computer environment. In the late 1960s, Volvo redesigned the nature of work to change (among other things) the massive control exerted by the assembly line pace. Rather than 45 second operations on endless lines of automobiles, they permitted work groups to work for longer periods of up to an hour on automobiles that the work group brought into the work area from a buffer line. The introduction of the manufacturing robots at the General Motor's (GM) Lordstown plant was a move in the other direction. It is generally accepted that the strain on Swedish workers in the Saab and Volvo plants reorganized along the lines of this new production model was reduced and the strain on the assemblers at the Lordstown facility of GM was increased. The problem, of course, is disentangling all of the many influences that define these distinctly different psychosocial environments. In addition to different cycles or work paces, there were also differences in physical environment, social systems, methods of supervision, and methods of payment.

In the new electronic workplace, work pace is often determined by system response time. Here, strain might be more closely associated with slow rather than fast cycle time. VDT operators often expect rapid response time from their equipment. When a key is pressed that initiates an action (e.g., summoning a search or replacement subroutine in word processing), the operator expects that action to be completed rapidly so that processing can continue. If the response time is too slow, strain results (Boucsein, 1987). Paradoxically, systems that respond too quickly also seem to have negative consequences. Boucsein (1987) conducted laboratory research that indicated that there are optimal system response times and that there may be individual difference parameters associated with these optimal times. The dependent variables in this research were electrodermal activity and other indicators of emotionality. Schleifer and his colleagues (1989, in press) have also studied system response time and used blood pressure and heart rate as their dependent variables of interest but found no direct influence of system response time on those physiological parameters. Landy, Rastegary, Thayer, and Colvin (1991) have suggested that an organismic variable—time urgency—may mediate strain in suboptimal response time circumstances.

From a practical perspective, in the design of work, one must recognize that systems seldom behave optimally. This is particularly true with respect to system response times. Systems frequently run slower than anticipated and often stop responding at all (e.g., in the case of a computer "crash"). Effective workers seem to anticipate such problems and create a series of "parallel" tasks that might be initiated when the primary tasks are tied up as a result of suboptimal system responses. The "good" word processing technician begins another task when waiting for a recently completed job to print. There is a strong flavor of parallel processing in the actions of this person.

The implication for work design is that work should be arranged in a way that permits the worker to move to alternative tasks under certain circumstances. In some senses, this is similar to the argument for task variety proposed by the job enrichment advocates (Hackman & Oldham, 1975) except that it does not necessarily imply a linear or sequential variety. Instead, it implies a choice that a worker has when obstacles appear in completion of the primary task. It is this choice that represents the exercise of control by the worker. This is compatible with the demand/resource explanation of strain proposed by Karasek (1979). In this case, the resource is the freedom to pursue alternative task completion when blocked on primary task completion.

Work scheduling. Another parameter of control at the workplace is the scheduling of work. The most onerous situation would be a rotating shift schedule with little information about impending shift changes or modifications. Or consider the situation of marginal and part-time workers who are not assigned regular hours but are expected to "check in" on a regular basis to see if they are scheduled for work. This is common for many classes of workers in the transportation industry (e.g., low seniority bus drivers). In contrast, although some systems might be characterized by rapidly changing human resource environments they nevertheless retain maximum control for the worker. For example, firefighters commonly work for one 24 hour period and are off for two 24 hour periods. Nevertheless, it is not uncommon for firefighters to work for two consecutive 24 hour periods or not to appear for work for one or two weeks. This is because they often have the autonomy to trade work with fellow firefighters. This permits them to hold second jobs and engage in other activities that might conflict with scheduled work in other occupational settings. Another example of schedule control by the worker is the concept of flex time where the worker is permitted discretion in arrival and departure time as long as he or she is at the workplace for a "core" period. It has been suggested (Landy, 1989) that flex time represents an excellent opportunity for workers to experience some control over their work lives. It is interesting to note that in many instances, there is little actual change in the average reporting or departing time for workers (Ronen, 1981). This is because the time at which an individual starts and stops work is correlated with other variables such as school schedules, spouse schedules, and transportation schedules. Nevertheless, several evaluative studies of flex time (Narayanan & Nath, 1982; Orpen, 1981) find that workers are generally happier with their lives in general after shifting to a flex time schedule. In light of the Ronen study, this would seem to be the result of the *possibility* of modifying a work schedule on a given day rather than the *reality* of that modification. In a flex time system, the individual is better able to cope with the unpredictable exigencies of familial responsibilities. The individual also has the option of altering a routine for the simple stimulation derived from change. Work schedules are potent forms of organizational control. To the extent possible, workers should be permitted to exercise some control over their work schedule. Organizations should maximize information to workers regarding schedules and potential schedule modifications. While a work force constantly on call might be effective from the operations perspective, it is also likely to lead to high strain. The just in time philosophy should not be extended to include the process of work scheduling.

Rewards, punishments, and performance monitoring. In Sweden, piece rate payment is frowned upon and permitted only under special circumstances. This is because it is considered a form of inappropriate control and associated with strain. In America, piece rate payment is often referred to as the "golden handcuffs" by workers implying that they are shackled to their machines by the piece rate scheme. In interviews with workers, it is common for older workers to express a preference for an hourly wage while younger workers opt for the potentially increased rewards of piece rate payment. The older workers express concern about being able to "make standard" on a day-after-day basis, particularly when the well-being of their family may be at stake. They seek more predictability in their income level and less pressure from the environment. The younger worker, with fewer responsibilities and the feeling of invulnerability that seems to come with youth, has no such concerns. Low pay received for a bad day can be offset by higher pay received a good day without difficulty.

In computer-based work, Schleifer (1989, in press) has demonstrated that piece rate payment schemes produce strain reactions in workers. This research monitored the heart rate and blood pressure of subjects completing a clerical task on a VDT and found elevated heart rate and blood pressure for subjects on incentive pay. Schleifer's work is part of a larger concern for the whole notion of performance monitoring at the workplace (Smith & Carayon, 1990; Sainfort & Smith, 1989). The new computer technology permits not only increased efficiency on the part of the worker in terms of information processing, but it permits more sophisticated measurement of work output by the employer as well as enhanced potential for turning hourly jobs into piece rate jobs. Thus, an employer monitors the quantity and error rate for a data input specialist and provides a "bonus" or a "penalty" for work that exceeds or falls short of standards. This is piece rate payment in everything but name and does not differ substantially from the principles proposed by Frederick W. Taylor in his theory of scientific management (1911). In fact, some observers have dubbed this form of performance monitoring the "new Taylorism." Garson (1988) refers to the VDT environment as the "electronic sweatshop" for similar reasons.

As was pointed out in an earlier section, however, it may not be electronic workplace monitoring (EWM) per se that is the culprit but rather the fact that the monitoring is introduced without a recognition of the larger sociotechnical issues. Thus, the Office of Technology Assessment suggests that EWM is less likely to result in strain when workers participate in the introduction of the monitoring system, when the standards for performance imposed are seen as fair, and when performance records are used to improve performance rather than to punish the performer. It is important to note that these are the same variables that are seen as crucial to the perception of the fairness and equity of *any* performance evaluation system (Landy, 1989). As described above, guidelines for the introduction and use of EWM may reduce the potential stress of the monitoring process (Schott, 1988).

In earlier years, this type of micromonitoring was characteristic of only a few occupations (e.g., telephone operators monitored by supervisors in interactions with customers) and was not possible on the massive and detailed basis provided by current technology. Although there is some evidence that computer monitoring is not yet widespread (Gutek & Winters, 1990), it will be tempting for employers to increase their surveillance of work behavior through this technology in the hope of reducing costs and increasing productive effort. Furthermore, as managers are boldened by the technological advances of the software systems engineers, it is likely that such monitoring will become more pervasive. For that reason, it is safe to predict that electronic performance monitoring is likely to become a substantial psychosocial variable in the work environment and that this monitoring will become more closely associated with monetary rewards. (For an opposing view, see Attewell, 1987.) This is a development that deserves considerable research and practitioner attention. Some have suggested that the very act of electronic monitoring heightens strain for workers. As cited previously, Schleifer (in press) found elevated heart rate and blood pressure in subjects exposed to such monitoring. As a result, he suggested that workers be given a "stress(or) allowance" in terms of production standards for working in environments that practice electronic performance monitoring.

It has been some time since methods of reward have received any serious attention. The early work of Rothe and Nye (1959) suggested that rate of production was more stable under incentive and piece rate plans than under conditions of hourly pay. This is not surprising. Skinner had demonstrated the effectiveness of contingent reward schedules many years earlier with rats and humans. Nevertheless, the emphasis of this research was on output not worker reactions. No one asked the production workers what type of schedule they preferred. Managers recognize the emotional difference between payment schemes. Workers will often be required to work on piece rate schemes until they "prove themselves" capable of maintaining steady and acceptable output rates. At that point, they are permitted to shift to an hourly, noncontingent pay scheme with the implied threat that they will be placed back on incentive pay should production fall off.

The emphasis of much of the research regarding remuneration has been on perceived equity (e.g., Birnbaum, 1983; Lawler, 1971; Lawler & Hackman, 1969; Mellers, 1982) or piece rate payment as a method for increasing effort expenditure (e.g., Latham & Dossett, 1978). With minor exceptions (e.g., Thierry, 1984), there has been little consideration of the direct role that remuneration systems might play as stressors in the workplace. A great deal more needs to be known about the role which a payment scheme may play in strain. By extension, more needs to be known about distinctions between generalized incentive and bonus systems, on the one hand, and piece rate systems on the other.

Social and Societal Control

Stereotypes. There are other forms of control that might add to the burden experienced by the worker. For example, there is the control implied in cultural expectations. In the workplace, as is true in other environments, biases and stereotypes influence the interactions among and between workers. These biases and stereotypes are associated with a wide variety of demographic characteristics, including age, gender, race, and educational level. These stereotypes and biases are perceived by many workers to limit access to employment, or if employed, to advancement (Morrison & von Glinow, 1990). In addition, they are thought to influence the nature of interpersonal interactions (Cleveland & Landy, 1981). Thus, an older Black woman is at a substantial disadvantage compared to a young White male in similar work environments. Not only may there be differences in access to positions but there may also be differences in reward and punishment systems. The enormous number of disparate treatment cases litigated under the mantle of Title VII provides ample testimony to the fact that there is at least the *perception* by demographically defined subgroups of workers of inequitable treatment.

It is common to find high levels of unhappiness by Black and White workers alike related to the concept of affirmative action. Similarly, the concept of a "glass ceiling" may soon become a reality if the Department of Labor pursues the initiative described recently of glass ceiling audits of private employers. This concept refers to the fact that although women may experience increased access to entry level positions in industries and job titles with historically limited access to women, they eventually discover that a ceiling has been put in place that prevents movement up the organizational ladder. To the worker, it is likely that these social and societal influences represent aspects of control—controlling access to positions and rewards. It is interesting to note that in 1975, 5% of new business start-ups were initiated by women. In 1985, that percentage had grown to 25%. This may be an indication of the desire to exercise control denied at traditional workplaces. These tend to be chronic and long lasting forms of control as well, and less amenable to modification than methods of payment, machine pace, or system response time. Employers must recognize that these perceptions exist and that they may be associated with increased strain in minority and female employees. These perceptions can be addressed through educational efforts. A good model for the employer is the educational system. At every level of the educational system from primary through postsecondary, diversification programs are being introduced. These programs are intended to educate and sensitize majority group members to the value systems, behavior patterns, and apprehensions of minority group members. Employers might reduce strain on minority and female employees by following a similar program or education and sensitization.

The more behaviorally aggressive form for these stereotypes is actual harassment. It seems clear, at least in the case of sexual harassment, that harassment is a stressor (Crull, 1982; Gutek, 1985). The same would certainly be true for harassment related to age, race, religion, handicap, and any other similar focus for ridicule or discrimination. To the extent that an individual must endure such ridicule and discriminatory and degrading treatment, strain is likely to result. Many of the Title VII cases of disparate treatment are driven by this sense of frustration by the person suffering the discrimination. These issues are seldom exclusively monetary.

It is likely that employers will realize themselves that in order to be competitive in the workplace of the future, diversity will be a sine qua non. Workforce demographics make that conclusion axiomatic. Nevertheless, those employers who do not embrace this diversity concept will be maintaining environments that foster the harassment that is fed by stereotypes and that leads to employee strain.

Regulatory control. To this point, we have been examining informal societal control but there are more formal parameters of social control as well and these are represented by the regulatory control present in the statutes and administrative procedures enforced by governmental bodies. Thus, nuclear power plant workers feel controlled and constrained by the regulations and standards of the NRC in the abstract and by resident inspectors of that agency in the concrete. Similarly, Environmental Protection Agency (EPA), OSHA, and Equal Employment Opportunity Commission (EEOC) exercise control over the various decisions made within organizations. Many middle level managers express frustration related to perceived over-control by these federal regulatory bodies. It is easy to see how this broad societal control reduces to individual worker constraints in terms of work-related decisions, particularly for managers and supervisors. It is an unusual supervisor who has not wondered at least once if he or she will be sued by a worker if that worker receives a poor performance evaluation. There is not much that an employer could or should do about formal regulatory control, per se. In all instances of regulatory control, a decision has been made that the public good demands control even though it may limit the activities of individuals and reduce feelings of personal control. Nevertheless, in some industries, organizations imply regulatory control when there is none there. They attempt to control and motivate workers by interpreting regulations in the broadest sense and implying that the standards being set are not those of the organization but rather the standards of the regulatory agency. As an example, many police officers believe that unless every "i" is dotted and every "t" is crossed in a criminal report, that it is possible that the case will be lost on a technicality. This belief has been fostered by supervisors who imply that such standards of excellence are demanded by judges when in fact, these are the personal standards of the supervisors. No one would disagree with the right of the organization to demand excellence. The point is that such tactics (i.e., implying "regulation" when none exists) may simply heighten the feelings of powerlessness on the part of the worker. It is best to distinguish between regulatory requirements and organizational expectations.

The Nature of Work Demands

To this point, we have been considering the context in which work is done but only indirectly the nature of the work itself. We will now address issues more closely tied to the actual tasks that comprise a job.

Task Demands

As we suggested earlier, tasks vary in terms of their individual and collective "load" on a worker. There are several aspects to that load. The first is the volume/intensity/duration combination. It is reasonable to assume that the greater this index, the greater the demand on the worker. Nevertheless, it is not simply load or demand that determines strain. Rather it is the combination of a perceived demand coupled with perceived resources. If an individual perceives a demand or load to exceed resources, regardless of the absolute level of that demand, it is likely that strain will result (Karasek, 1990). Nevertheless, all other things being equal, it is safe to say that increasing demands are likely to be positively correlated with increasing strain, regardless of the level of resources.

Another issue that is relevant in terms of task demands and strain is the variability of that load. In many jobs, there is wide variability in the demands experienced across a shift. To return to our example of firefighters, they may be minimally engaged in work for several hours and called upon to exert near maximal effort for some period. This may happen once a shift, several times on the shift, or not at all for several shifts. Similarly, many jobs require vigilance with occasional bursts of activity to correct or control an ongoing process or system. A good example of this is the reactor operator in the control room of a nuclear power plant. This individual may do nothing more than record values for an entire shift if all is running smoothly. On the other hand, in the midst of normal power production, a valve in the cooling system may begin to leak requiring rapid and coordinated action. Little is known about the strain associated with this demand variability but it is likely that a price is paid by the worker.

It seems clear that some tasks have a speed characteristic to them and others do not. For our firefighter, it is critical that a burning room or structure be ventilated immediately to prevent the explosion that will inevitably occur when heat and toxic gases build beyond some critical level. On the other hand, the speed with which that same firefighter lays out hoses to dry after a fire is largely irrelevant. In nursing, there is a speed parameter associated with work in the emergency room or operating room but little or no speed demand for work in the chemical dependency unit. Schriber and Gutek (1987) have identified a number of temporal dimensions that can be measured in organizational settings. The research literature tends to deal with time urgency as a property of a person (as seen in the Type A Behavior Pattern profile). It is likely that time urgency is also (and maybe predominantly) a property of the job. The work of Johansson (Johansson & Aronsson, 1984) indicates that VDT workers experience more time urgency in their jobs than do other occupational groups. Although we cannot determine yet if time urgent people may gravitate to particular occupations or if the occupations influence the experience of time urgency, simple job analysis (Gael, 1988; Landy, 1989) has demonstrated that differences in the time demands of tasks can be readily identified with large and homogeneous samples of industrial workers. Thus, it is likely that there is at least a main effect for the time demands of tasks on worker strain.

To be sure, there are likely to be environments in which supervisors create artificial time pressures as a way of "motivating" subordinates. In addition, it is possible that people (or at least some subset of people) create their own artificial time pressures. Much more needs to be known about time as a resource and its role in work strain.

A final issue relates to the stimulation value of tasks. In most of the situations sketched so far, we have been describing situations that might be labeled "over-stimulating." There is also the opposite problem. Many jobs are simply boring or monotonous. Garson (1975) provided rich detail about the nature of boring work in a book entitled *All the Livelong Day*. More recently, Kahn and Byosiere (in press) have identified monotony as a potential source of strain. The parameters of boredom would include the variety of tasks undertaken, and more directly, the variety of knowledge, skills, and abilities called on for the successful completion of those tasks. It is likely that there is an inverted-U relationship between experienced strain and task/skill variety with either very high levels of variety (e.g., the tasks of a police officer) or very low levels of variety (e.g., the package crimp inspector in a frozen foods assembly line) associated with high strain and intermediate levels associated with low strain.

It is axiomatic that work design should take boredom and monotony into account. The very fact that many of the most common systems of job evaluation (i.e., the methods by which dollar values are attached to jobs) provide extra compensation for boring work should be taken as an admission of design failure. From the strain perspective, one cannot make up for the physiological consequences of boring work with additional compensation. This was one of the primary principles of Taylorism. One might hope that we had progressed beyond that point in job design. For the employer, the implications are rather direct. Examine recent job evaluations and target all jobs that receive substantial numbers of points for the boredom/monotony factor for redesign. The implications for industrial engineers and industrial psychologists are equally direct. Pay close attention to the "monotony index" when designing work. The period 1940 through 1960 was replete with examinations of boredom in industrial settings (e.g., Ryan, 1947). For many jobs, there is no need for additional research on the conditions that comprise monotony or the experience of boredom. It is only necessary to use existing information in the redesign of current jobs. For other jobs, particularly those defining the new electronic workplace, more information may be needed on the contributors to boredom. In some respects, one of the advantages of the move to a service-based economy may be a reduction in general levels of monotony that characterize the workplace and increase strain on workers. With respect to pay levels, the increase in skill levels required by the newly designed jobs should offset any pay reduction from the elimination of the boredom factor.

Motivating Potential of Jobs

This discussion of task and skill variety brings us back to an earlier aspect of our discussion—the motivating potential of jobs. Hackman and his colleague (Hackman & Oldham, 1975) have proposed that jobs can be analyzed in terms of their capacity to motivate the job holder. They further proposed that the effect of the job depends, to some extent, on whether the job holder is intrinsically motivated, but that argument is problematic in some respects (Landy, 1985, 1989) and not particularly important for the present discussion so we will not consider that individual difference parameter here. The proposed aspects of a motivating job include autonomy in decision making and action, high levels of feedback, task complexity, task and skill variety, and task significance. It is inherent in the propositions of this approach that jobs can be designed in a manner that would maximize the values of these parameters. The question is the relationship of the motivating potential of a job to strain. At first blush one might expect that highly motivating jobs are low in strain but there are clear instances of jobs that place considerable strain on workers *because of* that motivating potential. In the popular literature, the notion of workaholism fits this pattern. The question for stress researchers is "how much is too much?" It is tempting to blame the victim for the disease by suggesting that there are some predispositions that lead to the syndrome that are brought to the situation by the person but it is clear that there must be an interaction between the nature of the tasks that make up work and the characteristics of the person. Trial lawyers are more likely to be motivated by the nature of the work they do than the attendants who park their cars in the parking garage they use or the bus drivers who transport them to their office. As a result, it is likely that more trial lawyers cancel social engagements to continue reading an interesting case than do parking lot attendants who want to park just a few more cars or bus drivers who want to run their routes a few more times. For purposes of application and intervention, it is important to know what situations lend themselves to overcommitment by workers, even if it represents a problem for only a subgroup of those workers.

Job Demands

We have been discussing task demands. It appears as if there may be characteristics of entire jobs that lead to strain. There is an accumulating literature on burnout that suggests that certain occupational groupings are more prone to strain than others (Maslach & Jackson, 1984). The active ingredient in this phenomenon seems to be dealing with the problems of others. Thus, people holding jobs in the medical professions seem to experience higher levels of emotional exhaustion, in comparison to other human service professionals (Maslach & Jackson, 1986). High levels of emotional exhaustion have also been found among police (Gaines & Jermier, 1987; Jackson & Maslach, 1982) social service administrators (Maslach & Jackson, 1984), and public defenders (Jackson, Turner, & Brief, 1987). It is also possible that there is simply a fundamental difference in jobs that deal with people versus jobs that deal with things. The behavior of people is infinitely more variable and less predictable than the behavior of mechanical and operating systems. But there is likely another issue involved, beyond simply dealing with people. That issue relates to the *effective* interaction with people. The problem faced by nurses, police officers, probation officers, lawyers, welfare counselors, and so forth is that often their efforts are to no avail. Even when someone is actually helped by their services, bureaucratic social service systems usually include no provisions for service providers to receive direct positive feedback from their clients. Feedback is usually about the continuing problems of their clients. The fact that a client does not return may be the only indication that a problem has been solved. People continue to die, commit crimes, violate regulations, ignore high quality advice, and so on. With respect to the issue of job design, it is that aspect that must be addressed. The epidemiologist can tell us what professions are likely to be most vulnerable to this type of strain but for effective treatment and job redesign, we need to know more about exactly what aspects of these occupational groups are problematic.

The notion of "overcommitment" implies a counterintuitive position for many managers. They spend a great deal of time developing systems of motivation and leadership that will engage the worker, that will maximize involvement and a sense of ownership, and that will send the worker home at night worrying about work-related problems. It may be difficult to accept the possibility that there can be too much of a good thing. The job design that maximizes motivation (i.e., the arrangement of structure and process that maximizes self-directed effort) may not be the job with the lowest associated worker strain. Karasek (1979) has suggested that increasing the demand of the job or role without increasing the resources or decision latitude is a prescription for worker strain. In one sense, increasing the motivating potential of a job by concentrating on feedback, significance, variety, and complexity but leaving autonomy untouched might result in such strain. The caution to employers is to make sure that to the extent possible, increased autonomy is central to any efforts to increase worker motivation through job enrichment.

Endogenous Variables

Although the primary goal of this panel is to deal with job and work design, some brief mention should be made of the possible endogenous variables that might interact with design characteristics. There are several different ways in which these variables might be arranged but for the purposes of the current discussion, two categories can be proposed—substances that alter internal metabolic states and chronic dispositions.

Substances

There is little dispute about the fact that physiological systems are implicated in strain. These systems can be thought of as either independent/antecedent or dependent/consequent systems. Here, we are concerned with the systems as antecedent or independent variables. The most common substances which are used by a large number of workers and are likely to interact with or contribute to job strain are coffee and cigarettes. Caffeine and nicotine are both stimulants that are likely to raise resting heart rate, blood pressure, and result in other autonomic changes that are associated with the physiological symptoms of strain. For many people, an excess of coffee can lead to disordered behavior and psychological reactions similar to those associated with anxiety. A large portion of the population "overdoses" on coffee on a regular basis. It is reasonable to assume that overstimulation from substances will combine unfavorably with the aspects of the work that also produce strain (e.g., task load or demand, machine pacing, etc.). The critical issues here are the "dose level" and the interacting task characteristics. For example, it is likely that such stimulants actually relieve strain in monotonous jobs in addition to improving vigilance. On the other hand, an excess of a stimulant in an environment characterized by high demand for information processing is likely to create problems in performance and strain reactions in the worker. In some people, coffee also results in a roller-coaster effect in terms of felt fatigue. The burst of energy that follows the ingestion is, in turn, followed by a period of fatigue and lethargy. This might suggest that there are periods of the day that are more likely to be vulnerable periods for the appearance of strain than others for those who have coffee for breakfast and lunch. The point is that there may very well be a periodicity to strain reactions, a possibility suggested long ago by Hersey in a study of German and American railway workers (Hersey, 1933, 1955). Nicotine might work similarly. Since it is clear that both neurotransmitters and hormones are influenced by caffeine and nicotine and it is clear that both neurotransmitters and hormones are implicated in strain reactions, it follows that it would be important to determine if the effects of these substances when coupled with design characteristics are additive or possibly superadditive (Landy, 1989). This is another item to add to the research agenda. We need to know more about the life style variables that might interact with stressors in the workplace.

Coffee is accepted at the workplace, whereas other substances causing similar effects are not yet accepted. For example, cigarettes have a direct effect on both the central nervous system and the autonomic nervous system through nicotine. Similarly, alcohol has complex effects on humans. Low doses act as stimulants while higher dosages act as a depressant. Thus, the consumption of alcohol on the job is likely to have complex interactions with task characteristics depending on the amount of alcohol and the demand level of the task. Various drugs are likely to have equally complex interactions depending on whether the drugs are depressants, stimulants, or opiates. If national statistics can be trusted, the use of substances like marijuana and cocaine in the workplace represents a substantial problem for performance. Although less is known about the exact dynamics, it is likely that substance abuse interacts with job characteristics and results in strain. From a research as well as a practical perspective, it is important to be able to separate the influences of work design from the influences of life style variables in understanding worker strain and the consequences of that strain. From a strain perspective, there are two points to be made. The first, and most obvious, is that changes in life style (e.g., cessation of smoking or reduction of coffee consumption) might reduce overall strain in an individual. The second point is somewhat less obvious. The very change in life style may represent a stressor in its own right. As a current example, consider the pressure placed on individuals to stop smoking by recently enacted legislation and changes in organizational policy. A common reaction among smokers is that they have been branded "unclean." In many organizations, the smokers huddle by a loading dock to smoke. It is likely that they are experiencing strain simply from the changed cultural expectations. Should they choose to stop smoking or drinking coffee, there is another form of strain that is likely to result from the process of physiological and psychological withdrawal. As we have pointed out earlier, the work environment is a complex social system. Changes in one aspect of that system (e.g., smoking policies) may have substantial ramifications in other parts of that system (e.g., strain experienced by smokers). Of course, we are not arguing that an increased strain from change will cancel out the reduced long-term strain implied by that life style change. We are simply pointing out that there are many secondary factors that must be taken into account in reshaping organizational policies. In the case of smoking, it would be wise to recognize the increased strain on smokers and to provide support systems that will help them make the transition from smoker to nonsmoker. Creating a smokers' ghetto is not likely to help in changing the target behavior in some people and is likely to increase strain in all smokers.

Dispositional

Dispositional characteristics might be thought of as trait-like and enduring. Often, these are considered personality characteristics implying a habitual pattern of behavior. The most prominent of these characteristics in the stress literature is the Type A Behavior Pattern (TABP). There is a great deal of debate with respect to what component of the TABP is most closely associated with strain. The two leading candidates are time urgency and hostility. The notion is that people whose behavior might be characterized as TABP are more likely to experience strain and the negative health consequences of that strain. Other variables that have been suggested as moderators of strain include the need for achievement (Jackson & Schuler, 1985), locus on control (Jackson, 1989; Kahn & Byosiere, in press), and self esteem/self efficacy (Kahn & Byosiere, in press). The point is that some people may be more prone to strain reactions than others. This might be considered as similar to an allergic reaction. In the absence of the allergic substance, no problems appear. On the other hand, when the substance is present, there is a negative interaction. In the case of job design, it may be that there are no particular problems experienced by TABP individuals or those with low self-esteem or those with a high need for achievement until and unless certain job design elements are present.

This dispositional/design interaction implies several potential courses of action. It implies a placement or diagnostic function so that individuals with these vulnerabilities are provided with information about how the vulnerability manifests itself and how best to cope with the vulnerability. Placement or selection might also be implied such that individuals with particular vulnerabilities are placed in jobs with design characteristics that do not create problems. There are also implications of design. Thus, it might be reasonable to think of modifying jobs to fit the vulnerabilities of those in them. As an example, Schleifer (in press) suggested a "stress(or) allowance" for individuals subject to electronic monitoring. This is a form of accommodation similar to that contemplated by the new Americans with Disabilities Act.

One final dispositional characteristic might be simple physical fitness, particularly cardiovascular fitness. Literature suggests that exercise can reduce resting heart rate and blood pressure. It follows that physically fit individuals (particularly those with fit cardiovascular systems) might be better able to withstand stressors in the environment. It also suggests a potential interaction between fitness levels and strain reactions. As was the case with other dispositional characteristics, such an interaction might imply counseling, placement, or design modifications.

Recommendations

Within the body of the paper itself, there are specific recommendations regarding intervention and research. Nevertheless, for the sake of closure, it might be helpful to pull those recommendations together in a summary statement.

It would appear that there are some major design variables that warrant attention. These variables include control, uncertainty, conflict, and task/job demands. These variables will now be examined independently.

Control: Intervention

1. Workers must be given the opportunity to control various aspects of the work and the workplace. These aspects might include work pace, task assignment, method of payment, task content, goal selection, and so forth. The most effective way to accomplish such control is through participative decision making. This control includes the capacity to shift from one task to another when obstacles to task completion arise.
2. Systems must have optimal response times or optimal response ranges. These optimal values should be built into machine and task design.
3. Performance monitoring must be introduced and implemented in an appropriate manner. It should be used as a source of relevant feedback to individuals in improving the quality and quantity of performance.

Control: Research

1. We need to know to what extent control in one aspect of the work environment (e.g., work schedule) can balance a lack of control in another aspect (e.g., task assignment).
2. We need to understand what the active ingredient of participative decision making is.
3. We need a clearer explication of the constructs of demands and resources.
4. We need a better understanding of the impact of methods of payment on strain.

Uncertainty: Intervention

1. Employees need to have information in as timely and complete a form as possible.
2. Work assignments need to be clear and unambiguous.
3. Shift change communication needs to be improved. In the manufacturing and process environment, shift changes are a particular time for uncertainty to emerge.
4. Organizations need to make clear policy statements and apply those policies in a consistent manner.
5. Employees need to have easy access to information sources.

Uncertainty: Research

1. Does everyone find uncertainty aversive?
2. Are some sources of uncertainty more potent than others?
3. What role does social support play in the experience of uncertainty?
4. How can one distinguish between uncertainty and stimulation?
5. What are the dimensions of uncertainty?
6. What occupations are characterized by high uncertainty?
7. What epidemiological data are available to tie uncertainty to strain?

Conflict: Intervention

1. Participative decision making should be used to reduce conflict.
2. Job descriptions and task assignments should be clear and stable.
3. Mechanisms should be introduced for the management of conflict.
4. There should be more open discussion of potential and real conflicts in organizational settings.
5. Supervisors should adopt supportive styles to reduce conflict.
6. Demands should not exceed resources.

Conflict: Research

1. What is the active ingredient of conflict?
2. Which types of conflict are most damaging?
3. Why does participative decision making reduce conflict?
4. What individual difference characteristics contribute to conflict at the workplace?

Task/Job Demands: Intervention

1. A variety of knowledges, skills, and abilities should be required by a job.
2. Workers should receive feedback about performance.
3. Organizations should stop paying people to endure boring work and set about making the work more interesting.
4. Service work should not be patterned after the assembly line.
5. Information based jobs should be enlarged rather than reduced in scope.
6. Feedback should be provided to service workers.

Task/Job Demands: Research

1. What are the implications of matches and mismatches between individual difference characteristics such as time urgency and task demands?
2. What is the optimal mix of new and practiced tasks as well as new or old skill demands?
3. What is the active ingredient in burnout?

To be sure, these recommendations simply touch the surface of the implications of the paper. Nevertheless, there seems to be general agreement on these points. In addition, the panelists have elaborated on several of these points. These elaborations appear in the following section of these proceedings.

References

Alfredsson, L., Karasek, R., & Theorell, T. (1982). Myocardial infarction risk and psycho-social risk— an analysis of the male Swedish workforce. *Social Science and Medicine, 3*, 463–467.

Argote, L., Goodman, P., & Schkade, D. (1983). The human side of robotics: How workers react to a robot. *Sloan Management Review, 24,* 31–41.

Argyris, C. (1980). *Inner contradictions of rigorous research.* New York: Academic Press.

Association of Schools of Public Health. (1988). *Proposed national strategies for the prevention of leading work-related diseases and injuries: Part 2.* Cincinnati, OH: National Institute for Occupational Safety and Health.

Attewell, P. (1987). Big brother and the sweatshop: Computer surveillance in the automated office. *Sociological Theory, 5,* 87–99.

Bandura, A. (1986). *Social foundation of thought and action: A social cognitive theory.* Englewood Cliffs, NJ: Prentice-Hall.

Barling, J., & Rosenbaum, A. (1986). Work stressors and spouse abuse. *Journal of Applied Psychology, 78,* 346–348.

Bennis, W., & Nanus, B. (1983). *Leaders: The strategies for taking charge.* New York: Harper and Row.

Berlinguer, G. (1990). Research strategies and preventive models in work. Paper presented at Work and Welfare Conference, Karlstad, Sweden.

Bertin, J. E., & Henifin, M. S. (1987). Legal issues in women's occupational health. In A. H. Stromberg, L. Larwood, & B. A. Gutek (Eds.), *Women and work: An annual review* (Vol. 2, pp. 93–116). Newbury Park, CA: Sage Publishers, Inc.

Birnbaum, M. H. (1983). Perceived equity of salary policies. *Journal of Applied Psychology, 68,* 49–59.

Boucsein, W. (1987). Psychophysiological investigation of stress induced by temporal factors in human-computer interaction. In M. Frese, E. Ulich, & W. Dzida (Eds.), *Psychological issues of human-computer interaction in the work place* (pp. 163–182). New York: North Holland.

Bowen, D. E., & Schneider, B. (1988). Services marketing and management: Implications for organizational behavior. In B. M. Staw & L. L. Cummings (Eds.), *Research in organizational behavior* (Vol. 10, pp. 43–80). Greenwich, CT: JAI Press.

Cleveland, J., & Landy, F. J. (1981). The influence of ratee age and rater age on two performance judgments. *Personnel Psychology, 34,* 19–29.

Colligan, M. J., Smith, M. J., & Hurrell, J. J. (1977). Occupational incidence of mental health disorders. *Journal of Human Stress, 3,* 11–26.

Crull, P. (1982). Stress effects of sexual harassment on the job: Implications for counseling. *American Journal of Orthopsychiatry, 52*(3), 539–594.

Curran, C. R., Minnick, A., & Moss, J. (1987). Who needs nurses. *American Journal of Nursing, 87,* 134–142.

Davis, S. (1987). *Future perfect.* Reading, MA: Addison-Wesley.

Dray, S. M. (1988). From tier to peer: Organizational adaptation to new computing architectures. *Ergonomics, 31*(5), 721–725.

Fiedler, F., & Garcia, J. E. (1967). *New approaches to effective leadership.* New York: Wiley.

Fleishman, E. A., & Harris, E. F. (1962). Patterns of leadership behavior related to employee grievances and turnover. *Personnel Psychology, 15,* 43–56.

Frankenhauser, M., Lundberg, U., Fredrikson, M., Melin, B., Tuomisto, M., Myrsten, A. L., Hedman, M., Bergman-Losman, B., & Wallin, L. (1989). Stress on and off the job as related to sex and occupational status in white collar workers. *Journal of Organizational Behavior, 10,* 321–346.

Frese, M. (1989). Theoretical models of control and health. In S. Sauter, J. Hurrell, & C. Cooper (Eds.), *Job control and worker health.* New York: Wiley.

Gael, S. (1988). *The job analysis handbook for business, industry and government.* New York: Wiley.

Gaines, J., & Jermier, J. M. (1987). Emotional exhaustion in a high stress occupation. *Academy of Management Journal, 26,* 567, 586.

Galegher, J., Kraut, R. E., & Egido, C. (Eds.). (1990). *Intellectual teamwork: Social and technological foundations of cooperative work.* Hillsdale, NJ: Lawrence Erlbaum Associates.

Garson, B. (1975). *All the livelong day.* New York: Doubleday.

Garson, B. (1988). *The electronic sweatshop.* New York: Simon and Schuster.

Goodman, P. S. (1974). An examination of referents used in the evaluation of pay. *Organizational Behavior and Human Performance, 12,* 170–195.

Greller, M. (1990). Managing careers with a changing work force. *Journal of Organizational Change Management, 3,* 2.

Gutek, B. (1985). *Sex and the workplace.* San Francisco: Jossey Bass.

Gutek, B. A., Bikson, T. K., & Mankin, D. (1984). Individual and organizational consequences of computer-based office information technology. In S. Oskamp (Ed.), *Applied social psychology annual: Applications in organizational settings* (Vol. 5, pp. 231–254). Newbury Park, CA: Sage Publishers, Inc.

Gutek, B. A., Repetti, R. L., & Silver, D. L. (1988). Nonwork roles and stress at work. In C. L. Cooper & R. Payne (Eds.), *Causes, coping, and consequences of stress at work* (pp. 141–173). New York: Wiley.

Gutek, B. A., & Winter, S. J. (1990). Computer use, control over computers, and job satisfaction. In S. Oskamp & S. Spacapan (Eds.), *People's reactions to technology in factories, offices, and aerospace: The Claremont Symposium on Applied Social Psychology* (pp. 121–144). Newbury Park, CA: Sage Publishers, Inc.

Hacker, W. (1985). Activity: A fruitful concept in industrial psychology. In M. Frese & J. Sabini (Eds.), *Goal directed behavior* (pp. 262–283). Hillsdale, NJ: Lawrence Erlbaum Associates.

Hackman, J. R., & Oldham, G. R. (1975). Development of the job diagnostic survey. *Journal of Applied Psychology, 60,* 159–170.

Hall, E. M., & Johnson, J. V. (1989). A case study of stress and mass psychogenic illness in industrial workers. *Journal of Occupational Medicine, 31*(3), 243–250.

Herold, D. M. (1990). Using technology to improve our management and labor market trends. *Journal of Organizational Change Management, 3*(2), 44–57.

Hersey, R. (1955). *Zest for work.* New York: Harper.

Herzberg, F., Mausner, B., Peterson, R. O., & Capwell, D. F. (1957). *Job attitudes: Review of research and opinion.* Pittsburgh: Pittsburgh Psychological Services.

Herzberg, F., Mausner, B., & Snyderman, B. (1959). *The motivation to work.* New York: Wiley.

Humphrey, J. H. (1988). *Stress in the nursing profession.* Springfield, IL: Charles C. Thomas.

Jackson, S. E. (1983). Participation in decision making as a strategy for reducing job-related strain. *Journal of Applied Psychology, 68*(1), 3–19.

Jackson, S. E. (1989). Does job control control job stress? In S. L. Sauter, J. J. Hurrell, Jr., & C. L. Cooper (Eds.), *Job control and worker health* (pp. 25–53). Wiley.

Jackson, S. E., & Maslach, C. (1982). After-effects of job-related stress: Families as victims. *Journal of Occupational Behavior, 3,* 63–77.

Jackson, S. E., & Schuler, R. S. (1985). A meta-analysis and conceptual critique of research on role ambiguity and role conflict in work settings. *Organizational Behavior and Human Decision Process, 36,* 16–78.

Jackson, S. E., Turner, J. A., & Brief, A. P. (1987). Correlates of burnout among public service lawyers. *Journal of Occupational Behavior, 8,* 339–349.

Johansson, G., & Aronsson, G. (1984). Stress reactions in computerized administrative work. *Journal of Occupational Behavior, 5,* 159–181.

Kahn, R. L. (1981). *Work and health.* New York: Wiley.

Kahn, R. L., & Byosiere, (in press). Stress in organizations. In M. Dunnette (Ed.), *Handbook of industrial and organizational psychology.* Chicago: Rand-McNally.

Kahn, R. L., Wolfe, D. M., Quinn, R. P., Snoek, J. D., & Rosenthal, R. A. (1964). *Organizational stress: Studies in role conflict and ambiguity.* New York: Wiley.

Karasek, R. (1990). Lower health risk with increased job control among white collar workers. *Journal of Organizational Behavior, 11,* 171–185.

Karasek, R. A., Jr. (1979). Job demands, job decision latitude, and mental strain: Implications for job redesign. *Administrative Science Quarterly, 24,* 285–308.

Konrad, A. M., & Gutek, B. A. (1987). Theory and research on group composition: Applications to the status of women and ethnic minorities. In S. Oskamp & S. Spacapan (Eds.), *Interpersonal processes: The Claremont Symposium on Applied Social Psychology* (pp. 85–121). Newbury Park, CA: Sage Publishers, Inc.

Kuhnert, K. W., & Vance, R. J. (1990). *Job security and moderators of the relationship between job security and employee adjustment.* Manuscript submitted for publication.

Landy, F. J. (1985). *The psychology of work behavior* (3rd ed.). Homewood, IL: Dorsey Press.

Landy, F. J. (1989). *The psychology of work behavior* (4th ed.). Monterey, CA: Brooks/Cole.

Landy, F. J., Rastegary, H., & Motowidlo, S. (1987). Human computer interactions in the work place: Psychosocial aspects of VDT use. In M. Frese, E. Ulich, & W. Dzida (Eds.), *Psychological issues of human-computer interaction in the workplace.* New York: North-Holland.

Landy, F. J., Rastegary, H., Thayer, J., & Colvin, C. (1991). Time urgency: The construct and its measurement. *Journal of Applied Psychology, 76,* 644–657.

Latham, G. P., & Dossett, D. L. (1978). Designing incentive plans for unionized employees: A comparison of continuous and variable reinforcement schedules. *Personnel Psychology, 31*, 47–61.

Lawler, E., & Hackman, J. R. (1969). Impact of employee participation in the development of pay incentive plans: A field experiment. *Journal of Applied Psychology, 53*, 467–471.

Lawler, F. E. (1971). *Pay and organizational effectiveness: A psychological review.* New York: McGraw-Hill.

Lawrence, P. R., & Dyer, D. (1983). *Renewing American industry.* New York: Free Press.

Majchrzak, A., & Davis, D. (1990). The human side of flexible factory automation: Research and management practice. In S. Oskamp & S. Spacapan (Eds.), *People's reactions to technology in factories, offices, and aerospace: The Claremont Symposium on Applied Social Psychology* (pp. 33–66). Newbury Park, CA: Sage Publishers, Inc.

Maslach, C., & Jackson, S. E. (1982). Burnout in health professions: A social psychological analysis. In G. S. Sanders & J. Suls (Eds.), *Social psychology of health and illness* (pp. 227–251). Hillsdale, NJ: Lawrence Erlbaum Associates.

Maslach, C., & Jackson, S. E. (1984). Burnout in organizational settings. In S. Oskamp (Ed.), *Applied social psychology annual, 5.* Beverly Hills, CA: Sage Publishers, Inc.

Maslach, C., & Jackson, S. E. (1984). Patterns of burnout among a national sample of public contact workers. *Journal of Health and Human Resources Administration, 7*, 189–212.

Mathieu, J. E., & Zajac, D. M. (1990). A review and meta-analysis of the antecedents, correlates, and consequences of organizational commitment. *Psychological Bulletin, 108*(2), 171–194.

Maurer, H. (1979). *Not working.* New York: Holt.

McClaney, M. A., & Hurrell, J. J. (1988). Control, stress, and job satisfaction. *Work and Stress, 2*, 217–224.

McGrath, J. E. (1976). Stress and behavior in organizations. In M. D. Dunnette (Ed.), *Handbook of industrial and organizational psychology.* Chicago: Rand-McNally.

Mellers, B. A. (1982). Equity judgment: A revision of Aristotelian views. *Journal of Experimental Psychology, 111*, 242–270.

Miceli, M. A. P., & Near, J. B. (1988). Individual and situational correlates of whistle-blowing. *Personnel Psychology, 41*, 267–281.

Ministry of Labor. (1987). *The Swedish work environment act (with amendments) and the Swedish work environment ordinance (with amendments).* Stockholm: Author.

Morrison, A. M., & von Glinow, M. A. (1990). Women and minorities in management. *American Psychologist, 45*(20), 200–208.

Moses, J., & Lyness, K. (1988). Individual and organizational responses to ambiguity. In F. D. Shoorman & B. Schneider (Eds.), *Facilitating work effectiveness.* New York: Free Press.

Narayanan, V. K., & Nath, R. (1982). A field test of some attitudinal and behavioral consequences of flexitime. *Journal of Applied Psychology, 67*, 214–218.

Near, J. P., & Miceli, M. A. P. (1987). Whistle-blowers in organizations: Dissidents or reformers? In L. L. Cummings & B. M. Staw (Ed.), *Research in organizational behavior* (Vol. 9, pp. 321–368). Greenwich, CT: JAI Press.

Nieva, V., Newman, P., & Bottlik, G. (1990). Factory automation and production jobs: A longitudinal study. In S. Oskamp & S. Spacapan (Eds.), *People's reactions to technology in factories, offices, and aerospace: The Claremont Symposium on Applied Social Psychology* (67–120). Newbury Park, CA: Sage Publishers, Inc.

Orpen, C. (1981). Effect of flexible working hours on employee satisfaction and performance. *Journal of Applied Psychology, 66*, 113–115.

Ouchi, W. G. (1981). *Theory Z.* Reading, MA: Addison-Wesley.

Parmalee, M. A., Near, J. P., & Jensen, T. C. (1982). Correlates of whistleblowers' perceptions of organizational retaliation. *Administrative Science Quarterly, 27*(1), 17–34.

Porter, L. W. (1990, April). *Commitment patterns in industrial organizations.* Paper presented at meetings of the Society for Industrial and Organizational Psychology, Miami Beach, FL.

Porter, L. W., & Lawler, E. E. (1968). *Managerial attitudes and performance.* Homewood, IL: Dorsey Press.

Randall, D. M. (1985). Women in toxic work environments: A case study and examination of policy impact. In L. Larwood, A. H. Stromberg, & B. A. Gutek (Eds.), *Women and work: An annual review* (Vol. 1, pp. 259–281). Newbury Park, CA: Sage Publishers, Inc.

Rothe, H. F., & Nye, C. T. (1959). Output rates among machine operators: consistency related to methods of pay. *Journal of Applied Psychology, 43*, 417–420.

Ryan, T. A. (1947). *Work and effort*. New York: Ronald.

Sainfort, P. C., & Smith, M. J. (1989). Job factors as predictors of stress outcomes among VDT users. In M. J. Smith & G. Salvendy (Eds.), *Work with computers: Organizational, management, stress, and health aspects* (pp. 233–240). Amsterdam: Elsevier Science Publishers.

Sauter, S., Hurrell, J. J., & Cooper, C. L. (1989). *Job control and worker health*. New York: Wiley.

Schleifer, L. M., & Amick, B. C., III. (1989). System response time and method of pay: Stress effects in computer-based tasks. *International Journal of Human-Computer Interaction, 1*(1), 23–39.

Schleifer, L. M., & Okogbaa, O. G. (in press). System response time and method of pay: Cardiovascular stress effects in computer-based tasks. *Ergonomics*.

Schlenker, J. A., & Gutek, B. A. (1987). Effects of role loss on work-related attitudes. *Journal of Applied Psychology, 72*, 287–293.

Schott, F., & Olson, M. (1988). Designing usability in systems: Driving for normalcy. *Datamation, 34*(10), 68–76.

Schriber, J. B., & Gutek, B. A. (1987). Some time dimensions of work: Measurement of an underlying aspect of organizational culture. *Journal of Applied Psychology, 72*, 642–650.

Schuler, R. S., & Jackson, S. E. (1986). Managing stress through PHRM practices: An uncertainty interpretation. *Research in Personnel and Human Resources Management, 4*, 183–224.

Smith, M., & Carayon, J. (1990). Electronic monitoring of worker performance: A review of the potential effects on job design and stress. Madison, WI: University of Wisconsin.

Smith, M. J., & Salvendy, G. (1989). *Work with computers: Organizational, management, stress, and health aspects*. New York: Elsevier Science Publishers.

Stahl, S. M., & Lebedun, M. (1974). Mystery gas: An analysis of mass hysteria. *Journal of Health and Social Behavior, 15*, 44–50.

Steers, R., & Porter, L. (1983). *Motivation and work behavior*. New York: McGraw-Hill.

Tarkel, S. (1974). *Working*. Pantheon: New York.

Taylor, F. W. (1911). *The principles of scientific management*. New York: Harper & Brothers.

Thierry, H. (1984). Systems of remuneration. In *Handbook of work and organizational psychology* (Vol. 2). New York: Wiley.

Thorndike, E. L. (1922). The psychology of labor. *Harper's Magazine, 144*, 799–806.

Vroom, V. (1964). *Work and motivation*. New York: Wiley.

Vroom, V., & Yetton, P. (1973). *Leadership and decision making*. Pittsburgh: Pittsburgh University Press.

Walton, R. E. (1987). *Innovating to compete*. San Francisco: Jossey-Bass.

Warr, P. B. (1987). *Work, unemployment and mental health*. Oxford: Clarendon Press.

Zuboff, S. (1982). New worlds of computer-mediated work. *Harvard Business Review, 60*(5), 142–152.

Zuboff, S. (1985). Automate/informate: The two faces of intelligent technology. *Organizational Dynamics, 14*(2), 5–18.

Zuboff, S. (1988). *In the age of the smart machine: The future of work and power*. New York: Basic Books.

Zuckerman, M. (1979). Sensation seeking and risk taking. In C. Izard (Ed.), *Emotions in personality and psychopathology* (pp. 163–197). New York: Plenum.

Zuckerman, M., Bone, R. N., Neary, R., Mangelsdorff, D., & Brustman, B. (1972). What is the sensation seeker? Personality trait and experience correlates of sensation seeking scales. *Journal of Consulting and Clinical Psychology, 39*, 308–321.

Panel Comments

Mirian M. Graddick

I have elected to elaborate on three major areas related to Landy's paper on work design and stress. These areas include the potential impact of globalization on the changing nature of work, research conducted at AT&T related to the impact of social variables on strain in the workplace, and the role of human resources (HR) planning as a way to potentially minimize worker strain.

Globalization

The paper tred lightly over the changing nature of work as it pertains to environmental changes such as intense international competition and corporate restructuring. We cannot underestimate the overall impact of globalization on the nature of work. As domestic and global competition increases, the number of business firms operating across national borders rises. Many United States based companies are now receiving over 50% of their revenues from outside the United States.

Multinational firms with a string of relatively unconnected operations in various countries are now moving towards becoming truly global. Global companies operate as though the world were one large market, weaving the individual operations into a strategic mosaic. Simply put, globalization refers to the millions of business transactions moving across the globe at an increasingly accelerated rate. It involves the movement of people, goods, services, and capital through mechanisms such as planes, ships, and electronic mail.

Operating in such an increasingly complex global environment surely has an impact on worker strain, particularly for those companies that have had to move with startling swiftness to combat competition. Not only will companies need global standards for quality, pricing, service, and design, but they must have a management team capable of executing a global strategy. Success will depend on several key factors, many of which can potentially induce strain in those responsible for implementation. Having a management team that is truly international is critical. Important skills required to perform effectively in the global marketplace include adaptability to different environments, cultural flexibility (to be comfortable as a global business person rather than a "stranger in a strange land"), and multilingual capability. Understanding the impact of world events, adaptation to policy-constrained environments, and an appreciation of governance in different national settings are key to success as well.

Global managers will also be required to build and support overseas operations by attracting, developing, and retaining a cadre of local nationals. These managers must find ways to coordinate the actions of people around the globe to exchange ideas, work, information, marketplace intelligence, and other business elements. Extensive international travel, the transfer of families into different cultural settings, and the reality of having a new boss, perhaps as a result of a merger or acquisition, who comes from or resides in a different country or culture can contribute greatly to strain.

The traditional model of success has clearly changed. In reality, many companies do not have leadership teams possessing these additional types of skills or experiences. Many Americans may be clearly hampered by the singularly domestic focus of our work, family, and educational experiences. The appropriate level of comfort for managing in a global environment will therefore be lacking until the focus changes and the skills expand to include the globalized set. A critical challenge more directly related to job design is how to structure tasks and ensure teamwork when groups are geographically dispersed around the world.

The Social Fabric of Work

Over the past decade, AT&T has undergone tremendous organizational changes resulting in massive downsizing, the introduction of new technology, redirection of the business, and redeployment of the workforce. During these turbulent times, our medical department initiated a health prevention program designed to ease worker strain. Key to implementing and tracking behavioral results is a thorough initial assessment of an array of individual and organizational problems, needs, interests, and resources. Traditional assessment methods have not addressed cultural, social, and environmental factors related to behavior change.

Scofield and Martin (1990) developed an instrument called the AT&T Health Audit which was designed to measure culturally-based health and risk variables within an organization. This 68-item instrument consists of organizational, environmental, and individual variables.

Thus far, the Health Audit has been completed by over 25,000 employees across 24 company locations. A rather surprising finding revealed that for the analysis of high stress and super stress employees, the most powerful predictor of stress was a lack of support from one's boss. The implications of these findings highlight the importance of the social context within which one works. Perceiving that a job is stressful, and being able to cope with that stress, may depend as much on employees' interaction with their bosses as on the job itself or the employee's coping skills (Scofield & Martin, 1990).

The Role of HR Planning as a Way to Potentially Minimize Worker Strain

Labor market trends suggest that the pool of available workers may be insufficient to meet future business needs and larger segments of this population may not have the appropriate skills for jobs which they are expected to fill. Various solutions have been identified for dealing with these issues such as increasing the skill levels through training, changing policies, laws and regulations which tend to restrict the availability of qualified labor (e.g., immigration laws), and use of segments of the labor pool which are currently underutilized (e.g., people with handicaps, part-timers). To date, very little has been done by way of using technology to address some of the human resource problems brought about by the changing demographics. In fact, when decisions are made regarding the introduction of technology in the work force, they are generally based on variables such as cost, quality improvement, accuracy, and safety, rather than labor pool issues. Herold (1990) proposes that labor market considerations may be as important for choosing technology as variables such as cost and quality improvement. In fact, he would argue that HR planners should evaluate the use of technology as it relates to the overall success of the company, rather than reacting to technological imperatives imposed by others in the organization.

Herold (1990) proposes that technology impacts workers in the following ways: (a) deskilling—when a lower-level worker can now do the job; (b) replacement—the introduction of technology eliminates the need for the worker; and (c) augmentation—a partnership between a skilled specialist and technology. When technology decisions are made independent of human resource issues, the impacts on the current work force can undermine effective human resource utilization and add significant stressors to the workplace. If HR planners were involved more in the initial decision making process, both cost and people implications could be considered simultaneously. A key issue is to thoroughly understand the impact of technology on future skill requirements. The choice of technology could potentially impact recruiting, selection, training, compensation, and development.

If technology, for example, were to result in a replacement of workers, key issues would be whether strategically those are the appropriate people to replace, and what the impact of the replacement will be, including both the management and economic implications. Conversely, one might intentionally introduce replacement technologies where shortages exist or are predicted to occur.

Herold suggests that one might consider different technological options for different labor market conditions (see Table 2). By examining five labor market conditions against the three technological options, it is possible to examine different strategies for dealing with particular conditions. By looking at the cells within a row, we can compare different strategies for dealing with a specific condition. By examining cells within a column, one can propose dynamic strategies which allow shifts between cells.

Having determined that a technological solution may be appropriate, several key questions need to be addressed:

- Is a technology solution available to implement?
- What is the state of development, cost, and rate of change for the technology?
- What human implementation problems are anticipated?

As you can see, the framework is useful in linking business planning, labor market conditions and technological options. Doing this type of an analysis for several jobs will lead to an organization-wide labor requirement, rather than a job-by-job design.

There are obviously a variety of important factors that would impact final

Table 2. A Framework for Considering Technological Options for Different Labor Market Conditions

Predicted Labor Condition	Technological Options		
	Replace	De-Skill	Augment
Shortages insufficient labor/ insufficient skill			
Short Falls sufficient labor/ insufficient skill			
Underprepared sufficient labor/ insufficient skill			
Adequate sufficient labor/ sufficient skill			
Surplus			

Note. From "Using Technology to Improve Our Management and Labor Market Trends" by D. M. Herold, 1990, *Journal of Organizational Change Management, 3*(2). Copyright 1990 by University Press, Ltd. Reprinted by permission.

decisions, such as nontechnological solutions to labor problems, or nonlabor elements in decision to choose new technologies. The significance of having HR planners partner with technology planners is that many of the potential impacts on the work environment and many of the potential stressors could be identified and possibly minimized.

References

Herold, D. M. (1990). Using technology to improve our management and labor market trends. *Journal of Organizational Change Management, 3*(2), 44–57.

Scofield, M. E., & Martin, W. (1990). Development of the AT&T health audit for measuring organizational health. In M. E. Scofield (Ed.), *Worksite health promotion* (Vol. 5, No. 4, pp. 755–766). Philadelphia, PA: Hanley and Belfus, Inc.

Panel Comments

Susan E. Jackson

Landy's review of the research on work design and stress provides voluminous evidence supporting the conclusion that control is a key determinant of experienced strain. When employees are given more control over aspects of their tasks and their environments, they experience less strain. When employees have little autonomy and control, they experience higher levels of strain. Despite what appears to be good scientific evidence about the linkage between the amount of control employees have and their experiences of strain, employing organizations have been slow to institute changes designed to give their employees more control. Our research seems to be having little impact on the way jobs are designed.

In this commentary, I will consider two possible reasons for why research showing the relationship between control and strain has not stimulated a revolution in job redesign, and I will suggest how we as researchers and interventionists could become catalysts in the future. Briefly, the two reasons that I believe explain why there has been no rush to redesign jobs in ways that give employees more control can be stated as follows:

1. Interventions designed to increase the control of any group of employees are likely to be perceived as diminishing the personal control of those at the next higher status level in the organization. Therefore, even if managers and supervisors were interested in finding ways to reduce the strain experienced by their subordinates, they are unlikely to favor job redesign efforts intended to give their subordinates greater control. Doing so would require that the supervisors and managers give up some control themselves. Our evidence clearly indicates that supervisors and managers should expect such changes to increase the strain they experience personally.
2. Managers and supervisors do not expect positive economic payoffs to follow from interventions designed to give employees more control or, more generally, from interventions designed to reduce employee strain. Instead, they assume that changes made for the purpose of reducing strain are also likely to reduce productivity and diminish the organization's profitability.

If these two assertions accurately describe the beliefs that managers hold about the consequences of increasing their subordinates' control in the workplace, it seems obvious that managers will ignore our pleas for increasing the degree of control their subordinates have over their work environment. It follows that psychologists will not be effective change agents in this domain unless and until we address these two issues. It is unrealistic to expect supervisors and managers to sacrifice both their own well-being and their firm's profitability for the sake of their subordinates' mental health. At the minimum, we must find job redesign strategies that (a) increase the control given to workers at lower levels in the organization without decreasing the control of those at higher organizational levels, and (b) do not have negative consequences for productivity. Ideally, we would develop job redesign strategies that (a) give greater control to organizational members at all levels and (b) increase productivity.

Conceptualizing Control in New Ways

To date, psychologists have largely ignored the issue of how changing the level of control exercised by employees at one level impacts the feelings of control for employees at higher levels. I suspect we have ignored this issue because we implicitly accept the view that control within an organization is finite. Conceptualizing control as finite implies that giving one group more control (e.g., subordinates) necessarily requires that control be taken away from another group (e.g., their supervisors). Accepting this view of control has clear implications for the types of arguments we are likely to make when trying to convince managers to redesign jobs, roles, and organizations in ways that give their subordinates more control. Because we accept the assumption, we attempt to convince managers that, although giving up their own control may be painful or distressing to them, in the long run it is better for the organization as a whole and for their subordinates in particular. Our approach is equivalent to the following scenario:

> Imagine that you own a large and beautiful shade tree. It is one of the few sources of pleasure in your otherwise dreary existence. You planted the tree 20 years ago; you have nurtured it and taken great pride in watching it grow. One day, you are approached by a member of the community and asked to cut down your tree and give the wood to some of your neighbors, who will use it as a source of energy. You are offered no payment for the wood, but you are assured that your generosity will be good for the community as a whole. You consider the request, but decide to refuse, noting that your neighbors show no obvious signs of serious distress and that you are not convinced your donation would substantially benefit the community as a whole. Instead, you feel certain that cutting down such a beautiful tree would have a negative impact on property values in the neighborhood! A creative solution is needed. How can you have your tree and let the community burn it too?

Consideration of this scenario suggests two reasons why psychologists have been unsuccessful in their attempts to convince managers and supervisors to give more control to their subordinates: (a) we ask people to give up control but offer them nothing in return, and (b) we argue that giving away control will benefit the organization but offer no evidence to document this point. If we are to ever be successful in convincing managers to initiate job and role redesign efforts intended to increase their subordinates' levels of control, we must address these two flaws in our sales pitch.

Correcting the first flaw in our argument will require that we think differently about the concept of control. We need new models of organizational life that disable our tendency to view control as finite and enable us to see ways to give more control to everyone in an organization simultaneously. For the scenario described above, one solution is to realize that judicious pruning of the tree will provide fuel for immediate use, encourage new and thicker growth for future energy needs, and at the same time actually improve the density of shade provided by the tree. If our organizational models enable us to convince managers that, by giving up some of their control over subordinates they would be freed to exert more control over other important aspects of their organizational environment, we might have some hope of effecting the redesign efforts called for by Landy. This is an area where theoretical work is badly needed.

Is Strain the Price of Productivity

Correcting the second flaw in our argument—that is, lack of evidence showing that organizational effectiveness can be improved by increasing the levels of control employees have and/or reducing their experienced strain—is equally important. What empirical evidence, if any, informs us about the relationship between control and performance? Most reviews of the research evidence have not found strong support for the assertion that increased productivity follows interventions intended to increase employees' influence or control in the workplace (Brett & Hammer, 1982; Guzzo, Jette, & Katzell, 1985; Hammer, 1983; Locke & Schweiger, 1979; but also see Berlinger, Glick, & Rodgers, 1988). On the other hand, numerous recent case studies of the experiences of large corporations such as Ford Motor Company (Banas, 1988), Xerox Corporation (Pace & Argona, 1991) and others (see Goodman, Devadas, & Hughson, 1988; Lawler, 1990; Whyte, 1991) reveal that top executives in some major corporations are now convinced that corporate productivity can be improved by giving more control to employees who work at lower levels in their organization. Social scientists often dismiss results reported in case studies of large-scale organizational change efforts, citing methodological problems that make it difficult to draw firm conclusions about cause-and-effect relationships. This is unfortunate because such vivid examples showing how major organizational change efforts can impact productivity are more likely to be convincing to managers than are small-scale, well-controlled experimental conducted in either in a laboratory setting or within an isolated unit of an organization. Furthermore, some researchers have argued that, in comparison to small-scale experiments, case studies such as those of Ford and Xerox actually provide much better scientific evidence about the consequences of introducing control-enhancing change into complex organizational systems (see Whyte, Greenwood, & Lazes, 1991, for an excellent discussion of the issues).

In order to convince employers to give workers greater control, we must convince them that doing so economically benefits their organizations. If we believe that control and strain are causally related, it is imperative that we develop interventions that enhance worker control while simultaneously improving the organizational bottom line. Numerous case studies are now available to instruct us in how to design and implement such interventions. If we reject the evidence from the case studies and ignore the lessons they have to offer, we are unlikely to be able to argue persuasively that control-enhancing interventions are worthwhile, and we are unlikely to be effective in implementing such interventions.

Without evidence that control-enhancing interventions improve productivity, psychologists must argue for such interventions as a means of reducing employee strain. While some people might argue that this objective should be sufficient reason for employees to make major organizational changes, it is difficult to imagine that American firms, which are facing increasingly intense competition and difficult economic conditions, will be willing to place the objective of reducing employee strain above the objective of improving productivity and organizational effectiveness. The problem we face is not simply that the objective of employee stress reduction has lower priority than the objective of productivity improvement.

I have asserted that managers typically assume that any changes they might make to reduce strain their subordinates will also lower productivity. This assumption follows naturally from our everyday experiences. When we are working hard, pushing ourselves to our maximum capacities, we experience feelings of strain and, it seems, we are more productive than usual. Managers are not alone in their assumption that strain is positively associated with productivity; this seems to be an implicit assumption of psychologists, as well.

A complete review of research relating experienced strain to performance levels is beyond the scope of this short commentary. However, it is probably safe to assume that a review of laboratory research on the relationship between experienced strain and performance would show a positive relationship between the two, at least when strain is operationalized as very short-term, the task would be a simple motor task, and quantity of performance would be measured rather than quality of performance. At work, people work on tasks for hours, weeks, and months rather than minutes. The simple motor tasks that many people previously worked at are now being done by machines so people are now doing more complex tasks (Johnson & Packer, 1987). Furthermore, performance quality is being increasingly attended to by American industry. Therefore, the laboratory research on strain and performance may be of questionable relevance to us here.

Some evidence regarding the relationship between strain and performance at work is also available. One review (Jackson & Schuler, 1985) found a weak relationship between objective performance and role strains and a stronger relationship between self-rated performance and role strains. Importantly, the direction of the relationships was negative, however, contradicting the assumption that high stress and high performance go together. For services jobs, where job performance is defined by quality of interpersonal interactions with customers, it seems highly likely that a stronger negative relationship would exist between experience strain and performance. Certainly, theory and research on burnout among human service professionals assumes this view. Jackson and Schuler's (1985) review of the role strain literature offers empirical support for the conclusion that job-related strain is especially detrimental to performance in service jobs.

The point of this brief commentary is simply to encourage psychologists interested in reducing work-related strain to pay more attention to the organizational implications of the interventions they suggest, especially when these interventions involve increasing employee's feelings of control. In particular, we need to (a) develop interventions that increase the control given to lower level employees without decreasing the control experienced by others in the organization, and (b) develop interventions that serve the dual purposes of strain reduction and productivity improvement. The former objective requires us to develop new conceptualizations of the concept of control, and these new conceptualizations must take a systems perspective. The latter objective may be most easily achieved when performance quality is a significant determinant of the organization's productivity and effectiveness. That excellence in product and service quality is now acknowledged as a major strategic objective of American firms, as evidenced by the large financial investments now being made in pursuit of the prestigious Baldrige Award for Quality, is a fact stress researchers may be able to use to their advantage. The increasing number of jobs that involve service provision also provide stress researchers and interventionists with new opportunities to demonstrate the organizational value of reducing employee strain.

References

Banas, P. A. (1988). Employee involvement: A sustained labor/management initiative at the Ford Motor Company. In J. P. Campbell & R. J. Campbell (Eds.), *Productivity in organizations*. San Francisco: Jossey-Bass.

Berlinger, L. R., Glick, W. H., & Rodgers, R. C. (1988). Job enrichment and performance improvement. In J. P. Campbell & R. J. Campbell (Eds.), *Productivity in organizations*. San Francisco: Jossey-Bass.

Brett, J. M., & Hammer, T. H. (1982). Organizational behavior and industrial relations. In T. Kochan, D. Mitchell, & L. Dyer (Eds.), *Industrial relations research in the 1970s: Review and appraisal*. Madison, WI: IRRA.

Goodman, P. S., Devadas, R., & Hughson, T. L. G. (1988). Groups and productivity: Analyzing the effectiveness of self-managing teams. In J. P. Campbell & R. J. Campbell (Eds.), *Productivity in organizations*. San Francisco: Jossey-Bass.

Guzzo, R. A., Jette, R. D., & Katzell, R. A. (1985). The effects of psychologically based intervention programs on worker productivity. *Personnel Psychology, 38*, 275–292.

Hammer, T. H. (183). Worker participation programs: Do they improve productivity? *ILR Report, 21*(1), 15–21.

Jackson, S. E., & Schuler, R. S. (1985). A meta-analysis and conceptual critique of research on role ambiguity and role conflict in work settings. *Organizational Behavior and Human Decision Process, 36*, 16–78.

Johnson, W. B., & Packer, A. E. (1987). *Workforce 2000: Work and workers for the 21st century*. Washington, DC: U.S. Department of Labor.

Lawler, E. E., III (1990, Autumn). The new plant revolution. *Organizational Dynamics, 19*(2), 5–14.

Locke, E. A., & Schweiger, D. M. (1979). Participation in decision making: One more look. In B. M. Staw (Ed.), *Research in organizational behavior: Vol. 1*. Greenwich, CT: JAI Press.

Pace, L. A., & Argona, D. R. (1991). Participatory action research: A view from Xerox. In W. F. Whyte (Ed.), *Participatory action research*. Newbury Park, CA: Sage Publishers, Inc.

Whyte, W. F. (1991). *Participatory action research*. Newbury Park, CA: Sage Publishers, Inc.

Whyte, W. F., Greenwood, D. J., & Lazes, P. (1991). Participatory action research: Through practice to science in social research. In W. F. Whyte (Ed.), *Participatory action research*. Newbury Park, CA: Sage Publishers, Inc.

Panel Comments

Robert L. Kahn

Landy's paper on work design and stress is comprehensive and well documented. In reviewing it, I found much to agree with and little to add. I will, therefore, use my time to do two things: first, attempt some integration of the main points around the concept of organizations as sociotechnical systems, and second, make some specific recommendations for action, both on the part of scholars and of practitioners who cannot wait for more definitive research but must act on the basis of what is now at hand.

Sociotechnics Revisited

The concept of productive organizations as sociotechnical system is almost 40 years old, and it has had a substantial influence on organizational theory and research. The basic idea, of course, is that any productive system includes both a technological organization—layout of equipment and specification of process—and a social organization that specifies individual tasks and the relationships of individuals who perform them. I once proposed to a colleague that we could state the sociotechnical position more succinctly by saying that every organization consists of tools and rules. Current practices in job design led us to consider extending the rhyme to include tools, rules, and fools, but neither of us was cynical enough to carry the verse that far.

The recognition of organizations as having this dual sociotechnical character raises two questions of goodness of fit: fit between the social and technical aspects of the organization, and fit between the resulting sociotechnical structure and the human characteristics of the people who must bring it to life in their daily work. Research in the sociotechnical tradition has addressed these questions by accepting the technology as given and then attempting to discover which of the social-organizational possibilities compatible with this technology was most acceptable to members of the organization.

The earliest work in the British coal mines, for example, compared two socially different ways of using the same then-new mechanized equipment for hewing coal from the mine face. Both methods were in use, and the research compared their effects on productivity, job satisfaction, and relationships among workers (Trist & Bamforth, 1951). Later work in the same tradition was more ambitious; research workers did not limit themselves to comparing organizational arrangements that were already in use; they proposed innovations in the design of jobs, the division of labor, and the nature of supervision. Research then compared the effects of such innovations on worker satisfaction and productivity with the more conventional arrangement (Davis and Cherns, 1975; Rice, 1958; Thorsrud, Sorensen, & Gustavsen, 1976).

This kind of research, important as it is, continues to take the existing technology as its starting point; it accepts the limitations which that technology imposes, and asks how fully the needs of individuals can be met within those technological limits. Cases in which major modifications in existing technologies have been made in order to increase worker well-being are rare, and cases in which wholly new technologies have been developed for that purpose are almost nonexistent. The introduction of an alternative to assemby-line production of automobiles in the Volvo plant at Kalmar (Sweden) during the 1970s generated sustained public interest precisely because it was a unique event: an attempt to invent and adapt technology to the needs of individuals (Aguren, Hansson, & Karlsson, 1976).

Decades of organizational research have documented quite thoroughly the conditions that determine the quality of working life—challenge, variety, autonomy, affiliative bonds, adequate material rewards, and job security (Kahn, 1981). Research on stress at work, well summarized in Landy's paper, has given us the mirror image, or rather the dark side, of these same job characteristics—fragmentation, monotony, powerlessness, isolation, inadequate wages, and pervasive uncertainty. The accumulation of such knowledge is far from complete, but it is sufficient to provide the basis for a new relationship between engineers and social scientists, between those who create the technology with which workers work and those who study the effects of technology on the health and well-being of workers. Collaborative relationships between engineers and social scientists in the design of jobs and technology itself are rare, but they are necessary to launch an era of experiments and demonstrations that will for the first time show us to what extent the goals of consumption and efficiency can be made to converge with those of worker well-being.

Recommendations

In the long run we can hope for a new breed of behavioral scientists/engineers who will bring to the task of job design the full range of expertise that it requires. We must live, however, in the short run, and my recommendations deal with actions that can be taken immediately. There are six of them, three that are based on research already in hand and three that involve research still to be done. They are as follows:

1. *Train people in the combined fields of social psychology and engineering/ergonomics.* This can be done in many ways. Predoctoral and postdoctoral fellowships, for example, can encourage the acquisition of such dual competencies. NIOSH fellowships in a few universities with already strong graduate programs in engineering and social science could start the process.

2. *Create interdisciplinary design teams to develop optimal job designs and organizational arrangements for current and emerging technologies.* These job designs could then serve as models for employing organizations that

utilize such technologies. For example, such job designs might be developed for the clerical uses of VDTs, for computer-assisted manufacturing processes, and the like. Sponsorship and support for interdisciplinary teams to create these designs could come appropriate from government agencies such as NIOSH and the Department of Labor, and from corporate membership associations such as The Conference Board, the American Management Association, and the National Association of Manufacturers.

3. *Develop goals and minimum standards for the psychosocial aspects of jobs.* Many organizations, inside and outside government, can contribute to this process, but it should ultimately be expressed in corporate practice, labor union programs, and the law itself. The missions of NIOSH, the Department of Labor, and the National Institutes of Health are appropriate to the task of developing and proposing such standards, but they have yet to assume it. By doing so they can accomplish for job design what is already done routinely for the toxicological aspects of work.

4. *Conduct field experiments in job design to test the compatibility of specific technologies with the health-enhancing attributes of work.* Such experiments could be considered replications of earlier studies in the sociotechnical tradition, but they are needed in connection with new technological developments. Universities and major corporations are the obvious agents for such research; foundations and government are the most likely sources of support.

5. *Get the results of such experiments into the mainstream of employing organizations.* This is perhaps the most difficult of my recommendations to carry out, and it points to the area of greatest failure thus far: Research findings and even successful experiments in job design and organization have not transformed managerial practice. If they are to do so, much as time and motion study did in an earlier generation and computer technology is doing now, a sustained effort at dissemination and management education will be required. Schools of business administration, professional societies, and government agencies—perhaps especially NIOSH and the Department of Labor—are vehicles of choice.

    More than effort is required, however. We need to understand the factors that facilitate or impede dissemination and research utilization, so that future effort can be more successful than past attempts. We need, therefore, to do research on the process of dissemination and organizational change itself, and that research should be specific to the domain of job design.

6. *Search for stress moderators.* All stress cannot be eliminated from working life, or from life in general for that matter. Along with the effort to reduce the incidence and intensity of stress, therefore, we need research to identify factors that intervene between the stressors and its effect on well-being, and that may act as buffers or moderators of stress.

Research workers who are interested in the possibility of such stress-buffering factors have been so captivated by one of them—social support—that they have given little attention to discovering others. Robert Sutton and I (1987) have suggested prediction, understanding, and control as stress moderators worthy of investigation, and others almost certainly await the attention of researchers.

When APA and NIOSH next convene a group to consider the state of work and health in the United States, I propose that we assess progress along the six lines that I have just described. Let us hope that it will be substantial.

References

Aguren, S., Hansson, R., & Karlsson, K. G. (1976). *The impact of new design on work organization.* Stockholm: The Rationalization Council (SAF-LO).

Davis, L. E., & Cherns, A. B. (1975). *The quality of working life* (Vols. 1–2). New York: Free Press.

Kahn, R. L. (1981). *Work and health.* New York: Wiley.

Rice, A. K. (1958). *Productivity and social organization: The Ahmedabad experiment.* London: Tavistock Publications.

Sutton, R. I., & Kahn, R. L. (1987). Prediction, understanding, and control as antidotes to organizational stress. In J. W. Lorsch (Ed.), *Handbook of organizational behavior.* Englewood Cliffs, NJ: Prentice Hall.

Thorsrud, E., Sorensen, B. S., & Gustavsen, B. (1976). Sociotechnical approach to industrial democracy in Norway. In R. Dubin (Ed.), *Handbook of work organization, and society.* Chicago: Rand McNally.

Trist, E. L., & Bamforth, K. W. (1951). Some social and psychological consequences of the long-wall method of coal-getting. *Human Relations, 4,* 3–38.

Panel Comments

David LeGrande

In 1986, NIOSH sponsored a symposium for the purpose of developing a national strategy for the prevention of psychological disorders. Inadequate funding for scientific research and direction have prevented the National Strategy from being implemented. The Communication Workers of America (CSA) is pleased that the *Work and Well-Being* Conference was conducted and we hope that all involved parties—labor, management, academia, and government—approached the conference with the commitment of not only pursuing and furthering the goals developed during the 1986 Symposium, but truly making psychological disorders an agenda item high on its collective priority list.

It strikes me that in order for the work design panel to assist in this process, it should:

- Emphasize the social and economic needs of further developing and implementing a national strategy on psychological disorders;
- Emphasize the social and economic costs of not further developing and implementing a national strategy on psychological disorders;
- Borrowing from the National Strategy formulated in 1986, the focus of this panel should be primarily upon psychosocial factors (i.e., variables specific to the social work environment, work organization, and job design). Work organization should be the point from which this work initiates. Included within the topic of work organizations are variables such as work pace, workload, monitoring, job security or uncertainty, training, and managerial style. This direction allows for adherence to a systems approach (as suggested by the 1986 Symposium).

It is imperative that such work investigate both psychological and physical health symptoms and their interrelationship specific to psychological disorders/occupational stress.

This work should also contain both research and implementation components. In instances where valid research has been conducted, intervention strategies need to be developed and implemented in an expeditious manner. Future research and intervention activities must involve participation by labor, management, academia, and government. NIOSH must take the lead in establishing agreed upon research and intervention activities. The Agency's carrying out of this role is essential if our parallel concerns are to be achieved.

Panel Comments

Gavriel Salvendy

In order to effectively achieve the objectives of the joint APA/NIOSH *Work and Well-Being* Conference it is recommended that the following actions be initiated:

1. *Create adaptive job designs.* Since individuals' preferences, likes and dislikes regarding the nature of the job which they like to perform varies, it is recommended that an advanced research and development study be undertaken which will result in the viability of having an adaptive job design for computerized work. In this design mode the software would be adapted to accommodate both differences which exist between people and the differences which exist within people over a period of time. In order to fully benefit from the utilization of an adaptive interface a flexible organizational design will need to be adopted.
2. *Make job designers slaves to technology.* Individuals engaged in the design of jobs take the availability of technology for granted. Yet, it is those who design jobs who should know best what new technologies ought to be developed in order to increase the effectiveness of jobs. Therefore, job designers should push the technology.
3. *Use systems approachs to optimize job design.* The emphasis to merely optimize or minimize stress in job design is inappropriate because that may have significant negative ramifications on productivity and international competitiveness. Therefore job designers should consider all variables including job satisfaction, job productivity, and job evaluation issues as part of the overall systems approach to optimizing job design, and not merely concentrating on the stress variables.
4. *Involve industrial and organizational psychologists.* Industrial and organizational psychologists responsible for job design should have some training in engineering and technology for which they design jobs. Since job design is a social/technical operation, it stands to reason that those who design jobs would be knowledgeable not only about the social but also about the technical aspects of jobs.

Panel Comments

Fred Schott

I approach the issue of stress and work design as an information technology (IT) professional concerned with the impact of IT on the people who use it to achieve business results. I've found the following conceptual framework (derived from Bikson, 1987) to be helpful.

In this framework, outcomes of interactions between people and their work environment are basically a function of the level of demands in relation to relevant resources at hand, given a baseline performance level. People can operate in the "comfort zone" when demands and resources are pretty much in balance. Over time, as part of a developmental process, people can boost their baseline performance

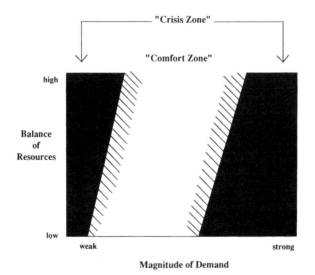

Figure 2. Framework for Conceptualizing Adaptation to Computer-Mediated Work.

Note. From "Social, Ergonomic, and Stress Aspects of Work With Computers" by S. L. Sauter and J. J. Hurrell, Jr., in G. Salvendy, S. L. Sauter, and J. J. Hurrell, Jr. (Eds.), *Advances in Human Factors/Ergonomics, 10A,* 1987, p. 354, Elsevier Science Publishers: The Netherlands. Copyright 1987 by Elsevier Science Publishers. Reprinted by permission.

I would like to acknowledge the following Aetna colleagues whose insights and comments have been helpful in preparing this paper: Dr. Joseph Eker and other members of the Aetna Employee Health Services staff, Laura Bennett, Nancy Conlan, Carol Sullivan, Rick Telesca, Donna Way, and last but far from least Emmett McTeague. The views in this paper are my own and should not be construed as a statement of Aetna Life and Casualty corporate policy.

level and consequently broaden the comfort zone. When there's a serious discrepancy between demands and resources, however, people find themselves thrown into the "crisis zone." Standard ways of working just will not do, and people have to go into problem-solving mode to find a way out. One of two things can happen: They can master the situation (with the result being positive affect and a boost in performance level) or they can fail to do so (with the result being impaired performance and negative affect, or strain).

For me, there are three key points here: First, people are capable of adapting to changing circumstances. Their comfort zone can be broadened. Second, significant imbalances between demand and resources (crises) are not necessarily things to be avoided at all costs. The Chinese have the right idea here: The ideogram they use to represent crisis is a composite of the ideograms for "opportunity" and "danger." When faced with crisis, we always want to maximize the opportunity and minimize the danger. That leads to the third key point, namely that strain is the result of *failure* to deal with stressors, and not the inevitable reaction to them.

Given this perspective on stress, I believe the objective of work design should be to create an environment that empowers workers, enabling them to deal with and master the varied and often unpredictable challenges that come their way, so that they can help achieve the mission of the organization to which they belong.

Production Versus Productive Capacity

Probably the most serious disagreement I have with the conference paper is in the section on supervisors and managers as they figure in the social fabric of work. There, the paper asserts that supervisors have limited appreciation for the importance of considerate and supportive interactions with their subordinates. Why? "This is, in part, the result of a concentration on productivity and output rather than worker well-being. It is clear that unhappy workers can still be productive and that happy workers can be unproductive. As a result, there is a tendency on the part of supervisors to see consideration and support as simply a reward or bonus that might be afforded workers" (p. 133). I think the paper is off the mark here.

What's missing here is an appreciation of the idea of "productive capacity" (Covey, 1983). To illustrate what's meant by productive capacity, it's helpful to draw an analogy. Let's say I run a delivery service. My minivan is a critical resource. I want it to be as productive as possible, so I keep it on the road as often as possible. I cannot bear the thought of unproductive downtime, so I do not bother with changing the oil, or rotating the tires, or doing a tune-up, or getting a brake job, or any of those other unproductive maintenance chores. I'm certainly maximizing the production I get out of my minivan, but I'm destroying its productive capacity. Before you know it, I'll be getting poor gas mileage, the front tires will be bald, and eventually the engine will die on me (preferably before I step on the brakes only to find they will not work anymore). I certainly will not be able to meet my organizational mission then, despite my effort to maximize resource productivity.

I submit it's no different with human resources. Managers who neglect the productive capacity of the people they support (their so-called "subordinates") will fail to achieve the organization's mission. In the long run, unhappy workers—people who are not committed to the success of their organization, who are not equipped to deal with the challenges they face in the course of their work—are never productive workers. There has been a steady stream of columns and feature stories with this theme in the business press the last few years—clear testimony to the fact that the American business community, having undergone its own form of perestroika, now realizes the importance of productive capacity.

The Importance and Value of a Sociotechnical Systems Approach

I fully agree with the paper's broad definition of what's involved in work design and with its endorsement of the sociotechnical systems (STS) approach. STS is a *purpose-oriented* approach to work design (Taylor, 1987). In contrast to a problem-oriented approach (which is concerned with solving a particular problem such as high production costs or poor delivery time) or a solution-oriented approach (which seeks to implement a particular technique such as quality circles or self-managing teams), a purpose-oriented approach starts with a definition of the organization's mission or purpose and then designs organizational structures, management systems, workflow, and technology to achieve that mission. A focus on purpose or mission can do much to reduce strain resulting from role ambiguity, role conflict, and uncertainty.

Let me illustrate how a purpose-oriented approach works by describing the Aetna Management Process (AMP). Aetna's president, Ron Compton, introduced AMP about 2 years ago with the intent of providing managers with a systematic way of thinking to facilitate sound decision making. It is currently being used at all levels of the company, from the individual contributor all the way to the president, and appears to be taking hold as part of the company culture. Indeed, a new verb has entered Aetna people's vocabulary: One of the first things we do when starting a new project is AMP it, that is, apply the seven steps of the Aetna Management Process. Those steps are as follows:

1. *Identify your mission.* This is a statement of purpose for whoever (an individual, a task force or project team, a department, a strategic business unit) is "AMPing." A mission statement has to define precisely *what* is to be done, *for whom*, and *to what end*. We have found that getting clarity on these three elements (what, for whom, to what end) can avoid significant problems with role ambiguity or role conflict further on down the line. For example, by asking "For whom?" you may find that your real customer may not be the one you always assumed it was, or you may find that you have multiple customers each of whom may need different treatment. By asking "To what end?" you begin the process of defining measures of success that are truly relevant and meaningful. You may even find you cannot answer the question, in which case you may need to ask yourself whether you should even be doing whatever it is you're doing or planning to do.

2. *Identify critical success factors.* Once the mission has been defined, the next step is to ask two questions: What must go right in order to accomplish the mission? What, if it went wrong, would jeopardize or even destroy the mission? The answers to these questions are called critical success factors (CSFs). There usually are about three to five CSFs for any mission. CSFs provide people with a screening mechanism, a way of focusing on what's truly important.

3. *Scan and describe the environment.* The third AMP step involves a scan of the external and internal environments for conditions that affect, or could affect, one or more CSFs. This sets the stage for the fourth step.

4. *Identify gaps.* Gaps are differences between the way things are, given the environment in which you operate, and the way things must be in order to achieve CSFs. Once identified, gaps need to be closed. Hence the next AMP step.

5. *Set objectives.* In the AMP framework, objectives must be well-stated. They must be specific and results-oriented, measurable, time-bound, and must identify people who are responsible for them. Clearly stated objectives reduce the likelihood of role conflict or role ambiguity. When you are trained in the use of AMP, you also learn the importance of setting objectives that are achievable and based on a realistic assessment of the environment; that allow room for change if unexpected threats or opportunities arise; that are sufficiently challenging so as to stretch performance capabilities but not out of reach; and that are set with the active participation of those responsible for achieving them. These considerations for setting objectives get at the issues of control and balance and demands and resources that are central to the discussion of stress and stain in the work environment.

6. *Develop action steps and implement.* Action plans should clearly specify responsibilities, milestones, target dates, resource requirements, and possible obstacles.

7. *Monitor performance.* This is the final AMP step. Significantly, the AMP framework itself generates the monitoring plan. That is, monitoring is done in terms of action steps that relate to specific objectives that have been set to close gaps that have been identified as a result of environmental scans done with respect to critical success factors for the mission, or basic purpose of the individual or organization. A performance monitoring system that is the result of a properly done AMP is much more likely to be seen as fair than one that is not.

As I mentioned earlier, AMP appears to be taking hold in the Aetna culture. Managers and supervisors are evaluated on the basis of a number of managerial "competencies." One of these competencies is direction-setting and the use of AMP.

In addition to providing a means for reducing the possibility of role ambiguity or role conflict, a process like AMP also provides a powerful tool for dealing with uncertainty. I may not know whether my competitors are going to roll out a new service, or what kind of standards government regulators will require me to meet, or who my new manager will be. I may not know how all these things will impact me. But if I know what I need to accomplish and what's critical to my success in accomplishing it, the uncertainty is much more manageable. The AMP or AMP-like process provides me a framework for problem-solving and mastery.

One final comment on this particular topic: The AMP process provides a general framework for doing purpose-oriented sociotechnical systems design, but it's not enough. There's still a need for a detailed systems engineering methodology within that framework. The methodology has to address simultaneous design of the social system and the technical system. Case studies of the STS approach will be very helpful, but if the STS approach is to be widespread system designers need to know *how* they can do it. There's some good, high-level guidance available on how to do STS design (cf. Berniker, 1983; Mumford, 1983; Pava, 1983). The next step is to translate it into pragmatic tools and techniques that system designers can apply in their daily work.

Dealing With Cognitive Press in Computer-Mediated Work

As the conference paper points out, we are seeing a broad shift to an information-based economy and workplace. Computers and communications technology are both enabling and driving this shift. Needless to say, over the course of the rest of this decade a significant portion, if not the majority, of the United States workforce will find itself engaged in some form of computer-mediated work.

Work in the electronic office is highly cognitive in nature. Physical objects such as documents or file folders disappear and are replaced by abstract representations on the computer's visual display screen. Shoshana Zuboff (1988) has described in considerable detail the cognitive demands that work in the electronic office makes on the people who perform it. These demands, which can be characterized as cognitive press, have been shown to be incremental, cumulative, and continuous (Bikson, 1987). I believe it's important, from a stress research and a stress intervention perspective, to pay more attention to this phenomenon. It's been my experience that cognitive press is best dealt with in a two-pronged manner: First, by incorporating usability engineering into the software development cycle and second, by providing ongoing training and support in the use of computer-based tools to get work done.

Software usability engineering is the discipline of creating computer applications that fit the tasks, personal characteristics, and working environment of the people who must use them. The emphasis is on meeting specific usability objectives such as learning time, task completion time, error rates, user satisfaction rating, or retention of knowledge over time. It is, in effect, software or cognitive ergonomics. It emphasizes use of design guidelines grounded in appropriate research and experience, iterative testing and refinement using prototypes, and most importantly active participation in the design, development, and testing process of the actual users of the software. Usability engineering has become a major element of the software development process for a growing number of organizations, my own among them.

The usability engineering process keeps users as the primary focus of the software development effort. Thus, the user interface is the main object of interest. There are three levels to the user interface: The first is what defines how the application "looks" to the user (i.e., graphics, screen layout, icons shapes, use of color, typography, etc.). The second is what defines how the application "feels" to the user (i.e., use of pull-down or pop-up menus, conventions for moving or copying objects on the screen, command syntax, etc.). The third, and from the perspective of cognitive press probably the most important, is the user's conceptual model. This can be defined as a "grammar of action-object relationships" (Rosenberg, 1989) that establishes the relationship between the abstract concepts presented by the software and the user's business tasks.

The usability engineering challenge with respect to the user's conceptual model is two-fold: First, the software must be designed so that this grammar is readily evident and easily learned. An effective way of doing this is incorporating metaphors into the software. The Apple Macintosh desktop metaphor is the most familiar example, but by no means the only one. Second, there must be congruence between the conceptual model embedded in the software and the conceptual model associated with the task domain. Bill Liddle, an alumnus of the Xerox Palo Alto Research Center (where many of the concepts subsequently incorporated into the Apple Macintosh interface were first developed), suggests this may be one of the most important—and most neglected—aspects of the user interface: "The user must not go through a Jekyll-and-Hyde cycle of switching from the concepts of the job to the concepts of computing and back again. Alternating between unrelated and mutually interfering tasks produces a conflict, debilitating to the mind and spirit, that causes the suffering user to shorten the creative application of the software" (Liddle, 1988). Specific design rules to guide software developers' efforts in this area are sparse (at least in comparison to other aspects of the user interface; see for example Rubinstein & Hersh, 1984), but I believe that as interest in this issue grows over the next few years the body of knowledge about specific techniques for creating congruent conceptual models will grow substantially.

There are a number of other ways application of usability engineering can help deal with cognitive press. One of these is the design of customizable software. For example, the Apple Macintosh has a "control panel" where users can set such system features as the mouse tracking and clicking rate, the background pattern of the "desktop," or the audio cue for special alert situations. "Task integrator" software such as Hewlett-Packard's NewWave allows users to define entire operation sequences, assign them to an icon, and then initiate them by clicking on the icon. Approaches such as this not only securely place the locus of control with the user, and not the software, but they also serve to reduce the level of cognitive demand being placed on users.

Forward-thinking computer scientists have recognized the stress implications of software user interface design (see for example Shneiderman, 1986). I urge stress researchers to work more closely with the computer science community so as to enrich the body of knowledge on how to address cognitive stress and press in the electronic office.

Good software design is a necessary but not sufficient condition for dealing with cognitive demands of computer-mediated work. Education in competent use of information technology to do work is also required. Increasingly, competence and mastery in the emerging information workplace depend on what has been referred to as "intellective skill" (Zuboff, 1988). Intellective skill has three components: the ability to think abstractly, inductive reasoning, and a theoretical conception of the process to which data refer. People who do not have this skill will quickly feel lost and are likely to experience strain. Needless to say, if we are to make recommendations about work design and stress, one of them would have to be that a substantial part of the training that workers receive in the use of computer technology should be devoted to the development of intellective skill.

How does one go about developing intellective skill? I do not have a ready answer, but I think an excellent starting point has been defined by Gloria Schuck

(1985). Schuck talks about the need to move from training information workers in objects and actions (i.e., what buttons to push) to enabling them to deal with the "field of meaning" through exercise of higher-order cognitive skills. Two of the most important conditions for this different kind of learning are play (any behavior that liberates a person from constraints of objects and actions and allows him or her to create, examine, or redefine meanings) and social mediation (where people learn through interactions with and assistance from other people). These conditions can be brought about through a "pedagogy of meaning," which Schuck says is not a single course or series of training but instead involves a reconceptualization of the workplace as a learning environment and a redefinition of the role of the manager in the learning process.

Other Comments

I have a few other comments to make about secondary (at least to me) points raised in the conference paper.

Other Challenges of the New Information-Based Service Economy

I agree with the paper's conclusion that we need to know much more about the active ingredients of burnout, especially in light of the emergency of a service economy. One service guru has talked about how successful customer service entails making a "bear any burden, pay any price" commitment to the customer (Zemke, 1989). At what point does the burden become too heavy or the price too high?

I agree that we need to know a lot more about time urgency, especially in the communications infrastructure of work. We're seeing the emergency of what can be called "acceleration syndrome"—the tendency to do things faster and faster. What does this do to people's ability to deliberate and make sense of things? (Weick, 1985).

I believe we need to know more about the effects of "telecommuting," specifically in terms of people's abilities to "compartmentalize" their lives. When people can stay in touch with the office from home, when they can do much of their work at home, the boundary between personal and work life becomes fuzzy. This can be a positive development (more flexibility, greater degree of personal commitment to work), but it also has a dark side (intrusiveness, disruption of family relationships). We need to understand the dark side better.

Employees' Perceptions and Beliefs Regarding Workplace Health and Safety

I agree this is an important issue. Concern that working conditions may not be healthy or safe can certainly be a stressor, regardles of whether the concern is founded in fact or in belief. Good managers should take employee fears and concerns seriously and respond to them openly and honestly.

My experience is that, at least in the context of a computerized office, health and safety concerns are often a "lightning rod" for other concerns having to do with the way change is introduced, how quickly it's introduced, and the underlying climate of trust in the office. People often feel it's not legitimate to express concerns about these kinds of things (they'll be viewed as chronic complainers), whereas it is acceptable to raise health and safety concerns. Good managers will probe to see if any of these factors are behind health and safety complaints and will deal with them accordingly.

Trust is a key issue here. Mangers can go out of their way to deal with health and safety concerns, but if workers do not trust them, their efforts will not get very far. Unfortunately, I think that overly sensational media accounts of health and safety issues may have made is difficult to maintain a climate of trust. After a while, the fashionable "cover-up" charges of some health and safety exposé journalism become so deeply rooted in some workers' consciousness that they'll discount what managers are telling them, even if it's the truth.

Linking Pay to Performance

The conference paper pretty much recommends against piece work payment plans. I can understand the rationale behind this position. I'm concerned, however, that this could lead to throwing out the baby with the bath water (i.e., attacking any attempts at linking pay to performance).

People want to do work that is central to the mission of the organization (Taylor, 1987). What better way of demonstrating centrality than by linking pay with performance? The issue here, I think, is not the link per se but rather the appropriateness of the performance measures. As I mentioned earlier in my discussion of the Aetna Management Process, if performance monitoring is done in accordance with a purpose-oriented process and is based on measures that relate to what is truly important for achievement of the organization's mission, the likelihood of strain will be minimized.

References

Berniker, E. (1983). Sociotechnical systems design: A glossary of terms. *American Productivity Center Productivity Brief, 25.*

Bikson, T. (1987). Cognitive press in computer-mediated work. In G. Salvendy & J. Hurrell (Eds.), *Social, ergonomic and stress aspects of work with computers* (pp. 353–365). Amsterdam: Elsevier Science Publishers.

Covey, S. (1983). Seven basic habits of highly effective people. Address to general meeting of Profit Oriented Systems Planning Programs, Inc., San Diego, CA.

Liddle, W. (1988). Challenge of the real world: How graphical user interfaces should be designed. *MacWeek,* December 6.

Mumford, E. (1983). *Designing human systems for new technology: The ETHICS method.* Manchester UK: Manchester Business School.

Pava, C. (1983). *Managing new office technology: An organizational strategy.* New York: Free Press.

Rosenberg, D. (1989). A cost benefit analysis for corporate user interfaces standards: What price to pay for a consistent "look and feel"? In J. Nielsen (Ed.), *Coordinating user interfaces for consistency* (pp. 21–34). San Diego, CA: Academic Press.

Rubinstein, R., & Hersh, H. (1984). *The human factor: Designing computer systems for people.* Burlington, MA: Digital Press.

Schuck, G. (1985). Intelligent technology, intelligent workers: A new pedagogy for the high-tech work-place. *Organizational Dynamics, 14*(2), 66–79.

Shneiderman, B. (1986). Seven plus or minus two central issues in human-computer interaction. In M. Mankei & P. Orbeton (Eds.), *Human factors in computing systems III: Proceedings of the CHI '86 Conference held Boston, MA, USA, 13–17 April 1986.* Amsterdam: North-Holland.

Taylor, J. (1987). Job design and quality of working life. In R. Kraut (Ed.), *Technology and the transformation of white-collar work* (pp. 211–235). Hillsdale, NJ: Lawrence Erlbaum Associates.

Weick, K. (1985). Cosmos versus chaos: Sense and nonsense in electronic contexts. *Organizational Dynamics, 14*(2), 51–64.

Zemke, R. (1989). Address to Aetna Executive Information Systems Conference, Sturbridge, MA.

Zuboff, S. (1988). *In the age of the smart machine: The future of work and power.* New York: Basic Books.

Panel Comments

Leon J. Warshaw

The following comments will address items that have been mentioned or alluded to in Landy's paper but which, at least in my view, deserve greater emphasis. The first, generally understood by stress researchers but which, nevertheless, always needs to be stated explicitly, is that the reactions to stressors which we have dubbed "strains" often act as stressors in their own right; and they may remain active long after the original stressors have been removed or controlled. Further, strained workers are often a stressor to coworkers and supervisors. This leads to the observation that treatment for workers suffering from strain may be considered "primary" prevention for their coworkers.

Second, while some strains are produced by particular stressors (e.g., ocular complaints produced by poor legibility, glare, etc.), they are nonspecific for the most part. They reflect an imbalance between the cumulative effects of stressors on and off the job and the individual's capacity to cope with them. Individuals may vary in their tolerance for particular stressors. In fact, in some cases, individuals beset by personal, off-the-job problems may find work therapeutic despite job-related stressors that may be troublesome to others.

These points are emphasized for two reasons. The first is to emphasize the complexity of stress as a continuing interplay among a group of moving variables. The second is to note that strains can be prevented by controlling stressors and/or enhancing coping mechanisms.

In alluding to the "phenomenon of corporate structuring," Landy's paper does not indicate either its frequency or its power as a stressor. For example, 68% of the companies responding to a nationwide survey of stress in the workplace conducted by the Gallup Organization for the New York Business Group on Health said there had been layoffs or talks of layoffs within the past year. Forty-one percent said there had been a plant or office closing.[2] Downsizing has become virtually a standard feature of American industry. Prior studies have demonstrated job loss and, even more, fear of job loss to be among the most potent work-related stressors. Downsizing is stressful also to those workers who remain and must maintain acceptable levels of productivity within an organization that usually has been disrupted and demoralized. Much of the difficulty can be obviated by proper handling of these situations.

In considering the psychological architecture of work, the paper focuses on tasks, jobs and the administrative and organizational environment in which they are carried out. For many, this architecture is complicated by the fact that their jobs

---

[2] Warshaw, L. J. (1989). *Stress, anxiety, and depression in the workplace: Report of the NYBGH/Gallup Survey*. New York: The New York Business Group on Health, Inc.

deal with people rather than things (e.g., sales persons, police officers, nurses, etc.). Perhaps the best example might be the urban bus driver who must meet the schedule and the monitoring of roving supervisors while driving the unwieldy vehicle through traffic, dealing with the riding public, and training bladder function to conform to rest stops.

Although not usually perceived as a part of work design, one of the more troublesome stressors for many workers is commuting to and from the job. Modifying the work schedule to minimize this burden will often prevent strain. A similar stressor is the requirement in many jobs for extensive travel away from home. This not only brings into play such stressors as jet lag and the inconvenience of travel but also the stressors of lack of familial and social support.

One dispositional characteristic worthy of mention is the individual who manifests little or no strain despite high levels of potent stressors. Whether they represent inherent personality characteristics, examples of job selection representing "one person's meat is another's poison," or "hardening" through acquired coping techniques is a question that calls for research.

A number of areas call for additional research:

- *Sleep disturbances*—these may be intrinsic or the consequence of disurpted circadian rhythms as in frequent shift changes or long distance travel across time zones. In either case, they may interfere with well-being and job performance and make ordinary tasks inordinately stressful.
- *Therapeutic value of work*—the therapeutic value of work is well documented in rehabilitation following serious illness or injury and less well studied in the relief of emotional/behavioral/psychosocial problems. Designing work to meet such needs is an area for study.
- *Adaptation to work*—inadequate educational background and lack of training in basic work discipline characterize too many young people entering the work force and are not only stressors to them and their supervisors but are frequently responsible for failure on the job. Development of improved elements of work design and supervisory training is needed along with adequate career counseling and proper placement.
- *Small organizations*—most stress research is conducted in large organizations where sophistication and expertise in personnel management, training, and support services are available. Yet, most of the working population is employed in small organizations where resource constraints and more informal, often ad hoc, approaches influence attempts to modify work design. The applicability of many of the solutions proposed for large organizations remains to be explored.
- *Executive stress*—in addition to such issues as "who bells the cat," the techniques of modifying the work patterns of executives call for research beyond the often self-serving pronouncements of writers of articles for business magazines.

Summary of Chair's Comments

Frank J. Landy

The conference paper was written with the assistance of the panel members. Their charge was to examine various drafts and save the chair from looking foolish. Nevertheless, they were not expected to be intellectually subordinate to the chair. As a result, they were invited to present individual comments on the main conference paper. These comments were to be critical, where appropriate, and elaborative, where appropriate. In the preceding section, you have had an opportunity to see those comments. As you would expect, many of their comments strike a responsive chord (as they should since they were stimulated by the conference paper). Nevertheless, there are some (few) areas that might benefit from additional comment by the chair. For the most part, these additional comments from the chair represent an opportunity to emphasize certain points rather than to disagree with them. Since the panel papers were not intended to flow together in any consistent manner, they cannot be easily combined. As a result, the comments that I will make will be topical and associated with particular panel members. Because this paper is already so long, I have tried to limit my additional comments. This should not be taken as dismissive of the panelist comments that I do not address. On the contrary, this means that there is nothing further that needs to be added. I will address the panelists' comments in alphabetical order. It should be noted that several panelists chose not to submit written comments so they are not represented in this section.

Mirian Graddick makes a strong argument for the consideration of global issues in the examination of sources of strain for managers. This is understandable given the organizational and functional unit that she represents. Nevertheless, this is not a major issue for the average American worker (or manager). Thus, I am not sure that the issue is a prominent one in a national agenda that attempts to increase well-being through work. For those organizations who do compete in this global arena, Graddick's insights are useful. In particular, she suggests that what is needed as a resource (or buffer) is not necessarily deep technical knowledge on the part of the manager but rather flexibility, adaptability, and general process (e.g., language) skills. These are capabilities that have been at the heart of multinational human resource success for a long time. It is useful to see the ability issue tied to stress and strain, however.

Susan Jackson makes an interesting point with respect to organizational politics. She is somewhat more forgiving than I might be. She suggests that we need to change the attitudes of managers toward the sharing of information and control. In some senses, Susan's manager is portrayed as somewhat rigid and out of touch. My experience with some managers is at odds with this view. It is my impression that managers can use uncertainty as a weapon in the battle for control. The less the subordinates know, the more powerful the manager is. Simply stating that managers covet power does not do justice to the intricacies of many of the strategies by which managers control information and consolidate this power. This is truly the dark side of organizational reality but we need to know a great deal more about it. To me, it is the elephant in the room with respect to the management of uncertainty.

Another point that Susan makes is worth repeating. Behavioral scientists know precious little about the reactions of managers to sharing power, perceptions of control in participative decision making environments, and so forth. As an example, a recent study conducted in Sweden (Sandin, 1990) in a wood processing plant demonstrated that increases in participative decision making led to decreases in perceived autonomy for operators who had primary responsibility for process decisions. In other words, the process operators did not *like* sharing the decisions with others and felt less competent as a result of that sharing. These were not managers, these were operational people! It is naive to think that the social system that we are considering is not affected by such perturbations in power and control distribution.

Robert Kahn's comments match nicely with those of Gavriel Salvendy in one important respect. They both note that in the consideration of sociotechnical systems, there has been a tendency to think of the technology as given or constant. Instead, they urge us to start thinking of both the social and the technical systems not as constants but as variables and amenable to change. As Gavriel points out, however, this may not occur until social scientists begin to develop a better appreciation of design principles. Many if not most industrial engineering students now take basic courses in behavioral sciences. It is not true, however, that most students interested in industrial psychology take courses in engineering design.

Although Robert Kahn's experience and insight into the Swedish system are substantial and stretch back over more than two decades, I must take exception to the unqualified acceptance of the Swedish experiments of Volvo and Saab. The reality is that much of the work in the auto factories has become routine once again: Actual cycle time is short and skills are limited in the workers. The only difference is that the workers have created this unenlightened system all on their own rather than having it superimposed by management. They have formed subgroups, each of which does a piece of the work using a particular skill set. Thus, the promise of "bigger" work and increased skill sets has not been realized to the extent that we would be led to believe by the popular press. It really is time to take a hard look at the 2-decade Swedish initiative and separate the good from the bad. Many aspects of worker alienation remain untouched. Absenteeism and satisfaction changes are variable and seem to depend on constructs beyond work design. There is no doubt that the Swedish experiment was a bold one and that there is much to be learned from it but there are also some less than desirable outcomes.

Finally, Kahn seems to be calling for regulations in his request for minimum sociotechnical standards for jobs. I am not sure that the regulatory context is conducive to careful and illuminating research. By imposing regulations precipitously, we may deny ourselves the opportunity to identify critical variables in the stress-strain relationship. This is the essence of the arguments for and against action research. I realize that as an impatient activist, Kahn is reluctant to permit aversive conditions to persist at work. My concern is that we be clear with respect to what needs regulation before we start down that slippery slope.

Fred Schott takes issue with the comments in the conference paper related to supportive behavior on the part of managers and supervisors and makes a distinction between production and productive capacity. This is not a distinction with which I disagree. In fact, he seems to be making the same point as was made in the body of the main paper—that it is dumb for managers and supervisors to ignore this critical aspect of the psychosocial environment. Nevertheless, they do! Constantly! They see considerate behavior as a form of reward rather than a necessary condition for certain outcomes. I agree with Schott that there has been a "steady stream" of pieces in the popular press pointing out the value of supervisor consideration. But it does not seem that the right folks are reading these pieces. Supervisors are not changing as rapidly as one might like. The fact is that many managers see subordinates not as valuable resources to be developed but as tools to be used and discarded when they do not work the way they should. It is simply Taylorism in fast forward.

Leon Warshaw makes an interesting point about the reduction of primary and secondary strain. He argues that we need to be more aware of the secondary affect of worker strain—it creates a potential stressor for fellow workers. This is a wholly unexplored area. It would be useful to know more about the effect of the strain experienced by one person on those around that person. It is clear that the impact is substantial in the nuclear family. It is likely that the impact is equally substantial on fellow workers.

Warshaw also makes the valuable point that we need to keep in mind that the effects of stressors are likely to be cumulative rather than stressor-specific. It is likely that each new stressor uses up a portion of a psychological safety margin and that the strain we examine is not just the result of the most recent exposure to a stressor but represents the cumulative effect of repeated exposures to many stressors. The model for examining this notion of cumulative effects is a traditional one in human factors research (e.g., Landy, 1989) and should be prominent in design and analysis of stress studies.

Finally, Warshaw emphasizes the importance of the fear of job loss in workers. This has been noted repeatedly by behavioral scientists over most of the 20th century. Whiting Williams identified this as a critical issue as early as 1920; Henrik DeMan repeated this insight again in 1930. More recently, people like Maurer and Warr have pointed out the impact of job loss on psychological well-being. Work is a central defining parameter for most people. The threat of job loss is a substantial one. We must help workers to cope more effectively with this threat.

References

Sandin, P. (1990). *Work in the control room.* Stockholm, Sweden: Department of Psychology.

Summary of Audience Comments

Neal Schmitt

The discussion of Landy's paper on "Work Design and Stress" was animated and the period of time allowed for discussion did not allow all individuals to express their reactions. Reactions to much of what was said in the paper were positive; the remarks I summarize below were almost all from individuals who felt that a particular viewpoint already expressed in the Landy paper should receive more emphasis. I have arranged comments by topic but in no particular order. I also hope that I have not distorted the intent of any of the participants.

One participant suggested that more attention should be devoted to the fact that there has been an increasing involvement of women in paid work roles. This change has brought about (or has the potential to influence) a number of other changes that can increase or decrease work-related stress. Women in paid work roles force organizations to consider and make adjustments to family responsibilities and concerns that impact and are influenced by work responsibilities. One outcome of this increased concern is that men may also be freer to express nonwork or family concerns and to expect some relief whereas in the past men were not expected to allow family concerns to impinge on work. Second, the increased involvement of women in work roles and the increased emphasis on the role of teams in organizations suggests that organizations and researchers should pay more attention to the effects of team composition (gender and ethnic diversity) on work performance and stress. Third, it was felt that some research activity should be devoted to how supervisor and coworker reactions to the need for flexible work schedules (because of family-related concerns) influence the use of those scheduling opportunities and the effects on the individual who takes these opportunities. Finally, there should be greater attention to worker needs for autonomy and control over their work schedules to allow for family responsibilities.

The audience in general felt that the emphasis on worker participation in decision making about work and its role in worker health in the Landy paper was appropriate, but various people expressed some caveats. One participant pointed out that while participative decision making (PDM) may have positive effects on worker health, its effects on supervisors who are charged with promoting greater PDM may be quite different. These supervisors must constantly confront others' viewpoints and reconcile those points of view with each other and the perceived needs of the organization. In addition, some others cited the need for research on how to encourage PDM in an unwelcome organizational culture. For example, what are the consequences of making an attempt to promote PDM in an organization in which conflict is avoided and diversity is not valued.

At least one group of participants also felt that the effects of the physical environment (i.e., aesthetics, noise, dirt, etc.) on person's affective responses to work and their work-related health had not received enough attention in the Landy paper and that relationship between the physical and the psychosocial environment should receive far more research attention than they have to date.

Another major source of work stress identified in the Landy paper was uncertainty. Landy suggested that there may be individual differences in reaction to stress and that individuals may have different reactions to different dimensions of uncertainty. One respondent questioned the utility of trying to identify additional dimensions of uncertainty. That person felt that there would be merit in treating uncertainty as an unidimensional construct and investigating the degree to which people have the ability to tolerate different ranges of uncertainty.

Another participant expressed concern that the paper seemed to be a laundry list of factors that affect work-related stress and that there was no integrative theory or framework by which research and interventions could be directed. Dr. Pot of the Netherlands suggested that most of the factors that had been discussed could have been related to the structure of the division of labor and some aspect of employment relationships. He described a model of worker health that integrated the traditional control-demand theory of work stress and aspects of a sociotechnical model.

It was also pointed out that organizations are increasing their use of work teams and that use of work teams generates a new set of issues relevant to work stress. Specifically, work teams should increase the attention devoted to the connection between work design and stress. Since workers will need to be concerned about and, to some degree, dependent on the performance of members of their work team, there may be increased uncertainty. And, finally members of work teams who must work closely together may experience greater conflict and less control over their work. These are concerns about which we have little research data and about which we have paid little attention in those instances in which work teams have been introduced in organizations.

A major group of workers that have almost never been studied in research on work stress are construction workers. One participant drew our attention to this group. He pointed out that construction work is labor-intensive, stressful, and that there is high risk of accident and injury.

Another question related to how workers who have role changes cope with the stress that occurs during these changes. The example to which this participant pointed was the subordinate who must adapt behaviors as a supervisor that contradict his/her earlier work-related roles. A police officer, for example, may have been taught to be directive, controlling and nonparticipative, but as a police sergeant he/she is suddenly expected to adopt very different behavior in a supervisory role. Finally, one participant felt that more attention should be directed to development of methods to teach people how to develop health-promoting skills and habits.

Probably relevant to all of the suggestions in the Landy paper as well as the audience concerns was the concern expressed by one person that more attention be given to ethical concerns in the implementation of interventions designed to reduce stress. As interventionists, we are often telling people that they should adapt a particular behavior when the research data are sparse or when they are not fully informed of the intended effects or the likelihood that certain behavior will promote health. These uncertainties and the lack of fully informed consent raise ethical concerns that have received little or no discussion.

Certainly, the Landy paper, the panel's response, as well as the participants' questions and reactions summarized here provide a full research agenda for psychologists and other behavioral and social scientists. In addition, they point the way to possible interventions designed to alleviate work stress and questions that relate to the implementation and effectiveness of those interventions.

Part IV _____

Invited Presentations

Lennart Levi

Psychosocial, Occupational, Environmental, and Health Concepts; Research Results; and Applications

Asked to identify crucially important prerequisites for a good life, Sigmund Freud (1856–1939) is said to have answered "Lieben und arbeiten" (to love and to work). However, what if a sizeable proportion of the work force lacks the opportunity for at least the latter prerequisite because of unemployment or underemployment? What if another sizeable proportion of those who *are* gainfully employed are so under conditions that do not promote health and well-being or that are even outright pathogenic?

In addition, these conditions are changing more rapidly than ever. Many of these changes are well-intended but still carry negative side effects. Others are unintentional and can also lead to unforeseeable noxious effects. Some of the changes are planned and intentional, and their noxious effects are easily foreseeable, as in the case of exploitation of other people. Or, eventually, problems are created, not by the change, but by the lack of change, for example, by permitting harmful conditions to persist. Both changes and lack of changes are influenced by and influence phenomena such as population growth, urbanization, computerization, robotization, environmental pollution, uneven distribution of resources, and shortages of food, water, jobs, education, and housing.

Rather than describing a smooth curve, these interactions tend to be discontinuous, besides being intertwined and uncontrolled. Their effects in terms of health and well-being are often dramatic and destructive. The Club of Rome correctly conceives such problems as an untidy tangle of interrelated issues (the "problematique world"). The interactions between the different "threads" are many and varied but only dimly understood.

Against this background, a fundamental issue is whether governments, with the support of scientists and planners in all sectors and disciplines and of an informed community, will be able (and willing) to use the new opportunities offered by advanced technologies to analyze deliberately and consciously this untidy tangle in order to try to shape a better society and working life. Or will they passively attempt mere adjustments, post facto, as a matter of current expediency (cf. King, 1986).

A Theoretical Model

The components of this untidy tangle of person–environment–ecosystem are more easily described, interrelated, analyzed, and chosen as targets for coordinated actions if they are introduced into the heuristic ecological model illustrated in Figure 1.

We are surrounded by *nature*. Man modifies nature through a variety of *social structures and processes* (Box 1). Examples of social structures are a place of work, a neighborhood, a family, a school, or a hospital. A social process is what takes place in such a structure, for example, work, dwelling, care of children, education, or medical care.

These structures and processes are perceived and *appraised*. If these appraisals indicate a pronounced or a persistent *discrepancy* between the subject's abilities, needs, and expectations, and his or her environmental demand, opportunities, and outcomes, then health, well-being, and opportunities for human development are influenced through psychosocial and other stimuli (Boxes 2 and 3) that evoke a number of *pathogenic mechanisms* (Box 4). The latter are of four types: emotional, cognitive, behavioral, and physiological reactions. These four types of closely interrelated and potentially pathogenic reactions (Box 5) may in turn lead to (a) transitory disturbances of a number of mental and physical functions (Box 6), or *precursors of disease* (i.e., malfunctions in mental or physical systems that have not yet resulted in disability but that, if they continue, will do so) and (b) functional and, eventually, organic damage (e.g., damage to the myocardium, or the vascular wall).

Examples of *emotional* pathogenic mechanisms are feelings of anxiety, depres-

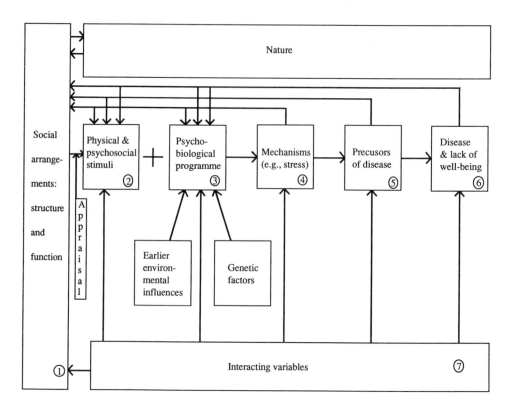

Figure 1. A heuristic model for individual-environment interaction as related to health.

Note. From "Health and Environment—Psychosocial Stimuli: A Review" by A. R. Kagan and L. Levi, in L. Levi (Ed.), *Society, Stress and Disease: Childhood and Adolescence*, 1975, London: Oxford University Press. Copyright 1975 by Oxford University Press. Adapted by permission.

sion or alienation, mental fatigue, apathy, and hypochondriasis. Examples of *cognitive* pathogenic mechanisms are restriction of the scope of perception (tunnel vision) or a lowered ability to concentrate, be creative, or make decisions. Examples of *behavioral* pathogenic mechanisms are the abuse of alcohol, tobacco, drugs, or certain foods, unnecessary risk-taking in working life and traffic, and unprovoked aggressive and violent behavior toward a fellow human being or toward oneself (suicidal behavior).

Some *physiological* pathogenic mechanisms are related to a specific situation, person, or disease; others are nonspecific, and these Selye (1936) termed *stress*. Technologically speaking, the term *stress* denotes "a force that deforms bodies." Translated into everyday language, this is more or less the same thing as load or pressure. In biology, however, the term stress often takes on a different meaning, being used in Selye's sense to signify stereotypic physiological "strain" reactions in the organism when it is exposed to various occupational and other environmental stimuli, or *stressors* (e.g., a change in, or pressures and demands for adjustment from, the environment). The propensity to react (or not react) with pathogenic processes depends on the organism's psychobiological *programming* (Box 3), which is conditioned by genetic factors and previous environmental influences.

The pathogenic process is modified by interacting variables (Box 7), for example, one's coping repertoire or the availability and utilization of social support. The process is cybernetic. A person who sustains, say, a depression, or a myocardial infarction, influences people around him or her, who in turn influence him or her in a different way from previously. The propensity to react and the quality of the reactions (i.e., the individual's programming) also change. In the worst case, a vicious circle develops, with successive reinforcement of the pathogenic process, and, consequently, negative effects on health and well-being.

Health is seen here not merely as an "absence of disease or infirmity" but also "a state of physical, mental, and social well-being" (WHO, 1986). *Well-being* is a dynamic state of mind characterized by reasonable harmony between a person's abilities, needs, and expectations and environmental demands and opportunities. The individual's subjective assessment is the only valid measurement of well-being available, even though it may not coincide with the objective views of others; for example, he or she may experience a sense of well-being while performing a monotonous or even potentially dangerous task.

Closely related to well-being is the concept of *quality of life*. This is a composite measure of physical, mental, and social well-being. When assessing the factors affecting well-being, it must be recognized that the same factor may be good for some individuals but bad for others, or good in some situations and bad in others. Failure to recognize this and to consider the entire pattern of complex and nonlinear interactions is probably one explanation for much of the confusion and controversy in this field.

What we need to know is: What is in each "box"? Which influences are pathogenic, in which individuals, by which mechanisms, which disease does this lead to, and which interacting variables modify the pathogenic process? Which are the *interactions* between the different "boxes," and how do we best comprehend the function of the whole complex system in order to identify critically important system components that are: (a) necessary, (b) sufficient, or (c) contributory in causing one or more diseases, accelerating its/their course, or triggering its/their symptoms?

Research Approaches

To obtain the necessary data, our first approach often comprises the three following consecutive, epidemiological, and experimental steps (Levi, 1987):

- determination of environmental and health problems and their interrelationships, using survey techniques and morbidity and/or mortality data;
- intensive, longitudinal, multidisciplinary, controlled field studies of high and/or low risk situations and high and/or low risk groups and the ways in which they interact; and
- controlled interventions, which include both laboratory experiments and evaluation of therapeutic and/or preventive interventions in real-life settings (evaluation of occupational and other health action) in natural and/or real experiments, utilizing results from the other two steps.

Our second, complementary, approach would be to test key hypotheses, leading to an increased understanding of the psychosocial factors and health concept in general (Kagan & Levi, 1975).

The ideal strategy would, therefore, be to select situations where the two can be combined efficiently, making it possible to engage in basic research and, simultaneously, address the enhancement of occupational health care, the prevention of occupational ill health, and promotion of occupational well-being, using no more resources for the four combined than if each were to be addressed on its own. Within the framework of a combined evaluative and hypothesis testing study, it should also be possible (for little additional cost) to obtain information on the quantitative relationships between factors or elements in the working environment-stress-health system thought to be relevant to the outcome.

Our three main objectives are:

- to carry out research aimed at *promoting* mental, physical, and social health and well-being at the workplace;
- to further the integration of psychosocial skills and knowledge into all levels of occupational and public health service provision; and
- to provide reliable and valid information on the role and implications of psychosocial factors in the planning of occupational health and health care to decision makers and all persons concerned.

Against this background, our group has proposed and embarked upon a long-term program for the study of the "psychosocial occupational environment-pathogenic mechanisms-health" system. The objectives are to establish:

- which psychosocial occupational structures and processes ("high-risk situations"), and their appraisals are of etiological significance, under what circumstances, and for whom ("high-risk groups");
- which emotional, cognitive, behavioral, and physiological mechanisms— ensuing from psychosocial stimuli ("high-risk reactions")—are implicated in the pathogenesis of various diseases;

- which interacting variables modify the health and well-being outcome, and how, why, and in whom; and
- which modifications of the occupational environment and/or of workers' behavior will promote health and well-being, and which should be avoided, and by whom (evaluation of occupational health action).

With such knowledge as a basis, environmental and/or individual measures are proposed that may be presumed to prevent disease and promote health. These are evaluated using an interdisciplinary approach, on a model scale. Relevant information is then fed back to decision makers, care providers, society planners, managers, labor unions, and the general public.

Research into the stress-related aspects of occupational social structures and process can be approached with reference to one or more of the following four value concerns (Gardell, 1980; Levi, Frankenhaeuser, & Gardell, 1982): (a) a humanistic-idealistic desire for a good society and a good working life; (b) a drive for health and well-being; (c) a belief in worker participation, influence, and control at the individual level; and (d) economic interest in competitiveness and profits of business organization and the economic system. To a large extent, the impact of stress research depends on the political priorities that these four value areas obtain. Thus, knowledge about working life usually has been applied to problems relating to economic goals and organizational efficiency (cf. the "total quality control programs" commonly applied in Japanese industries). Less attention has been paid to research that is oriented toward promoting workers' health, well-being, and personal development as values in their own right. Furthermore, the effort typically is to help workers adapt to existing conditions rather than to adapt such conditions to individual abilities and needs (cf. Cohen, Levi, Pardon, & Kalimo, 1986; Kalimo, El-Batawi, & Cooper 1987; Levi, 1979, 1981a, 1981b, 1984; Murphy & Schoenborn, 1987).

The ultimate aim of the research activities, and of the work environment and workers' health action that should be based on the results, is to make the workplace less stress and ill-health provoking while enhancing individuals' abilities to cope, thrive, and be productive (Adams, 1987). Research and health programs should focus on both the individual and on having the system remove unnecessary stressors and teach workers how to effectively cope with unavoidable stressors (or those that the individual chooses not to avoid).

Martin (1987) called attention to the need to consider background stressors such as international tensions, socioeconomic pressures, high unemployment, intergroup tensions, racial and sexual discrimination, objective concern about aging, and stigmatized stressors that originate in taboo issues that many individuals either prefer not to think about or hesitate to raise in any but the safest or most intimate contexts. When these and related types of stressors are omitted, stress research and stress management programs lose much of their relevance, effectiveness, and ultimately, acceptance.

Against this background, Martin (1987) rightly classified approaches into: (a) personal strategies attempting to make changes in the individual, (b) interpersonal strategies aimed at improving the relationships between individuals, and (c) external strategies focusing on the improvement of the environmental and organizational situation. Using these categories, our overall occupational environmental and health program should aim to be:

1. *systems-oriented*—addressing health-related interactions in the worker-workplace ecosystem;
2. *interdisciplinary*—covering medical, physiological, emotional, cognitive, behavioral, social, and economic aspects of these interactions;
3. *problem-solving oriented*—integrating complementary approaches;
4. *health oriented* (not only disease oriented)—trying to identify what constitutes and promotes positive health and counteracts ill health even in the presence of noxious exposures;
5. *intersectorial*—evaluating health actions administered in other sectors (e.g., work, housing, nutrition, traffic, education);
6. *international*—including multicenter collaborative projects carried out in different cultural and sociopolitical settings; and
7. *participative*—trying to involve not only occupational health professionals and management but the individual workers and their representatives as well.

Such a program would be of great benefit in making distinctions among stressful social structures and processes in the workplace, reactions to such stressors, the health- and wellness-related consequences of such reactions, and the modifiers of this flow of events.

Examples of Projects and Results

Staffing Levels at Day Nurseries—Effects on Children and Personnel

With a view to improving the health and well-being of 3-year-olds attending day nurseries, a study was undertaken to establish and evaluate an optimal level of staffing (Kagan et al., 1978). The stratified sample comprised 10 day nursery sections in Greater Stockholm, using a total of 100 children aged 2–4 years. At five sections (50 children) staffing was reinforced to a degree that permitted staff-child relationships of a more personal and emotional nature. The other five sections (50 children) continued with the lower staffing level recommended by the National Swedish Board of Health and Welfare. After 2.5 months, the staffing situation was reversed by transferring the additional personnel (cross-over). The higher staffing level was accompanied by a significant reduction of observed behavioral disturbances in the children, a significant increase in their well-being, and a significant decrease in their excretion of adrenaline. Among the staff, sick absence dropped 51%.

The reinforcement of present staffing levels, recommended by the study, is precluded by the present economic situation in Sweden, but the findings are frequently utilized as an argument against exceeding the recommended number of children per day nursery section.

Youth Unemployment and Ill Health

With a view to studying social and medical consequences of youth unemployment, a prospective study (Hammarström, 1986) was carried out in the town of Lulea in northern Sweden, covering all pupils attending the final year of compulsory education (15–16-year-old; $n = 1,083$). After 2 years, a follow-up was undertaken with an extensive questionnaire. The hypothesis was that those who became unemployed would have the most unfavorable sociomedical development and that a similar, less marked tendency would be found among those who went on to upper secondary school although they would have preferred to start work (concealed unemployed). The results confirmed the expected relation between unemployment, potentially pathogenic behavior (e.g., increased consumption of alcohol), and ill-health. Effects of "concealed" unemployment were similar, though less pronounced.

The study illustrates the importance of ensuring that school leavers are placed in the labor market without delay, unless they actively and voluntarily choose further training. Such training, however, is not a suitable alternative for those who choose it simply because they cannot get a job.

Unemployment and Ill Health

A job can help to make life meaningful and structured. It can give a person identity and self-esteem, friends and acquaintances, and, of course, material assets. Unemployment does away with much of this (Jahoda, 1979). In a controlled intervention (Brenner, Petterson, Levi, & Arnetz, 1988; Levi et al., 1984) with 200 unemployed female factory workers in Olofström in the south of Sweden, a multidisciplinary longitudinal evaluation was made of efforts to make good this loss and prevent its possible effects by finding or creating new jobs cooperatively or individually and with meaningful unpaid, self-administered, collective activities.

Results from this study demonstrate (a) pronounced mental and physiological stress reactions (high blood levels of cortisol) 1 month preceding job loss, (b) a diminution of these reactions in the first month of actual unemployment, (c) a subsequent, successive rise in self-rated depression and in cortisol levels over the first year of unemployment, following the initial period of relaxation and relative optimism, and (d) high levels of depression and cortisol and decreased immune function 1 year after the beginning of unemployment. This study illustrated what to expect before and after the onset of unemployment and provided health reasons for promoting gainful employment for all.

Eliminating Night Shifts for Industrial Workers

Another study (Akerstedt & Torsvall, 1978) concerned 400 industrial workers on a three-shift rotation. For half of them, the night shift was eliminated—some switched to a two-shift system, others to continuous day-shift—and the other half went on as before.

In a follow-up study 1 year later, those workers who changed from working three or four shifts to working two shifts (i.e., without night work) showed a sig-

nificant increase in well-being with respect to sleep, mood, gastrointestinal functioning, and social factors, along with an improvement in attitude to their work
schedules. Those who were switched from shift to day work reported greatly increased social well-being, a shortening of sleep-length during free days, and considerably improved attitudes towards their work schedule; their sickness absence
rates were also reduced. Questionnaire scores remained at their original levels in
those workers whose schedules were left unchanged. It is concluded that the abolition of night work results in a substantial improvement in mental, physical, and
social well-being.

Effects of Introducing Night Work

Two groups of middle-aged, male track workers (n = 16 and n = 17) at Swedish
Rail were bound by contract to switch to night shift for 1 month each summer. This
multidisciplinary cross-over study focused on the impact, after 1 and 3 weeks, of
switching from day to night shift and back to day shift (Akerstedt & Torsvall, 1978).

After 1 and 3 weeks, changing to night shift involved circadian rhythm disturbances in alertness and adrenaline excretion, accompanied by sleep disturbances,
gastrointestinal complaints, and significant elevations in the serum levels of cho-
lesterol, uric acid, and potassium. The change back to day shift caused these reactions to subside. The findings illustrated (a) difficulties in adapting biological
circadian rhythms to social demands, (b) biochemical and clinical stress reactions
to such changes in working hours, and (c) the possibility that these reactions, if
long-lasting and/or often repeated, may in time elicit ill-health. Following the study,
consultations between Swedish Rail and the trade union resulted in the abolition
of the night shift requirement for this particular group.

Altered Shift Rotation for Police Duty

The traditional duty rotation for the police force in Stockholm involves a daily,
counterclockwise change in working hours. Our research prompted the hypothesis
that clockwise rotation would be preferable because it should harmonize better with
human biology. In a multidisciplinary cross-over study (Orth-Gomér, 1983), about
40 police officers spent 4 weeks on each of the two rotations.

Clockwise rotation was associated with improved sleep, less fatigue, lower systolic blood pressure, and lower blood levels of triglycerides and glucose (i.e., positive
effects on risk factors for ischemic heart disease). A further evaluation—lasting 6
months with police officers in a nonmetropolitan area—also demonstrated decreased
fatigue and less stress disorders as well as improved sleep and health. However,
the model had a social drawback in that it reduced the opportunities for getting
prolonged, unbroken leisure periods.

The police officers therefore decided to go back to counterclockwise rotation.
However, after 9 months of this system they found that the last-named advantages
were outweighed by the drawbacks which we had documented. Despite the impairment regarding unbroken leisure time, the police officers therefore decided to return
once more to clockwise rotation. The study illustrated the possibility—in occupa-

tions where night work is unavoidable—of improving conditions by arriving at a more natural arrangement of working hours.

Counteracting Loneliness Among Pensioners

Elderly, single, female pensioners ($n = 35$) queuing for a retired people's hostel were offered group meetings with peers, while a comparable control group ($n = 22$) received no such offer (Andersson, 1984). After 6 months, the former group displayed significantly less feelings of loneliness and alienation, greater self-confidence, more social contacts and interactions, and a significant lowering of systolic and diastolic blood pressure. These desirable effects of an intervention that was simple to administer and inexpensive, led to the results being spread and the routines introduced in Stockholm's municipal program for care for the elderly.

Increased Autonomy and Social Interaction for Institutionalized Pensioners

Thirty pensioners in one section of a senior citizen apartment building were encouraged to take control of themselves to a greater extent with the hope that this would lead to an increase in their social activities (Arnetz, 1983). As a result of the intervention, social activities (planned and spontaneous) increased threefold, restlessness decreased, carbohydrate turnover (hemoglobin A_{1c}) improved, and anabolic hormones (plasma testosterone, estradiol, and dehydroepiandrosterone) increased. The study demonstrated the importance of active participation in care programs and showed that simple measures to this end, besides having social and psychological benefits, favor health and well-being.

Health Promotion

To promote a good working environment and occupational health, the Swedish Government Bill 1976/77:149 on work environment states that " . . . work should be safe both physically and mentally, *but also* provide opportunities for involvement, job satisfaction, and personal development."

   More than a decade later, the Swedish Governmental Commission on the Work Environment (1990) presented a series of proposed amendments to the Swedish Work Environment Act, stipulating more clearly than existing provisions *that*:

- Working conditions are to be adapted to people's physical and psychological conditions.
- Employees are to be given opportunities of participating in the arrangement of their own work situation, its transformation and development.
- Technology, the organization of work and job contents are to be designed so that the employee is not exposed to physical or mental loads that may lead to ill-health or accidents.
- Forms of remuneration and work schedules that involve an appreciable risk of ill-health or accidents are not to be used.
- Strictly controlled or tied work is to be avoided or restricted.

- Work should afford opportunities for variety, social contacts, cooperation, and a connection between individual tasks.
- Working conditions should provide opportunities for personal and occupational development, as well as for self-determination and professional responsibility.

In March 1991, the Swedish Government presented such a Bill (1990/91:140) to the Swedish Parliament, who passed the Bill in late May 1991.

To promote practical work along these lines, the Swedish Working Life Fund was set up by a decree from the Swedish Parliament. It distributes a total of 15 billion Swedish kronor (nearly 3 billion United States dollars), for a total labor force of 4.32 million (3.5% of that of the United States) over a 6-year period, aiming at a radical renewal of Swedish working life. The money has been collected from Swedish employers through a special charge. Through financial grants to the employers, the Fund will promote a healthy work environment and work organization as well as active rehabilitation programs in workplaces. This approach illustrates how research results can be, and actually are, translated into legislation and practical health action (cf. also Cohen et al., 1986; Kalimo et al., 1987; Levi, 1979, 1981a, 1981b, 1984; Levi et al., 1984).

Summary

Work-related psychosocial stressors originate in social structures and processes, affect the human organism through psychological processes, and influence health through four types of closely interrelated mechanisms—emotional, cognitive, behavioral, and physiological. The health outcome is modified by situational (e.g., social support) and individual factors (e.g., personality, coping repertoire). The work-environment-stress-health system is a dynamic one with many feedback loops. There is little but increasing direct evidence of a causal relationship between work-related psychosocial stressors and the incidence of occupational morbidity and mortality. But, a substantial body of indirect evidence strongly suggests that such associations exist and emphasizes the need to better understand their role. Accordingly, research and health action should aim at being systems-oriented, interdisciplinary, intersectorial, health (and not only disease) oriented, and participative.

Interventions for which supportive evidence suggests the value of application and evaluation are:

- increasing a worker's control of work arrangements and organization;
- avoiding monotonous, machine-paced, and short but frequent work actions;
- optimizing automation;
- helping workers see their specific task in relation to the total product;
- avoiding quantitative work overload or underload; and
- facilitating communication and support systems among work mates and others.

In Sweden, most of these ideas have now been incorporated into the new Work

Environment Act, and very substantial economic support is being made available to Swedish employers to promote improvements in work environment and workers' health through a newly created Working Life Fund. This serves as a beautiful illustration of fruitful interactions between researchers, legislators, and the parties on the labor market.

References

Adams, J. (1987). Creating and maintaining comprehensive stress management training. In L. R. Murphy & T. F. Schoenborn (Eds.), *Stress management in work settings* (pp. 93–107). Cincinnati, OH: National Institute of Occupational Safety and Health.

Åkerstedt, T. (1977). Inversion of the sleep wakefulness pattern: Effects on circadian variations in psychophysiological activation. *Ergonomics, 20,* 459–474.

Åkerstedt, T., & Torsvall, L. (1978). Experimental changes in shift schedules— their effects on well-being. *Ergonomics, 21,* 849–856.

Andersson, L. (1984). *Aging and loneliness—An interventional study of a group of elderly women.* Unpublished doctoral dissertation, Karolinska Institutet, Department of Stress Research, Stockholm, Sweden.

Arnetz, B. (1983). *Psychophysiological effects of social understimulation in old age.* Unpublished Doctoral Dissertation. Karolinska Institutet, Department of Stress Research, Stockholm, Sweden.

Brenner, S. O., Petterson, L. L., Levi, L., & Arnetz, B. (1988). *Stress reactions in response to threat of, and exposure to unemployment* (Stress Research Rep. No. 210). Stockholm, Sweden: Karolinska Institutet, Department of Stress Research). (In Swedish)

Cohen, A., Levi, L., Pardon, N., & Kalimo, R. (1986). *Psychosocial factors at work: Recognition and control.* Geneva, Switzerland: International Labour Office.

Gardell, B. (1980, September). *Scandinavian research on stress in working life.* Paper presented at the IRRA Symposium on Stress in Working Life, Denver, CO.

Hammarström, A. (1986). Youth unemployment and ill health: Results from a 2-year follow-up study. Unpublished doctoral dissertation, Karolinska Institutet, Stockholm, Sweden.

Jahoda, M. (1979). The impact of unemployment in the 1930s and the 1970s. *British Psychological Society Bulletin, 32,* 309–314.

Kagan, A. R., & Levi, L. (1975). Health and environment—Psychosocial stimuli: A review. In L. Levi (Ed.), *Society, stress and disease: Childhood and adolescence: Vol. 2* (pp. 241–260). London: Oxford University Press.

Kagan, A. R., Cederblad, M., Höök, B., & Levi, L. (1978). *Evaluation of the effect of increasing the number of nurses on health and behavior of 3-year-old children in day care, satisfaction of their parents, and health and satisfaction of their nurses* (Rep. No. 89). Stockholm: Laboratory for Clinical Stress Research.

Kalimo, R., El-Batawi, M. A., & Cooper, C. L. (Eds.). (1987). *Psychosocial factors at work and their relation to health.* Geneva, Switzerland: World Health Organization.

King, A. (1986). The great transition. *World Academy of Art and Science Newsletter, July,* 1–6.

Levi, L. (1979). Psychosocial factors in preventive medicine. In D. A. Hamburg, E. C. Nightingale, & V. Kalmar (Eds.), *Healthy people: The Surgeon General's report on health promotion and disease prevention: Background papers* (pp. 207–252). Washington, DC: U.S. Department of Health, Education and Welfare/Public Health Service.

Levi, L. (1981). *Preventing work stress.* Reading, MA: Addison-Wesley.

Levi, L. (Ed.). (1981b). *Society, stress and disease: Working life.* Oxford, England: Oxford University Press.

Levi, L. (1984). *Stress in industry.* Geneva, Switzerland: International Labour Office.

Levi, L. (1987). Future research. In R. Kalimo, M. A. El-Batawi, & C. L. Cooper (Eds.), *Psychosocial factors at work* (pp. 239–245). Geneva: World Health Oranization.

Levi, L., Brenner, S. O., Hall, E. M., Hjelm, R., Salovaara, H., Arnetz, B., & Petterson, L. L. (1984). The psychological, social, and biochemical impacts of unemployment in Sweden. *International Journal of Mental Health, 13,* 1–2, 18–34.

Levi, L., Frankenhaeuser, M., & Gardell, B. (1982). Work stress related to social structures and process. In G. R. Elliott & Eisdorfer (Eds.), *Stress and human health: Analysis and implications of research* (pp. 119–146). New York: Springer.

Martin, E. V. (1987) Worker stress: A practitioner's perspective. In L. R. Murphy & T. F. Schoenborn, (Eds.), *Stress management in work settings* (pp. 149–172). Cincinnati, OH: National Institute for Occupational Safety and Health.

Murphy, L. R., & Schoenborn, T. F. (Eds.). (1987). *Stress management in work settings.* Cincinnati, OH: National Institute for Occupational Safety and Health.

Orth-Gomér, K. (1983). Intervention on coronary risk factors by adapting a shift work schedule to biologic rhythmicity. *Psychosomatic Medicine, 45,* 5, 407–415.

Selye, H. (1936). A syndrome produced by diverse nocuous agents. *Nature, 138,* 32.

Swedish Government Commission on Work Environment and Health. (1990). *Arbeten utsatta för särskilda hälsorisker* [Jobs exposed to special health risks]. Stockholm, Sweden: Allmänna Förlaget.

World Health Organization. (1986). Constitution of the World Health Organization. In *Basic documents* (36th ed.). Geneva: World Health Organization.

About the Author

Lennart Levi

Dr. Levi is the Chair of the Department of Stress Research at the Karolinska Institutet in Stockholm, Professor of Psychosocial Medicine at the Karolinska Institutet, the Director of the National Swedish Institute for Psychosocial Factors and Health, and has recently been named Chair of the World Health Organization (WHO) expert group on psychosocial occupational health in Europe. Under his leadership, the Karolinska Institutet was chosen as the WHO Collaborating Research and Training Centre on Psychosocial Factors and Health.

Dr. Levi received his MD in 1959, and his PhD in 1972, both from the Karolinska Institutet in Stockholm. He began his career as a physician with the National Rehabilitation Clinic in Stockholm (1956–1958). From there he became assistant physician and researcher physician in the Departments of Internal Medicine and Psychiatry at the Karolinska University Hospital. In 1959 he became Director and Founder of the Department of Stress Research (formerly Laboratory for Clinical Stress Research) at the Karolinska Institutet. For over 15 years of his career, Dr. Levi has served as the designatee to the WHO Collaborating Research and Training Centre on Psychosocial Factors and Health.

Dr. Levi's professional career covers 35 years of dedication, determination, and commitment to the field of occupational health. His exemplary research in the occupational and public health field includes foci on stress-related symptoms of workers and the effect of the work environment on health and mental health. In addition, he is a member of a wide variety of professional organizations, including: WHO Expert Panel on Mental Health, the Swedish Medical Society, the International College of Psychosomatic Medicine (a founding fellow), the Society for Psychophysiological Research, the World Psychiatric Association (WPA) Section of Occupational Psychiatry (Chairperson), WHO, United Nations International Children's Emergency Fund (UNICEF), United Nations Educational, Scientific, and Cultural Organization (UNESCO), International Labor Organization (ILO), and the International Society of Psychoneuroedocrinology.

Dr. Levi was the keynote speaker at the APA/NIOSH conference. He is currently a member of the APA/NIOSH Planning Committee for the International APA/NIOSH Conference scheduled for fall of 1992.

"Sharon's Monologue"
From *The Department*

Barbara Garson

You know what the cages are like in this bank? [Sharon is asking the other women in her new department.] Yeah, the rooms with the bars where they send the animals.

Well somehow if you're my color, in this equal opportunity establishment, you take your slip from personnel, you show it to the guard and he points to a gray metal door that no one's ever been in. It's kind of like Dorothy going into Oz. Only this door you open and the whole movie turns black and white.

Inside is a huge room with no windows and no air and hundreds of women sitting in long lines all keying with three fingers of one hand, and turning over little slips as fast as they can with the other hand. Thousands of women; three shifts; all day, all night; and nobody knows they're there.

So they sit you down, point you to the numbers on the slips and say: "this is your cusip, this is your due date, and this is your subaccount."

"Huh?"

"Don't worry, you don't have to know anything. It's all in the machine."

And sure enough, 10 minutes later you're keying as fast as the rest of them: subaccount, cusip, due date: subaccount, cusip, due date: subaccount, cusip, due date. [She's miming the three fingered keying motions with one hand and turning slips of paper with the other.] And they're right, you don't have to know a thing. You sit there rolling the numbers across your eyeballs and out through your fingers . . . subaccount, cusip, due date; subaccount, cusip, due date.

The only break you get is to get up and get a new batch of work out of a bin . . . and the only word you hear is when you stop to stretch the cramp out of your neck and the supervisor passes behind you and says "What's a matter Sharon, you out of work?"

> Subaccount J0823, cusip 295236, due date 11/06/83: subaccount J0826, cusip 295263, due date 07/22/84.

After a while you start playing weird little games in your head like, next cusip with two first numbers that add up to six—I'm gonna have a Lifesaver®. Or, soon as I get a due date with the month and day the same as one of my kid's birthdays— I'm just gonna get up and go to the bathroom!

So I'm sitting there longing for a 3—3 or a 2—4 and thinking am I the only crazy one. Are the rest of these women playing games with their cusips?

[Once again she mimes the three fingered keying, growing weary as the time passes.] You look up after an hour's work and it's 4 minutes later.

And just when you think it couldn't get any worse they say "Ladies, we're going to put in some new machines that will make your job easier."

So they give you a clean Darth Vadar TV screen and sure enough, it's easier. 'Cause now you don't have to get up for new batches; they're in the machine. And there's no more due dates to play crazy games with because they're automatically on the form. I never realized how much I'd miss my due date. And now you don't even have to press a return key. Because each time you come to the end of a screen another blank form drops in front of your face. It's so much easier that your quota is up to 180 an hour. It's so easy you could do it in a straight jacket.

Two weeks after they put in the screens they called me to a glass room on the twelfth floor. This White kid with a leather blazer says "Sharon, are you having any problems at home?" "No, what do you mean?" He pushes a few buttons on his keyboard and he shows me a screen full of numbers. "Well as you can see from your chart, both yesterday and today, your production fell to less than nine thousand key strokes an hour after lunch. And look at all these errors and strike overs." Four floors away he could count every mistake and tell me the exact second when I stopped to scratch my nose. "If you want to stay here you'll have to come up to your quota" "Quota, what quota?" "By now you should be up to 15,000 keystrokes an hour. Are you sure you have no problems at home?"

15,000 keystrokes an hour! You sit there in one position all day staring into the screen. Your neck aches, your eyes burn, and you can't even turn your head. I never had headaches before. My kid says "Ma, what'd we do? You're always angry." I catch myself in the mirror and I see—I'm not angry, my face is just always set.

15,000 keystrokes an hour and the damn racist manager wants me to stay till 10:00 pm, 11:00 pm, whatever they say, to finish all the data.

But I have kids!

[Imitating the supervisor] "If you have special problems at home, Sharon, perhaps you should think of a more suitable job."

Not problems, kids you racist moron!

Not racist? [Shrugs] He's got two kids and a wife in the suburbs. He goes to open school night; he drives them to the Scouts. But me, I got three kids and I can stay till 10:00 pm. All that year I never once helped them with their homework. I didn't even know what was in their notebooks.

They stick us down there because we're not human. So what if our kids are sick? You can't even get a phone call if your kid is sick.

Now it's coming up here. Promoted. I should have known. If they let a Black move in, it's because the neighborhood is already changing.

About the Author

Barbara Garson

Barbara Garson is the playwright of *Macbird* which sold over .5 million copies as a book. Her other plays include: *Going Co-Op, The Department, The Dinosaur Door*, and *The Latest Security*. She is the author of two classic books about Americans at work: *All the Livelong Day: The Meaning and Demeaning of Routine Work* (1988) and the *Electronic Sweatshop* (1989). Her articles and stories have appeared in the *New York Times*, the *LA Times*, the *Washington Post, The Village Voice, Harpers, McCalls*, and *Mother Jones*. Garson's writing skills have earned her a Guggenheim Fellowship, a National Press Club Citation, and an Obie Award.

Conference Participants

Georgia Allen, *The Mediplex Corporation, Inc., Newbury Port, MA*
Toni Alterman, *Health Science Center at Houston, Houston, TX*
Thomas A. Annestrand, *Exxon Chemical Corporation, Baton Rouge, LA*
Michele A. Armitage, *Washington, DC*
Majorie Armstrong-Stassen, *University of Windsor, Windsor, Ontario, Canada*
Michael D. Atella, *Argonne, IL*
Sally S. Atkins, *Appalachian State University, Boone, NC*
Elizabeth Averill, *Workplace Health Fund, Washington, DC*
Robert K. Ax, *U.S. Department of Justice, Midlothian, VA*
Anita S. Back, *ISA Associates, Washington, DC*
Colin Baigel, *White Plains, NY*
Frank Baker, *Johns Hopkins University, Baltimore, MD*
Jordan Barab, *American Federation of County, State and Municipal Employees, Washington, DC*
Julian Barling, *Queen's University, Kingston, Ontario, Canada*
Beth Barnes, *Radford, VA*
Rosalind Barnett, *Wellesley College, Wellesley, MA*
Linda Batley, *Alexandria, VA*
Michael N. Baxley, *Pittsburgh, PA*
Faye Belgrave, *George Washington University, Washington, DC*
Judith D. Berman, *U.S. Department of State, Washington, DC*
Steven Besing, *Indiana Center for Rehabilitation Medicine, Indianapolis, IN*
Robert Biersner, *National Institute for Occupational Safety and Health, Cincinnati, OH*
Barbara E. Biesenbach, *Hay Systems, Inc., Washington, DC*
Richard G. Bishop, *Xenia, OH*
Niall Bolger, *University of Denver, Denver, CO*
Angela S. Bonds, *Radford University, Radford, VA*
Saletta M. Boni, *New York, NY*
Edward Foster Bourg, *Alametta, CA*
Michael W. Boye, *London House, Inc., Park Ridge, IL*
Gall A. Braun, *County of Sonoma, Sonoma, CA*
Mark Braverman, *Crisis Management Groups, Inc., Watertown, MA*
Christa Brett, *Washington, DC*
Albert Brockwell, *Fairfax, VA*
Janet Cahill, *Glassboro State College, Glassboro, NJ*
Barrett S. Caldwell, *University of Wisconsin, Madison, WI*
Wayne Camara, *American Psychological Association, Washington, DC*
John H. Chamberlin, *Psychological Services, Los Angeles, CA*
Arlena V. Chaney, *Washington, DC*
Gretchen G. Chase, *Howard University, Washington, DC*

Rupert F. Chisholm, *Pennsylvania State University Harrisburg, Middletown, PA*
Carol Cober, *American Association for Retired Persons, Washington, DC*
Richard Cohen, *Linwood, NJ*
Alexander Cohen, *National Institute for Occupational Safety and Health, Cincinnati, OH*
J. P. Connolly, *Orange, CT*
Royer F. Cook, *ISA, Washington, DC*
Chester D. Copemann, *Caribbean Behavioral Institute, Inc., U.S. Virgin Islands*
David M. Corey, *Wolf-Corey, Inc., Napa, CA*
Wayne Corneil, *Employee Assistance Services, Health and Welfare, Canada, Ottawa, Canada*
Paul T. Cornell, *Grand Rapids, MI*
Eleanor C. Crocker, *Charlottesville, VA*
Barbara Curbow, *The Johns Hopkins University, Baltimore, MD*
E. Carroll Curtis, *Westinghouse Corporation, Pittsburgh, PA*
Robert S. Czeh, *Silver Spring, MD*
Isabel Davidoff, *National Institute of Mental Health, Rockville, MD*
Dennis M. Dennis, *Seattle, WA*
O. Bruce Dickerson, *Dickerson Occupational Health Services, New York, NY*
Diane Dietz, *Cornell University, New York, NY*
Charlene Douglas, *Baltimore, MD*
Barbara Dubuc, *Health & Welfare, Canada, Ottawa, Ontario, Canada*
Nancy E. Durbin, *Batelle Human Affairs Research Centers, Seattle, WA*
William Eaton, *Johns Hopkins University, Baltimore, MD*
Jeff Edwards, *Darden—University of Virginia Charlottesville, Charlottesville, VA*
Donald Ellsburg, *Occupational Health Foundation, Washington, DC*
Katherine W. Ellison, *Montclair State College, Upper Montclair, NY*
Henry H. Emurian, *The University of Maryland, Baltimore, MD*
Lorraine D. Eyde, *U.S. Office of Personnel Mgmt., Washington, DC*
Julia Faucett, *University of California, San Francisco, CA*
Michael Feurerstein, *University of Rochester Medical Center, Rochester, NY*
Lawrence J. Fine, *National Institute for Occupational Safety and Health, Cincinnati, OH*
Lynda Firment, *American Association of Occupational Health Nurses, Inc., Atlanta, GA*
Sheila Fitzgerald, *Johns Hopkins School of Public Health, Baltimore, MD*
Sheila T. Fitzgerald, *Reston, VA*
Terence Fitzgerald, *University of Rochester, Rochester, NY*
Liz Fitzpatrick, *Kentwood, MI*
Catherine Flanagan, *Seaford, NY*
Robin F. Foust, *Health Management Corporation, Richmond, VA*
Marion Frank, *Dr. Marion Frank and Associates, Philadelphia, PA*
Julia Frank-McNeil, *American Psychological Association, Arlington, VA*
Jerri L. Frantzve, *Radford University, Radford, VA*
Diana Freeland, *Houston, TX*
Jeannie Gaines, *Tampa, FL*
Barbara Garson, *New York, NY*
Sheila Gehlmann, *Jersey City, NJ*

Mary Giallorenzi, *U.S. Office of Personnel Management, Washington, DC*
Robin Gillespie, *Service Employees International Union, New York, NY*
Kathleen O. Glaus, *Wright State University, Dayton, OH*
Kelli J. Godfrey, *Radford, VA*
Gloria Gordon, *St. Louis, MO*
Horst S. Gottschalk, *Health Administration, Arlington, VA*
Mirian Graddick, *AT & T International, Morristown, NJ*
Martin M. Greller, *Watchung, NJ*
Donald W. Grimm, Jr., *New York, NY*
Stephen J. Guastello, *Marquette University, Milwaukee, WI*
Britton, Guerrina, *Washington, DC*
Barbara A. Gutek, *University of Arizona, Tucson, AZ*
Janet C. Haartz, *National Institute for Occupational Safety and Health C-22,
    Cincinnati, OH*
Donald A. Hantula, *St. Joseph's University, Philadelphia, PA*
Allen R. Harkness, *University of Tulsa, Tulsa, OK*
Kathleen Delaplane Harris, *Wayne State University, Detroit, MI*
William T. Harris, *Occupational Health and Environmental Services, Washing-
    ton, DC*
Sandra Hauck, *American Psychological Association, Arlington, VA*
Alan Hedge, *Cornell University, Ithaca, NY*
Glenn Hernandez, *Exxon Chemical, Baton Rouge, LA*
Robert Hogan, *University of Tulsa, Tulsa, OK*
Nora Howley, *University of Maryland, College Park, MD*
Diane Hughes, *New York University, New York, NY*
Patrick J. Hunt, *Washington, DC*
Joseph J. Hurrell, Jr., *National Institute for Occupational Safety and Health,
    Cincinnati, OH*
Valerie A. Imburgia, *Rochester, NY*
Barbara A. Israel, *Ann Arbor, MI*
Susan Jackson, *New York University, New York, NY*
James Jones, *American Psychological Association, Washington, DC*
Robert Kahn, *Ann Arbor, MI*
Raija Kallmo, *Institute of Occupational Health, Helsinki, Finland*
John Kamp, *St. Paul Fire and Marine Insurance Company, St. Paul, MN*
Lisa A. Kanner, *Office of Disease Prevention and Health Promotion, Washington,
    DC*
Stanislav Kasl, *Yale University, New Haven, CT*
Thomas Keefe, *Louisville, KY*
Edward J. Kelty, *National Institutes for Mental Health, Rockville, MD*
Francis X. King, *Metropolitan Life, New York, NY*
Ellen Kirschman, *Sacramento, CA*
Stacey Kohler, *State College, PA*
Michael Kompier, *TNO Institute of Preventive Health Care, The Netherlands*
John D. Kraft, *U.S. Office of Personnel Management, Washington, DC*
Marilyn E. Krouse, *Radford, VA*
Karl W. Kuhnert, *Athens, GA*
Paul Landisbergis, *Empire State College, New York, NY*

Frank Landy, *Pennsylvania State University, University Park, PA*
Bryan Lawton, *Wells Fargo Bank, San Francisco, CA*
JoAnn Lee, *Sub-Committee on Senate Labor & Human Resources, Washington, DC*
David LeGrande, *Communication Workers of America, Occupational Safety and Health, Washington, DC*
Michael P. Leiter, *Acadia University, Wolfville, Nova Scotia*
Lennart Levi, *World Health Organization, Stockholm, Sweden*
Joan D. Levin, *Washington, DC*
Donald B. Levitt, *Ford Motor Company, Dearborn, MI*
Melania N. Liberto, *Doylestown, PA*
Kari J. Lindstrom, *Helsinki, Finland*
James Lipari, *National Institute of Drug Abuse, Rockville, MD*
Dianne Chasen Lipsey, *Washington, DC*
Edward H. Loveland, *Georgia Institute of Technology, Atlanta, GA*
Sally L. Lusk, *University of Michigan, Ann Arbor, MI*
John A. Lust, *Bloomington, IL*
Maurya Mac Neil, *Columbus, OH*
Beryce W. MacLennan, *Washington Business Group on Health, Washington, DC*
Judy Maggard, *American Psychological Association, Arlington, VA*
Mark J. Maggio, *Severn, MD*
Nancy J. Maintosh, *Seminole, FL*
Ronald W. Manderscheid, *National Institute of Mental Health, Rockville, MD*
Ann C. Maney, *National Institute of Mental Health, Rockville, MD*
A. David Mangelsdorff, *U.S. Army Health Care Studies and Clinical Investigation Activity, Fort Sam Houston, TX*
Michael R. Manning, *New Mexico State University, Las Cruces, NM*
Irwin J. Mansdorf, *Professional Health Associates, Inc., Elmurst, NY*
Carol Marcy, *Montgomery County Police Department, Rockville, MD*
Nancy L. Marshall, *Wellesley College, Wellesley, MA*
Eugene V. Martin, *Washington, DC*
Susan E. Martin, *Chevy Chase, MD*
William Martin, *New Orleans, LA*
Sheryl A. Martinson, *St. Paul, MN*
Lisa May, *Oil, Chemical, and Atomic Workers*
Michael G. McKee, *Cleveland, OH*
Gail H. McKee, *Roanoke College, Salem, VA*
Louis C. Milanesi, *University of California, Irvine, Irvine, CA*
Lyle H. Miller, *Brookline, MA*
Suzanne Miller, *Princeton, NJ*
Kim Morris, *Newcastle, DE*
Eileen Morrison, *Carrollton, TX*
John D. Morrison, Jr., *Tulsa, OK*
John K. Mulholland, *Rosemead, CA*
Lawrence Murphy, *National Institute for Occupational Safety and Health, Cincinnati, OH*
Catharine M. Napolitano, *Franklin Lakes, NJ*
Debra L. Nelson, *Oklahoma State University, Stillwater, OK*

Patricia M. Nio, *Radford University, Radford, VA*
Brigid Noonan, *COPE Incorporated, Washington, DC*
Katherine Nordal, *Washington, DC*
Peggy O'Hara, *University of Miami, Miami, FL*
Lynn Offerman, *George Washington University, Washington, DC*
Suzyn Ornstein, *Boston, MA*
I. Keith Orton, *Health Services, Portland, OR*
Daniel Owens, *Lynchburg, VA*
Angel M. Pacheco, *Servicios Professionales y Cientificos, Inc., Rio Piedras, Puerto Rico*
Lynda J. Page, *Consolidated Freightways, Mira Loma, CA*
Beth Page, *Steelcase, Inc., Grand Rapids, MI*
Anthony S. Papciak, *Center for Occupational Rehabilitation, Rochester, NY*
Katharine R. Parkes, *University of Oxford, Oxford, England*
S. Gail Pearl, *University of North Carolina, Chapel Hill, NC*
Kenneth R. Pelletier, *Institute for the Advancement of Health, San Francisco, CA*
James R. Petrie, *Arlington, VA*
Stephen Pfeiffer, *A Psychological Corp., San Diego, CA*
Ann T. Phelps, *Los Angeles, CA*
Sally B. Philips, *Metropolitan Life Insurance Company, New York, NY*
Kelly L. Phillips, *Aetna Life Insurance Company, Washington, DC*
Cindy Piltch, *Brookline, MA*
Chaya S. Piotrkowski, *National Council for Jewish Women, New York, NY*
David G. Poland, *Metropolitan Washington Airports Authority, Alexandria, VA*
Frank D. Pot, *TNO Institute of Preventive Health Care, Leiden, The Netherlands*
Glenn Pransky, *University of Massachusetts, Worcester, MA*
Sonja M. Preston, *American Psychological Association, Washington, DC*
Gwendolyn Puryear Keita, *American Psychological Association, Washington, DC*
James Campbell Quick, *University of Texas, Arlington, Arlington, TX*
Sally Radmacher, *Canden Point, MO*
Haleh Rastegary, *Pennsylvania State University, University Park, PA*
Jonathan Raymond, *Gordon College, Wenham, MA*
Marie-Claude Rigaud, *University of Illinois at Chicago, Chicago, IL*
John D. Riley, *San Francisco, CA*
Ismael Rivera, *American Psychological Association, Arlington, VA*
Lillian Robbins, *Rutgers University, Newark, NJ*
Edwin Robbins, *New York, NY*
Virginia A. Rockhill, *Behavioral Management Associates, Inc., Pawtucket, RI*
Joseph Rogers, *Rehabilitation Hospital of the Pacific, Honolulu, HI*
Robert Rosen, *Healthy Companies, Inc., Arlington, VA*
Ann Rubin, *Los Angeles Department of Water and Power, Los Angeles, CA*
Pascale C. Sainfort, *University of Wisconsin-Madison, Madison, WI*
Gavriel Salvendy, *School of Industrial Engineering, West Lafayette, IN*
Sue Sand, *Waban, MA*
Steven L. Sauter, *National Institute for Occupational Safety and Health, Cincinnati, OH*
Ted Scharf, *University of California-Irvine, Irvine, CA*

Ron Schell, *Arlington, VA*
Ruth M. Schimel, *Washington, DC*
Lawrence Schiefler, *National Institute for Occupational Safety and Health, Cincinnati, OH*
Neal Schmitt, *Michigan State University, East Lansing, MI*
Peter Schnall, *New York Hospital-Cornell Medical Center, New York, NY*
Irvin Schonfeld, *Eden City College of New York, New York, NY*
Fred Schott, *Aetna Life and Casualty, Hartford, CN*
Ellen Scrivner, *Prince George's County Police Department, Upper Marlboro, MD*
Lee Sharp, *Santa Rosa, CA*
Sonya I. Shelley, *Baltimore, MD*
Phil A. Shellhaas, *Machines Corporation, Washington, DC*
Bruce W. Shockleton, *Wayland, MA*
Jefferson A. Singer, *Connecticut College, New London, CT*
Karen B. Slora, *London House/SBA, Park Ridge, IL*
Michael Smith, *University of Wisconsin, Madison, WI*
Alma Dell Smith, *Brookline, MA*
Harold R. Smith, *Washington, DC*
Daniel C. Smith, *McDonnell-Douglas, Corp., Bridegton, MO*
Marc B. Sokol, *Iselin, NJ*
Mark E. Solomons, *Ater and Hadden, Washington, DC*
Charles D. Speilberger, *University of South Florida-Tampa, Tampa, FL*
Sara Staats, *Newark Campus, Newark, OH*
Graham Staines, *National Council of Jewish Women, New York, NY*
John S. Stern, *Washington University, St. Louis, MO*
Fran Stillman, *Johns Hopkins Medical Institutions, Baltimore, MD*
Joan Storey, *New York, NY*
James R. Striker, *Washington, DC*
Naomi Swanson, *National Institute for Occupational Safety and Health, Cincinnati, OH*
Mary Tatum, *Falls Church, VA*
Robert C. Temer, *Larkspue, CA*
Lois E. Tetrick, *Wayne State University, Detroit, MI*
Elayne F. Theriault, *Liberty Mutual, Atlanta, GA*
Paul R. Tobias, *Santa Monica, CA*
Cheryl Toth, *Radford, VA*
Will Turner, *Richmond, VA*
Craig T. Twentyman, *Social Sciences Research Institute, Honolulu, HI*
Veronica Vaccaro, *The Washington Business Group on Health, Washington, DC*
Robert J. Vance, *Pennsylvania State University, University Park, PA*
Gary R. VandenBos, *American Psychological Association, Washington, DC*
Christine VanDosen, *Wayne State University, Detroit, MI*
Joseph Vasey, *Pennsylvania State University, University Park, PA*
Dianne K. Wagener, *National Center for Health Statistics, Hyattsville, MD*
Elinor Walker, *Gaithersburg, MD*
Jacqueline R. Wall, *Morris and Associates, Jackson, Mississippi*
David Wall, *Weyerhaeuser Paper Company, Jackson, MS*
Katherine Warren, *Hypertension Center Starr Pavillion, New York, NY*

Leon Warshaw, *New York Business Group on Health, New York, NY*
David Watterson, Jr., *WLR, Chagrin Falls, OH*
Danny Wedding, *Arlington, VA*
Robert L. Weisman, *San Francisco, CA*
Stephen Weiss, *National Heart, Lung, and Blood Institute, Bethesda, MD*
Cindy Welch, *Radford University, Radford, VA*
Mary Werwath, *Milwaukee, WI*
Mila Wiener, *Radford University, Radford, VA*
Gordon D. Wolf, *Corey-Wolf Associates, Napa, CA*
Tom Ziegler, *National Institute of Occupational Safety & Health, Cincinnati, OH*

Index